101 751 559 X

IES IN
IMPERIALISM

general editor John M. MacKenzie

Established in the belief that imperialism as a cultural
phenomenon had as significant an effect on the dominant as
on the subordinate societies, Studies in Imperialism seeks to
develop the new socio-cultural approach which has emerged
through cross-disciplinary work on popular culture, media
studies, art history, the study of education and religion,
sport   children's literature. The cultural
em   ies of migration and race, while the
                    al, economic and military
                        rporates comparative
                        -building, with the
                    exclusive
                es, when these c
            most powerfully at work.

imperial persuaders

MANCHESTER
UNIVERSITY PRESS

D1380029

AVAILABLE IN THE SERIES

Imperial persuaders

IMAGES OF AFRICA AND ASIA IN BRITISH ADVERTISING

Anandi Ramamurthy

MANCHESTER UNIVERSITY PRESS

Manchester and New York

distributed exclusively in the USA by Palgrave

Published by **MANCHESTER UNIVERSITY PRESS**
OXFORD ROAD, MANCHESTER M13 9NR, UK
and ROOM 400, 175 FIFTH AVENUE, NEW YORK, NY 10010, USA
www.manchesteruniversitypress.co.uk

Distributed exclusively in the USA by
PALGRAVE, 175 FIFTH AVENUE, NEW YORK, NY 10010, USA

Distributed exclusively in Canada by
UBC PRESS, UNIVERSITY OF BRITISH COLUMBIA,
2029 WEST MALL, VANCOUVER, BC, CANADA V6T 1Z2

British Library Cataloguing-in-Publication Data
A catalogue record for this book is available from the British Library

Library of Congress Cataloging-in-Publication Data applied for

ISBN   0 7190 6378 7 hardback
       0 7190 6379 5 paperback

First published 2003

10 09 08 07 06 05 04 03   10 9 8 7 6 5 4 3 2 1

Typeset in Trump Mediaeval
by Graphicraft Limited, Hong Kong
Printed in Great Britain
by Biddles Ltd, Guildford and King's Lynn

In memory of my daughter
Amiya NASEEM Mehmood

CONTENTS

ILLUSTRATIONS

LIST OF ILLUSTRATIONS

GENERAL EDITOR'S INTRODUCTION

We live in an age in which advertising is part of the fabric of our lives. It comes at us from radio, television, newspapers, journals, billboards, footballers' jerseys, and a host of other places. To grab our attention, it has to be mildly dangerous, near an edge. Boring or restrained advertising is ineffective advertising, at least so the practitioners tell us. Because of this need to shock or amuse, to irritate or titillate, advertising often operates at the edge of acceptability, which is why advertising standards have become a feature of the modern age. But advertising also demarcates areas of acceptability, the margins of consensus, the limits of received ideas.

Advertising in its modern form largely has its origins in the later nineteenth century. Therefore, in common with a number of academic disciplines and influential cultural forms, its development was coterminous with the age of high imperialism. Inevitably, perhaps, it utilised, and fed off, many of the characteristics of the expansion of imperial power – military activities, explorers, politicians, technology, and of course race. In my *Propaganda and Empire* (1984), I noted the role of advertising in bringing aspects of imperialism to the cultural foreground in the consciousness of the British. But now Anandi Ramamurthy has examined these issues in far greater depth.

Images are often analysed 'cold', as it were, floating free from their essential contexts. The great strength of this book is that it places advertising images in historical contexts. By focusing on the advertising of specific products, like soap, cocoa, tea, and tobacco, all inseparably bound up with the imperial economy – and therefore also with its politics and its ideologies – advertisements with a racial content can be placed firmly at the intersection of capitalism and culture. These products sought to sell themselves on the basis of their exotic origins. They were used to illustrate the importance of empire to the British. And the depictions of other races were designed to produce a *frisson* of recognition, of difference, of power, and of that dangerous edge through which advertising secures its influence. Too many scholars have concentrated on high culture in the examination of representations of the Other. With advertising, we have a field in which the intention was to influence everyone, and to which all supposedly had access. It was also a field in which specific companies developed distinctive styles, setting out to associate their products with an imperial enterprise which not only had a high 'newsworthy' profile, but which was also perceived to be an acceptable one to their consumers.

It gives me particular pleasure to introduce Anandi Ramamurthy's important work. The first version was compiled as a PhD thesis under my supervision, and this significant research always needed to reach a wider audience. Dr Ramamurthy brings a remarkable range of expertise to bear upon this field. As a former curator in the museum and gallery world, as a historian, and as a practising academic in the realm of media studies, she is uniquely qualified to interpret images of other races in this key period in the development of advertising. Moreover, she recognises the extraordinary longevity of this kind of material. We are familiar with the concept of neo-colonialism in the economic sphere, as we are with notions of 'decolonising the mind'. Advertising neatly represents the manner in which various forms of racial images continued into the supposedly post-colonial world. This important conclusion is not the least of the many highly significant insights to be found in this book.

John M. MacKenzie

ACKNOWLEDGEMENTS

Firstly, I would like to thank Professor John MacKenzie for his support through-out the development of my Ph.D. thesis on which this book is based. Next, I must thank my friend and colleague Paul Keleman, who gave me valuable guidance in the development of my theoretical perspective. Other people who helped me at various points in the development of my work include Paul Greenhalgh, Michael Pickering, Tunde Zack-Williams, Simon Faulkner, Stephanie Ramamurthy and Krishna Ramamurthy. I would also like to thank all the archivists and librarians who helped me in the various institutions that I visited. I am not going to try to name them all for fear of forgetting a name. I would, however, like to give special thanks to the librarians at Man-chester Central Reference Library, who made my perusal of *The Graphic* and *Illustrated London News* especially easy by allowing me to have large numbers at once and to photocopy images at will, and provided me with trolleys to carry the heavy volumes during my pregnancies. I would also like to thank them for their support and permission to photograph the large number of images from *The Graphic* and *Illustrated London News* that are reproduced here without charge. I should also like to thank the libraries that reduced or waived fees for permissions in order to make it financially possible to repro-duce the number of images that I have included. Several company archives were also generous in providing me with photographs for reproduction here. A special thanks to the Barry Amiel and Norman Melburn Trust for financial support in paying for the photographs and reproductions fees which I could not get out of! Thanks to Steve Yates for his photographic skills and help. Particular thanks must go to Diane Frost, who helped me not only academic-ally, but also emotionally. The support you have given me over the last few years will always be valued beyond words. I must also thank my husband, Tariq, for supporting me both during the writing of my thesis and in the last few years after the death of our daughter. Without his belief in me I could never have got this far.

CHAPTER ONE

Advertising and colonial discourse

Images are historical documents. They do not simply reflect the ideological perspectives of an era, but form part of the process through which these ideologies are produced. This book traces the relationships between companies, governments and emerging racist, colonial and imperialist ideologies through their production of images. It reveals the way in which companies and institutions employed images of black people at given historical moments, in order to represent ideological perspectives which promoted their interests.

The book highlights the way in which racist representations continually developed and shifted throughout the nineteenth and twentieth centuries, depending on the particular political and economic interests of the producers of these images. The aim has not been simply to analyse these images as dehumanising, but to reveal the purposes to which these images of dehumanisation and exploitation were employed. These meanings can only be unravelled through a detailed historical and political contextualisation. It is hoped that this book will contribute to Douglas Kellner's request for a 'critical cultural studies' that situates culture within 'a socio-historical context' and 'criticises forms of culture that foster subordination'.[1]

The choice of advertising has not been accidental. Advertising is a form of cultural production that permeates every aspect of our lives. Advertising bombards us from every direction, on the streets, in our homes and in the magazines we buy and read. Although the level of bombardment has increased throughout the twentieth century, it is clear that by the late nineteenth century, advertising had begun to take on an increasingly ubiquitous form. The power of advertising lies not simply in its quantity, but also in its use of the latest technology to bamboozle us with brilliant images. Advertisers have always had access to the most advanced technology, since for the most part they represent the dominant classes, who have both capital and control over production. While the historical images under study may now appear like simple colour prints, we have to assess the novelty of them in the way we would assess digital images today. As John MacKenzie notes:

> It is perhaps difficult for us, jaded by the printed word and the omni-present electronic media, to comprehend fully the impact of these materials. There seems to have been a craving for visual representations of the world, of events, and of the great and famous, which a large number of agencies and commercial companies sought to satisfy in the period from the 1870s to the First World War. New advertising techniques were central to all this activity, and companies creating and supplying the new tastes were concerned to sell not just their own product, but also the world system which produced it.[2]

It is not just the power of these often ephemeral images that makes analysing these advertisements valuable. In the nineteenth and twentieth centuries discourses on 'race' and colonialism found articulation in exhibitions, music hall, painting, literature, film and all forms of cultural expression. Advertisements, however, not only highlight general cultural perspectives but often reveal political positions that reflect particular company interests. Advertising provides a context which is economic and political as well as cultural. The book hopes to assert the value of understanding the economic and material context of cultural production, while also appreciating the way in which all aspects of culture are affected by other cultural messages.

My interest in this subject first arose through the organisation of an exhibition entitled 'Black Markets: Images of Black People in British Advertising and Packaging from 1880 to 1990'. The primary aim of the exhibition was to look at contemporary and historical advertisements in order to trace the roots of racism in contemporary imagery. By displaying a large body of images, it highlighted the pervasive and seductive qualities of advertising and concentrated on the method of exposure to reveal the racism within advertising. The exhibition was divided into five sections, the first of which, 'Domestic Products – Domestic Spaces', concentrated on images which would have been received in the home, while the second one, 'Social Products – Social Spaces', dealt with those received in more public social interactions. After establishing these two spheres, the third section, 'Global Consumption', tried to place commodities and companies within an increasingly dominant global/transnational perspective, in order to express visually the hegemony of Europe in relation to the non-European world. The fourth section, 'State Advertising', tried to draw a sense of relationship between capital and the state, through the state's use of similar racist ideologies. The final section, 'The Black Consumer', raised questions about black people's reception of advertisements directed at a predominantly white audience.[3] While the exhibition did highlight dominant racist representations of the past and their frequent transmutation into present-day seemingly innocent images, it was unable to visually decode the images in a way which could make the visitor aware of how ideologies worked. It only expressed in a summary way issues about advertising's role not simply in reflecting dominant ideologies but also in perpetuating and creating them. Only a contextual approach to the advertising imagery could make this possible.

The study of black representations in historical popular culture

Much of the literature which has considered historical printed ephemera has taken a survey approach to the subject. It is interesting that many of the books on the subject are associated with specific exhibitions hosted in Europe and America during the 1980s. By the 1980s, anti-racist struggles across Europe and America had made the use of overtly dehumanising images less easy for advertisers and others to employ. It also became apparent that museums and libraries needed to critically evaluate their own collections. Most of the exhibitions that took place were related to examining specific collections.[4] All these exhibitions attempted to highlight the racism and dehumanisation of black people in Western popular culture, yet at the same time the display of such items of popular culture with the limited text that is possible in an exhibition did not always give a sense of the abhorrent nature of these images. It was easy for them to retain an element of entertaining fun, which was not in most cases the intention of the organisers. All of the exhibitions, apart from 'Black Markets', concentrated on representations of African people. In this exhibition I chose to use the term 'black' as a political term to signify people of colour who had undergone processes of direct or indirect colonisation by Europe, with particular reference to British colonies. This definition is in keeping with the political use of this term by anti-racist groups in Britain from the 1970s onwards. The exhibition attempted to highlight the links between the oppression of Asian and African people in Britain, although there were clearly certain themes which demanded a more specific location. I will continue to pursue these relationships and differences in this book and shall therefore use the term 'black' within the above political framework and the terms Asian or African when referring to a particular ethnicity.

[3]

Most of the exhibitions mentioned above produced catalogues of varying sizes, but the catalogue for 'White on Black: Images of Africa and Blacks in Western Popular Culture', held at the anthropological museum in Amsterdam, was particularly extensive and has since been reproduced in English as a book in its own right.[5] 'White on Black' was also the largest of the exhibitions noted and considered a trans-atlantic representation, whereas most of the others, including 'Black Markets', looked at images within the respective countries of produc-tion. The scope of 'White on Black' makes it the most appropriate exhibition and book through which to explore some of the recent trends and approaches to analysing these images in popular culture.

'White on Black' documents the changing representations of black people in Western popular culture and places these images within a socio-political context. The research for both exhibition and book was based on a collection started by Rufus Collins, an African-American theatre director who used the collection as an educational aid during rehearsals to try to make actors more aware of the absurd stereotypes to which they were conforming. The collection was expanded later by the Cosmic Illusion Productions Foundation. Jan Nederveen Pieterse's book deals with images which stretch over ten centuries. While he tries to evaluate and contextualise the historical images, it is difficult to do this effectively because of the scope of the book. The book is divided into three parts: the first deals with images of Africa, the second deals with images of black people in the West, and the third considers questions relating to issues about images and social repres-entations in general. The section 'Africa' gives a historical overview of various processes and events which affected the representation of black people particularly over the past two hundred years. Separate chapters explore the Eurocentric image of the 'savage' and 'heathen', the period of slavery, European exploration and missionary activity, as well as the colonisation of Africa in the nineteenth century. The last two chapters in this section break from the historical approach and look at the themes of apartheid and boys' adventure stories. While slavery and abolitionism are dealt with in this section, the images discussed do not strictly represent Africa but rather black people in America and the Caribbean in the eighteenth century. It could be argued that slaves represented images of Africa to Europeans at that period, but then so did black servants in the West whose images are discussed in section two.

The section titled 'In the West', however, is organised thematically around either stereotypes or specific contexts in which images may have been encountered. Representations of the servant, the entertainer, and the exotic man or woman with a rampant sexuality are each given a chapter. Pieterse also allocates a chapter to 'popular types' to consider images like the golliwog or Banania which emerged out of either literature or advertising, but took on meanings and socio-historical relations outside of their original sphere and in time began to be recognised as part of a national culture.[6] Other chapters consider the context of images; these include one on advertising and another on 'Kidstuff'. The thematic approach of the second section must explain why Pieterse chose to situate the chapter on slavery within a historical development. This confusion, however, is testimony to the problems of dividing the images geographically, especially since they were all consumed in Europe, and all acted to represent Africa to a European audience. The purpose of this geographical pigeonholing is Pieterse's assertion that the stereotype of 'the savage' was used to represent black people in Africa in contrast to domesticated images that dominate representations of Africans in the West. Although there is some just-ification for this analysis, I think it leads to a discussion about imagery that does not consider images as constantly negotiating meanings produced within arenas of conflict. The image of Africans as savage was constantly evoked whenever black people resisted their oppression, whether in Europe or Africa.

An issue which Pieterse never discusses is the resistance by black people to slavery, colonialism and exploitation and its affect on repre-sentation. This is the result of addressing the issue as that of 'white on black'. It is an approach which does not allow a full analysis of the dynamics of class, gender or nationhood, of oppressor versus oppressed, and the dynamics and conflicts which exist internally to them. How did these unequal and constantly conflicting relationships affect the production of representations? Christine Bolt's *Victorian Attitudes to Race* analyses the way in which the resistance of Indians to the Brit-ish in the so-called 'Indian Mutiny' and the resistance of Jamaicans in the 1865 revolt (to give just two examples) were interpreted and constructed as proof of their 'racial' inferiority and savagery.[7] While Pieterse does comment on the contending images of abolitionist pro-paganda and counter-propaganda by Southern planters, he does not discuss the crucial conflict between oppressor and oppressed and its effect on representations.[8]

The hegemony of the West and of Western culture, however, has conditioned most representations – even images of resistance – as Bolt's analysis shows. If Pieterse had taken this approach, he might have analysed an image from *Le Rire* of 18 April 1896 slightly dif-ferently.[9] Based on a Fuseli painting, this engraving depicts a savage and old-looking Africa sitting threateningly on top of a young woman who represents Europe. She is lying on a bed, her head and arms hanging down in a posture which suggests both sexual availability and death. Africa is old and decaying; Europe is young. Africa is not represented here as the white man's burden, but as a threat to what appears to be a vulnerable Europe. This scene, depicting the potential rape of a voluptuous yet seemingly innocent white woman, graphically legitimises the colonial rampage. The resistance that Africans put up at the time of 'the scramble', one example of which is beautifully documented in Med Hondo's film *Sarraounia* (1986), is represented in this late-nineteenth-century image so as to assert the dominant racist notions with which the public were familiar. This hegemony conditions representations of both black and white people. Pieterse, however, describes the image in *Le Rire* as peculiar, as the representation of 'the world turned upside down'. He comments only on the fact that the victim is blamed. What is also important in the image's construction is the resistance to oppression, which was a threat to British interests, and the interpretation of this threat as arising out of savagery in order to legitimate the colonial rampage. The main difficulty with Pieterse's text is its almost exclusive focus on stereotyping theory, an approach which, although valuable in exposing the gross distortions of racist representations, does not enable us to consider the ambiguities, conflicts and nuances of particular contexts.

Theorising representations of racism and difference

The key strategy with which images of black people from the colonial period have been considered is that of stereotyping. As Pieterse and all the exhibitions highlighted, black people were reduced to a few simple, essential characteristics, which were represented as fixed by nature. The most recent contribution to this argument is William O'Barr's *Culture and the Ad: Exploring Otherness in the World of Advertising*.[10]

The stereotype, as Richard Dyer argues, essentialises, naturalises and fixes difference. In this way, images or characteristics which do not fit with constructed stereotypes are constantly excluded from representations. The stereotype maintains a particular social and symbolic order which identifies what belongs and what does not – what is 'us' and what is 'them'. Finally, the stereotype tends to occur where there are gross inequalities of power. In this sense the production of the stereotype is part of what Foucault has defined as the relationship between knowledge and power. However, the stereotype only operates effectively through a general level of consent and indicates the way in which Gramsci's concept of hegemony operates in the cultural arena. As Dyer outlines:

[6]

The establishment of normalcy (i.e. what is accepted as 'normal') through social- and stereo-types is one aspect of the habit of ruling groups to attempt to fashion the whole of society according to their own world view, value system, sensibility and ideology. So right is this world view for the ruling groups that they make it appear (as it does appear to them) as 'natural' and inevitable – and for everyone – and in so far as they succeed, they establish their hegemony.[11]

Racist ideologies in the nineteenth century, produced as part of the imperial and colonising mission, defined blacks and whites as innately different. Pseudo-scientific theories had created a whole hierarchy of racial differences, using cultural and social factors, as well as physical characteristics, including colour, to define differences and legitimise notions of supremacy.[12] These theories were translated visually through a variety of mediums including photography, film, the music hall and all kinds of ephemera including advertising.[13] All these cultural forms acted to develop a discourse that constructed black people as intellectually, morally and socially less developed beings designed to serve the white man.

Within colonial discourse there is a clear connection between the representation of difference and power. Edward Said has argued this relationship excellently in *Orientalism*, his groundbreaking text on representations of the Arab world by the West.[14] Said's text illuminates the way in which knowledge about the 'other' was constructed as much from previous European literatures about 'the Orient' (a geographical location which was very loosely defined) as it was from actual experience. Observation was used to affirm already confirmed conclusions about 'the Orient'. In this way the literature, paintings and photographs produced about 'the Orient' produced a whole discourse, or body of ideas, to form a racialised knowledge of the Orient.[15] Although Said's text slips at certain points into generalisations about all knowledge of the Orient produced by the West from the earliest times, the most convincing and satisfying parts of his argument relate to his discussions about post-eighteenth-century Orientalism and its relationship, although not equation, with 'political power in the raw'.

Said's book has had a profound impact on the development of colonial discourse theory. The growing body of literature that analyses aspects of colonial discourses is heavily influenced by his work. Lynda Nochlin's 'The Imaginary Orient' ushered art historians to reconsider Orientalist paintings in relation to Said's work.[16] Others considered the way in which colonial discourse operated in relation to museums, photography, film, government institutions and literature. Malek Alloula's *The Colonial Harem*, for example, focused on colonial Algerian postcards to expose the way in which the photographs they depicted were constructed from the male European's imagination and previous writings about the 'Oriental' woman.[17] James Ryan's *Picturing Empire* has explored the way in which various genres of photography affirmed particular 'regimes of truth' that operated about Africa, including the notion of an untamed savage and exotic land. He also discusses the way in which the presence of photography as a technical and mechanical medium was viewed as representing the superiority of Western culture.[18] Ella Shohat and Robert Stam's *Unthinking Eurocentricism*, although much broader than a discussion about colonial and racist representations, considers the operation of colonial discourses in Western films.[19] Annie Coombes's *Reinventing Africa*, in its turn, establishes the relationship between colonial discourses and the museum.[20]

Said's text, however, has been criticised for his representation of colonial discourse as a form of power that is totalising. Aijaz Ahmed, who has argued for a greater analysis of colonial people's agency in resisting or negotiating colonial authority, has challenged this.[21] This issue of agency and of the idea of power as circulating has been important in the context of representation, in order to understand colonial peoples as not simply victims of a process. However, while this is an important issue in an analysis of colonial photography, for example, where the subjects may have been able to negotiate aspects of their representation, it has less bearing on advertising imagery, which in the process of construction at least is entirely controlled by the advertisers. Even in this context, however, campaigns of resistance to colonial rule clearly influenced changing representations, as I shall discuss.

While Ahmed has criticised Said with regards to the issue of colonial subjects' agency, others such as Homi Bhabha have argued from a psychoanalytic perspective that the stereotype needs to be read as ambivalent, since it relies both on its fixity as well as its need to be anxiously repeated in order to retain its authority. Bhabha's critique is a call for an approach to imagery which does not simply define images as positive or negative, but involves a greater understanding of subjectification.[22] While the work of Bhabha and others has developed increasingly sophisticated ways of reading imagery,[23] the focus on textual analysis has meant that local examples have sometimes acted as evidence of the operations of colonial power *per se*. As Benita Parry has remarked when discussing the writings on colonial discourse within literature: 'Colonialism as a specific, and the most spectacular, mode of imperialism's many and mutable states . . . is treated as identical with all the variable forms'.[24] Laura Chrisman discusses how even the 'exemplary criticism of Spivak' collapses themes of

imperialism and colonialism at times and colludes with the establishment of an Oriental/occidental binarism.[25] As Nicholas Thomas has
noted: 'Colonialism is not a unitary project but a fractured one, riddled
with contradictions and exhausted as much by its own internal debates
as by the resistance of the colonised.'[26]

These issues have been of particular concern to me. Without recognising their importance it would only be possible to understand the
relationship between stereotypes and the production of the most general colonial ideologies. Yet black representations were employed more
strategically in advertising to represent company interests in specific
colonial ideologies and policies. The value of looking at stereotypes
must be in order to analyse the ways in which they were employed to
service specific colonial ideologies – that is, to service specific power
interests.

Understanding the ways in which images operated and were constructed to serve specific interests can only be achieved through effective historical contextualisation. More recently a number of texts have
begun to try to provide greater historical context to an evaluation of
imagery. Annie Coombes's *Reinventing Africa* is one such text. It not
only discusses the general colonial discourses influencing representations in museums, but also focuses on particular military campaigns
and their consequences for the way in which cultural expressions
were interpreted. Two recent examples of an attempt to provide a
contextual approach to advertising can be seen in Thomas Richards's
chapter on 'Selling Darkest Africa' in his book on Victorian advertising and Anne McClintock's essay 'Soft Soaping Empire' in *Imperial
Leather*.[27] Richards provides an account of advertising images that
were used in the aftermath of Henry Stanley's expedition to Africa in
1890 and focuses on the way in which the images eulogised Stanley's
view of the commodity as a civilising source which would promote capitalism. McClintock comments on the relationship between
the image of black people and whiteness in soap advertising and the
denial of women's labour on these newly branded products. Neither
author, however, attempts to link the material interests of particular
companies to their use of the black figure.

Reading advertising imagery

Arguing for greater historical and economic contextualisations of the
advertising imagery should not suggest that close textual readings of
advertising imagery are not useful. The work of writers such as Roland
Barthes and Judith Williamson as well as the more recent work of
scholars such as Robert Goldman has shown the value of exploring

the social and cultural meanings of contemporary advertising through textual analysis.[28] To understand fully the mythologies created by advertisers and to be able to interpret fully the referent systems that Williamson discusses, however, we must research into the specific political, economic and cultural contexts of the imagery we discuss. This is an issue that Don Slater raised as early as 1983:

> Over the past two decades, the structuralist tradition has been the most progressive and fertile strategy for engaging cultural processes. It has now become a barrier to further progress. Though it does not consciously exclude as irrelevant the political economy of media and social relations within which they are consumed, it has ultimately consigned them to theoretical limbo. The structuralist tradition takes as assumed, as given, precisely what needs to be explained: the relations and practices within which discourses are formed and operated. It would like to specify the transactions and mutual constitution of subject and representation within the processes of signification, but to do this by appealing to discourses which are inexplicable in the terms of its theoretical apparatus. To use a vocabulary it would not recognise, the structuralist tradition aims to analyse 'ideological effect', yet takes as given precisely those discourses whose effect it would like to trace . . . The historic and dynamic construction of discourses within a force-field of social practices is obscured and ignored in order to focus on the negotiations of meaning carried out within the ambit of text and the moment of reading.[29]

I hope this book will address Slater's criticism and remove the political economy of the media and social relations in image analysis from its theoretical limbo. The historian David Nye's book *Image Worlds*[30] is a lucid example of the value of placing images within their historical, political and economic contexts, as well as viewing them as part of a series of images, since images, especially commercial ones, are not produced in isolation. Nye recognised the importance of understanding who the producer of these images saw as the consumer. He rightly privileges the meanings which the producer of these images intended, in order to understand the impact of General Electric's photographic persuasion as a whole. Nye's book is a rare example of the value of researching and understanding advertising or marketing imagery from the context of its production. While historians such as Roland Marchand in *Advertising the American Dream* have provided detailed analyses of the advertisers' general support for the concept of modernity, the location of advertisements within their context of production is rare. Apart from Nye's book, there are only a few short articles such as Cathy Squires's 'The Corporate Year in Pictures' and Sally Stein's 'The Composite Photographic Image and the Composition of Consumer Ideology' which consider the relationship of the images to political economy.[31] There are no texts which treat the representation of black people within advertising in this way.

This apparent lack of interest in understanding the representation of black people from the point of view of political economy seems even stranger when we consider that black people were not the consumers whom advertisers were trying to reach through these images in the late nineteenth and early twentieth centuries. We were labourers involved in the production of raw materials. It is therefore not surprising that a thorough investigation should reveal that many images of black people represented forms of labour relations which companies desired. Other images represented racist and colonial ideologies to support colonial policies that companies wished to foster. In the words of Marx and Engels:

> The class which has the means of material production at its disposal has control at the same time over the means of mental production, so that thereby, generally speaking, the ideas of those who lack the means of mental production are subject to it ... In so far, therefore, as they rule as a class and determine the extent and compass of an epoch, it is self-evident that they ... among other things ... regulate the production and distribution of ideas of their age: thus their ideas are the ruling ideas of the epoch.[32]

This approach need not suggest rigid economic determinism, but should aid us in understanding economic, political, social and ideological formations as interacting with each other in ways which are complex but not necessarily equal. In this way, it is possible to understand how racist ideologies, operating as part of a variety of colonial discourses, shifted constantly depending on advertisers' interests. This highlights the importance of understanding the political economy of advertising.

The political economy of advertising

Advertising, as has already been noted, provides a specific economic and political context for study. It is not simply linked to processes of production and consumption within capitalism, but constitutes a part of both processes. Thomas Richards has recently described advertising as a 'capitalist form of representation'[33] and as the culture of capitalism. It may be more accurate to describe it as a cultural representation of imperialism. Its pervasiveness after 1880, its intrinsic link to conglomeration and the importance of financial institutions, in terms of its role in 'cornering markets' etc., make it imperative that we understand it in relation to the monopoly stage of capitalism.

Raymond Williams and others have taken a similar analysis. As Williams wrote:

> The formation of modern advertising has to be traced essentially to certain characteristics of the new 'monopoly' (corporate) capitalism, first clearly evident . . . [at] the end and turn of the nineteenth century. The Great Depression . . . marked the turning point between two modes of industrial organisation and two basically different approaches to distribution. After the Depression, and its big fall in prices, there was a more general and growing fear of productive capacity, a marked tendency to reorganise industrial ownership into larger units and combines, and a growing desire, by different methods, to organise and where possible control the market. Among the means of achieving the latter purposes, advertising on a new scale, and applied to an increasing range of products, took an important place.
>
> Modern advertising, that is to say, belongs to the system of market-control, which at its full development includes the growth of tariffs and privileged areas, cartel quotas, trade campaigns, price-fixing by manufactures, and that form of economic imperialism which assured certain markets overseas by political control of their territories.[34]

In their analysis of the American economic and social order, Paul Baran and Paul Sweezy comment on not only how manufacturers had begun to exploit advertising as a means of securing consumer demand for their products, but also how by the 1890s 'both the volume and tone of advertising changed. Expenditures upon advertising in 1890 amounted to $360 million, some seven times more than in 1864. By 1929 this figure had been multiplied by nearly ten reaching $3,426 million.'[35] Although mine is a study of a British context, these figures give us an indication of the developments in the capitalist mode of production during this period. While many corporations may have first seen both advertising and marketing as a deplorable cost to be held down as much as possible, they were eventually recognised as 'a must for survival' by most organisations within this economic system.[36] In a market where price competition has declined, as within monopoly capitalism, advertising had become essential to encourage consumption, not simply between products, but also as a whole. Baran and Sweezy also comment on how, as monopoly capitalism reached a state of maturity, advertising not only burgeoned in quantity but also entered 'the state of persuasion, as distinct from proclamation or iteration'.[37] Burgeoning during the decade before the Great Depression, and playing a crucial role and influence by this period on other communications media,[38] advertising was now more than just a publicity tool to disperse information. It was a means of persuasion and a crucial tool in the constant drive towards accumulation. In selling commodities, in entering the arena of persuasion in particular, advertising also sells us the ideologies of its producers, namely imperialist ideologies. Bruce Macdonald, Director of BBDO Marketing, Moscow, in 1994 acknowledged: 'There is a very fine line between propaganda and advertising'.[39] Perhaps there is no line at all. It is this context, sometimes providing what appears an almost transparent representation of imperialist ideologies, including its use of racism, which will be explored in this book.

Here, it is essential to define my use of the term imperialism. I believe it is important to retain a definition of the term which is principally, although not exclusively, economic in order to describe the new phase of capitalist development which was clearly recognisable by 1900. Marxists have described this as 'monopoly capitalism'. Others have quibbled over the term. However, as Hobsbawm has pointed out:

> It does not much matter what we call it ('corporate capitalism', 'organised capitalism', etc.) so long as it is agreed – and it must be that combination advanced at the expense of market competition, business corporation at the expense of private firms, big business and large enterprise at the expense of smaller; and that this concentration implied a tendency towards oligopoly.[40]

In using the term monopoly it is also important to remember that bourgeois economists have used the term 'monopoly' to mean a single seller with no rival, whereas Marxists have used it to refer to a major departure from a 'free market'.[41] It is in the latter sense that I will use the term. Within the process of imperialism, Hilferding, Bukharin and Lenin also noted the rise of finance capital – i.e. the rise of a merging and intensified relationship between the banks and industrial capitalists.[42] They discussed the increase of combines and agreements between major powers that share the world markets amongst themselves. The G8 summits in Seattle and Genoa in recent years have seen these processes continue at the expense of the poor and the third world. In discussing representation, understanding the economic context of imagery is just as relevant as exploring the political and social contexts. The three are inextricably entwined.

Defining imperialism as principally economic is not to suggest that it has no relationship to political formations such as Empire, but rather to perceive the importance of having a terminology which will allow us to distinguish between economic and political formations. All three writers mentioned above have noted the relationship between economic, political and social formations in their analyses. As Hilferding wrote in 1910:

The demand for an expansionist policy overthrows the entire world view of the bourgeoisie. It ceases to be pacific and humanitarian. The old free-traders saw in free-trade not only the most just economic policy, but also the basis for an era of peace. Finance capital gave up this belief long ago. It does not believe in the harmony of capitalist interests, but knows that the competitive struggle becomes more and more a political struggle. The ideal of peace fades, and the idea of humanity is replaced by the ideal of the grandeur and power of the state.[43]

Hilferding's analysis highlighted the increasing role of finance capital, but also recognised the crucial changes of conglomeration in the industrial sector which aided this dominance. The ideals to which he refers need to be understood in the context of capitalism as a whole. These ideals are clearly perceptible in late-nineteenth-century advertising, most of which promoted the commodity rather than financial services, since in this era it was the rise of mass-produced goods which affected the average householder. The main clients of the financial service sector were big business and therefore it did not need consumer advertising. Recently P. J. Cain and A. G. Hopkins have reasserted the importance of finance capitalism.[44] However, they adopt what could be described as a culturalist approach, by attributing a cultural characteristic like that of the English gentleman to the dominance of an economic sector. They do not use the term imperialism to define a phase of capitalism but see it as a broad-based term which defines a branch of international relations within which they perceive a relationship of hegemony.

Within Baran and Sweezy's examination of the political economy, advertising's structural link to imperialism is made clear, but they do not explore the ideology of imperialism within advertising as a mode of representation, since their text is principally economic. Advertising as a manifestation of imperialist culture is not the only visual form which could be explored to express the values of a capitalist and imperialist culture, but its direct relationship to production provides us with a form of capitalist/imperialist representation in the raw. The representation of black people within this particular form of cultural production should also provide us with a context within which to explore the relationship between racism and imperialism, which Hilferding referred to as early as 1910:

The ideal is to insure for one's own nation the domination of the world . . . Founded in economic needs, it finds its justification in this remarkable reversal of national consciousness . . . [R]acial ideology is thus a rationalisation, disguised as science, of the ambitions of finance capital.[45]

One phenomenon within advertising which can be seen as directly related to this new phase is that of branding. It emerged during the last two decades of the nineteenth century, precisely at the time when manufacturers needed to distinguish between a range of similar products that were flooding the market. This process created identities for products, many of which were animated with human characteristics or imbued with social values, as we shall see in the chapter on soap advertising. W. F. Haug has described this process of branding as the 'aesthetic monopolisation of use value'. He discusses how branding is used to establish a monopolistic situation with 'all available aesthetic devices [being] employed to further this end'.[46] What is useful about Haug's comments is the way he draws together economic and aesthetic debates:

> What does it mean when competition limits itself to the competition of impression? Evidently it is not the objective features of the rival offers which are in competition. Thus there is no competition of use values. Primarily, the contest is between the images of the competing offers and those who offer them.[47]

Haug's comments make an analysis of advertising's representations central to a critique of the industry. He acknowledges their ideological power.

The process of branding is also important in terms of the study of black representation. Many of the images which will be explored highlight the 'racialisation' of brand identities created in the late nineteenth and twentieth centuries. The extent of 'racialisation' of course alters over time for each product, depending on specific economic and political interests within companies, as we shall see through the chapters. While some brands used racist images and images of black people in the construction of a broader identity (e.g. Pears), for others the product was entirely 'racialised' (e.g. the perfume Shem-el-Nessim in the early twentieth century; the sweet 'Black Jack' which is still sold today but with a different image from its previous caricature of an African face; or the toothpaste 'Darkie' sold by Colgate in the Far East until its name was changed to Darlie in 1989).

Haug's critique of 'commodity aesthetics' draws on Marx's earlier writings on the fetishism of commodities. It is worth considering Marx's writings and the way in which advertising has exacerbated the processes which he discussed. Even in an age prior to the burgeoning of advertising, Marx was aware of the way in which commodities were fetishised through the process of exchange. As Marx wrote:

A commodity appears at first sight a very trivial thing, and is easily understood, its analysis shows that it is in reality, a very queer thing, abounding in metaphysical subtleties and theological niceties.[48]

Marx continued by highlighting how commodities assume a social character because of the labour they contain, yet the social character of men's labour is no longer understood within the production process because the products of their labour interact in the market place:

a commodity is therefore a mysterious thing, simply because in it the social character of men's labour appears to them as an objective character stamped upon the product of that labour; because the relation of the producers to the sum of their own labour is presented to them as a social relation, existing not between themselves, but between the products of their labour.[49]

However, it is not the presentation of social relations through commodities which fetishises them, since commodities have always represented social relations, but it is the appearance of this process as 'natural' and almost god-given which fetishises and mystifies. This process of naturalisation has been enhanced by both advertising and branding. The naturalisation of value within commodities also fetishises the product further, since within the commodity form, labour and labour power are not distinguished. This not only dehumanises a worker's input, but also makes it difficult for the worker to distinguish between socially necessary labour-time and surplus labour-time.[50] It is this which fetishises the product and also oppresses the worker. Advertising enhances the appearance of things, while hiding the reality of commodity production.[51]

While Marx discussed the fetishism of exchange-value, it is clear that advertising, in amplifying the process, leads to the fetishisation of use-value too, as Haug hinted at in his text. The creation of brand 'personalities' is one way in which this takes place. In imbuing a product with imperial significance, for example, the use of the product seems to suggest the consumers' partaking in the imperial exercise. Sut Jhally in *Codes of Advertising* develops this discussion while highlighting the importance of not suggesting an infinite number of use-values as Baudrillard and Sahlins have done.[52] Such an approach would deny any materialist basis to the analysis of advertising images. Yet if we consider the products with the loudest imperial message, they were also often benefiting from this political and economic framework. The images do not simply highlight the adoption of ideologies from the superstructure but echo a relationship to the material base. The construction of imperialistic characteristics for brands was often in response to companies' economic concerns.

Thomas Richards has also discussed branding and fetishism as a process by which commodities 'came alive'.[53] Richards begins his book by discussing how the commodity in the early nineteenth century was simple in form 'like one of Adam Smith's pins', but how by the late nineteenth century the commodity had 'a world historical role to play'. Richards notes how even the vocabulary for things in the nineteenth century increased: 'gadget, dingus, thingamijig, jigger'. He also describes how the commodities' increasingly complex form even led Marx in his short chapter on commodity fetishism to 'shift metaphors every few sentences to do justice to its ubiquity as a form of representation'.[54] Richards continues his introduction by attempting to search for what he calls 'a stable system of representation for commodities', although it is difficult to understand why since he is talking about a capitalist form of representation. Since capitalism is structured on chaos, the system of representation itself must surely be unstable. However, he finds this system in the idea of 'spectacle' which Guy Debord developed in *The Society of Spectacle*. Debord discusses Western societies' post-television revolution and the bombardment of information and goods post-1966 as a method of dramatising events to the masses to prevent rebellion. Richards makes use of the concept of spectacle to express the Victorians' changing attitude to the commodity in the first period of mass production. He describes how even as early as the 1850s the commodity had become the focal point and the arbiter of all representation. He uses the Great Exhibition of 1851 to express the way in which the commodity was not only placed at the centre of the stage but was also infused with the ideology of Empire and monarchy. Interestingly he describes the commodities as 'the minstrels of capitalism', already racialising their existence. Richards continues, however, not simply by suggesting and emphasising the role of spectacle and drama but by presenting this spectacle as the mode of capitalist production. 'What it produces so deliriously', he writes 'are signs, signs taken for wonders, signs signifying consumption.' While spectacle may be a form of capitalist representation, it cannot be described as the mode of capitalist production. Richards fails to link his analysis of representations to the production of the goods he discusses. He collapses the useful work of industrial production and the parasitic work of industries like the advertising industry into one process. His analysis of representations almost suggests that the goods did actually come alive, rather than seeing this as a capitalist metaphor and representation. The conflict between appearance and reality so important in Marxist critique gets lost. The fetishism of commodities, or what Raymond Williams once described as the 'magic' in the market place, does not get analysed. The importance of linking a discussion of production and consumption to an understanding of how goods are fetishised within the capitalist process is pointed out by Jhally:

> What commodities fail to communicate to consumers is information about the processes of production. Unlike goods in earlier societies, they do not bear the signature of their makers, whose motives and actions we might access because we knew who they were. Specifically, the following kinds of information are systematically hidden in capitalist society: the process of planning and designing products; the actual relations of production that operate in particular factories; the level of wages and benefits of workers; whether labour is unionised or non-unionised; quality checks and the level of automation; market research on consumers; the effect on the environment of producing goods through particular industrial processes; the renewable and non-renewable nature of the raw materials used; and the relations of production that prevail in the extraction of raw materials around the world. All of these things constitute the meaning (information) that is embedded in products.[55]

Advertising from whatever period enhances the falsity of meanings within the fetishisation process, as it naturalises social relations. These images can deny or rework the relations of production. They are part of a process which fragments and hides information. Within capitalist social relations, it is difficult to acquire information about production in a systematic way. As Jhally continues:

> The real and full meaning of production is hidden beneath the empty appearance in exchange. Only once the real meaning has been systematically emptied out of commodities does advertising then refill this void with its own symbols. Thus when products appear in the market place, although we may be well aware of them as products of human labour, because there is no specific social meaning accompanying this awareness, the symbolisation of advertising appears as more real and concrete. The fetishism of commodities consists in the first place of emptying them of meaning, of hiding the real social relations objectified in them through human labour, to make it possible for the imaginary/symbolic social relations to be injected into the construction of meaning at a secondary level. Production empties. Advertising fills. The real is hidden by the imaginary.[56]

What is real and what is imaginary become confused. What is imagined has a physical presence, which makes it seem more real than the actuality of social relations – at least to the consumer of the products. In what way have advertisers used the image of black people to enhance these processes of fragmentation and falsification? Many products in the late nineteenth and early twentieth centuries depicted labour, especially scenes that represented black workers. This is not to contradict Jhally's important point, but to understand the processes of representation within a framework which is more complex than that of denial or affirmation. Within this, racism plays an important role. Black people were naturalised as labourers for the white man. To show the black man or even black child working was not seen as a symbol of exploitation, since it 'appeared' to be their 'natural' place. To understand the meanings, origins and symbolism within the representation of black people, to understand the nuances of meaning within a series of images, which often appear relatively similar (such as those of the black labourer), we have to consider them within their specific political, social and economic contexts of production. We cannot approach this deconstruction like an undiscerning consumer who makes no distinction between appearance and reality, when we are aware of the distinction. To decode these images directed at a white consumer without considering the role of black people within both the production and consumption of these products and images when they were far more integrally associated with the former cannot give us a fully round picture. Of course, as Jhally has noted, the systematic hiding of information means that we are forced to interpret this process through fragments.

Sahlins and Baudrillard, as Jhally notes, succumb to the mystification of commodity fetishism – they make a fetish out of consumption. What they see is vast proliferations of commodities capable of taking and reflecting multiple symbolic forms and they look exclusively to consumption to explain this multiplicity, forgetting the deeper reality of commodity production. In separating commodities from their material basis in production, they drift off into the idealist 'iconosphere' of the 'code' or 'culture'. Thomas Richards confuses the division between appearance and reality too, by substituting the production of signs for a mode of production.

My emphasis on the importance of understanding the context of production led me to take a product focus for the chapters, in order to analyse the interests of particular manufacturers' uses of black people's images. In their text *Social Communication in Advertising*,[57] Leiss, Kline and Jhally describe the earliest phase of advertising from 1880 to 1925 as one that was particularly product-orientated. This has made the product orientation of the early chapters particularly appropriate. The products discussed also complement each other in terms of the issues they raise. Soap provides an example of an ordinary product which was branded for the first time in the late nineteenth century; cocoa and tea provide examples of 'exotic' products which were consumed increasingly during this period. The former gives an opportunity to explore an image of the African and of Africa, while the latter gives scope to explore the image of the 'Orient'. The two products also provide examples of different methods of production and how this affected the representation of black labour.

The second phase identified by Leiss *et al.* is what they call the 'product symbols' phase (1920–44), in which products were symbolically associated with particular symbolic attributes which the consumer would find alluring. Recognising a move away from the product-oriented approach justifies concentration on an image of whiteness during this period. The third phase, 'personalisation' (1945–65), indicates why the image of black people is restricted to corporate companies by this stage, since our image was not one with which the white consumer public, fed on a diet of Empire, was keen to identify.

Finally, it is important to emphasise that while key advertising campaigns have been discussed in the book, there are other series of images which, although interesting, were excluded. For example, in the first decade of the twentieth century there was a fascinating series of images produced by Grossmiths for a number of exotic perfumes, including Shem-el-Nessim, Phul-nana and Wana-Ranee. These images exploited the interest in an Orientalist exoticism, but they are also interesting for the shifts in the image of the black woman that are represented. For example, the early Shem-el-Nessim images depict harem-like settings with white women in exotically dressed clothes as the protagonists. Through the 1900s and 1910s, however, the image continuously changes, as the advertisements focus more and more on the black servant/slave who was in the background of the previous images. She becomes Shem-el-Nessim, first carrying the bottle to the white woman, but finally standing on her own as the embodiment of the perfume and its exotic scent. While it would have been interesting to pursue a discussion of these images, the case studies in the following chapters were chosen to emphasise the value of uncovering the production contexts of images, although I realise that it is not always possible to analyse advertising images in this way.

Soap advertising enables an exploration of the soap companies' interests in the palm oil resources of West Africa. Cocoa advertising reveals company interests in raw materials, as well as specific kinds of labour conditions. Tea marketing enables company interests in particular kinds of production methods to be explored as well as the way in which an identity for Empire tea was formed. Tobacco advertising reveals the government's increasing involvement in pushing commercial companies to support Empire buying, as well as the response of commercial companies to the promotion of Empire. Finally the corporate advertising chapter reveals the interests of developing corporate firms and their anxiety over the loss of Empire markets.

The decision to end the evaluation of images in 1960 is due to the fact that advertising changed dramatically after this period. The civil rights movement in America and anti-colonial struggles had also produced a variety of new images that make it essential to discuss a series of other issues for which there was no space in the book. In spite of these changes, the conclusion argues for the value of giving attention to the production context of images today.

Notes

1 D. Kellner, *Media Culture: Cultural Studies, Identity and Politics Between the Modern and the Postmodern* (London, 1995), p. 32.
2 J. MacKenzie, *Propaganda and Empire: The Manipulation of British Public Opinion 1880–1960* (Manchester, 1984), p. 16.
3 *Black Markets: Images of Black People in Advertising and Packaging in Britain 1880–1990* (Manchester, 1990).
4 The exhibitions included: 'Ethnic Notions: Black Images in the White Mind', Berkeley Arts Centre, Berkeley, California, 1982; 'Ethnic Images in Advertising', Balch Institute for Ethnic Studies, Pennsylvania, 1984; 'Les Noirs, Tête d'affiches à partir de la collection de Marie-Christine Peyiere et Jean-Barthelemi Debost', Nanterre, 1985; 'Zaire 1885–1985: Cents ans de regards Belges', Bruxelles, 1985; 'Das Exotische Plakat – Exotische Welten, Europaische Phantasien', Gallerie de Ville de Stuttgart, 1987; 'Négripub: L'Image des Noirs dans la publicité depuis un siècle', Bibliothèque Forney, Paris, 1987; 'White on Black: Images of Blacks in Western Popular Culture', Koninklijk Institut voor de Tropen, Amsterdam, 1989; and 'Black Markets: Images of Black People in Advertising and Packaging 1880–1990', Cornerhouse, Manchester, 1990.
5 J. N. Pieterse, *White on Black: Images of Africa and Blacks in Western Popular Culture* (New Haven, 1992).
6 The golliwog, for example, was referred to as part of Britain's national heritage by the marketing director of Robertson's after a Greater London Council campaign against it in 1985.
7 C. Bolt, *Victorian Attitudes to Race* (London, 1971).
8 Pieterse, *White on Black*, see Chapter 3: 'Slavery and Abolitionism'.
9 *Ibid.*, p. 86.
10 W. O'Barr, *Culture and the Ad: Exploring Otherness in the World of Advertising* (Boulder, 1994).
11 R. Dyer (ed.), *Gays and Film* (London, 1977), p. 30.
12 For discussions of racism and 'race' theory, see R. Miles, *Racism* (London, 1989); for details about 'race' theory in the Victorian era and its relationship to Victorian attitudes to class, see D. Lorimer, *Colour, Class and the Victorians: English Attitudes to the Negro in the Mid-Nineteenth Century* (Leicester, 1978); for details about the way in which racism is articulated in post-war Britain, see P. Gilroy, *There Ain't no Black in the Union Jack* (London, 1987).
13 For general historical surveys of Empire and popular culture see MacKenzie, *Propaganda and Empire*, and J. MacKenzie (ed.), *Imperialism and Popular Culture* (Manchester, 1987).
14 E. Said, *Orientalism* (London, 1978). Although Said's text is often heralded as a new direction in thinking, scholars such as V. Kiernan and K. M. Pannikar had already discussed the relationship between representation and power. Said referred to Pannikar in both *Orientalism* and his lecture and essay 'Orientalism Reconsidered'. What was new in Said's book was his use of Foucault in developing an understanding of the relationship between knowledge and power.

15 J. MacKenzie's critique of Said in *Orientalism: History, Theory and the Arts* (Manchester, 1997) unfortunately does not address this crucial issue of the relationship between knowledge and power and has been challenged by sociologists.

16 L. Nochlin, 'The Imaginary Orient', *Art in America* (May 1983). Other texts on Orientalist imagery that have been influenced by Said's approach include R. Kabbani, *Europe's Myth of Orient* (London, 1986); G. Tawadros, 'Foreign Bodies: Art History and the Discourse of Nineteenth-Century Orientalist Art', *Third Text*, 3/4 (Spring/ Summer 1988), pp. 51–68; A. Ramamurthy, 'Orientalism and the Paisley Pattern', in C. Boydell and M. Schoeser (eds), *Disentangling Textiles* (London, 2003).

17 M. Alloula, *The Colonial Harem* (Manchester, 1987).

18 J. Ryan, *Picturing Empire: Photography and the Visualisation of the British Empire* (London, 1997). A variety of texts discuss colonial photography, including E. Edwards, *Anthropology and Photography 1860–1920* (New Haven, 1992); D. Bate, 'Photography and the Colonial Vision', *Third Text*, 10 (Spring 1990), pp. 53–60; J. Ryan, 'Imperial Landscapes: Photography, Geography and British Overseas Exploration 1858–1872', in M. Bell *et al.* (eds), *Geography and Imperialism* (Manchester, 1995); D. Green, 'Photography and Anthropology: The Technology of Power', *Ten 8*, 1:14 (1984), pp. 30–7; also see special issue on photography, *African Arts* (October 1990).

19 E. Shohat and R. Stam, *Unthinking Eurocentrism: Multiculturalism and the Media* (London, 1994).

20 A. Coombes, *Reinventing Africa: Museum, Material Culture and the Popular Imagination* (New Haven, 1994); also see A. Coombes, 'For God and England: Contributions to an Image of Africa in the First Decade of the Twentieth Century', *Art History*, 8:4 (December 1985), pp. 453–66.

21 A. Ahmad, 'Orientalism and After: Ambivalence and Metropolitan Location in the Work of Edward Said', in *In Theory: Classes, Nations, Literature* (London, 1992). Also see work by Ranajit Guha and the Subaltern Studies collective, and B. Parry, 'Resistance Theory: Theorising Resistance', in F. Barker *et al.* (eds), *Colonial Discourse/Postcolonial Theory* (Manchester, 1994), pp. 172–6.

22 H. Bhabha, 'The Other Question: Stereotype, Discrimination and the Discourse of Colonialism', in *The Location of Culture* (London, 1994), p. 66.

23 D. Bailey, 'Re-thinking Black Representations', *Ten 8*, 31 (1988), pp. 36–49 and S. Hall, 'The Spectacle of the "Other"', in S. Hall (ed.), *Representation: Cultural Representations and Signifying Practices* (London, 1997) provide useful introductions to this issue.

24 B. Parry, 'Problems in Current Theories of Colonial Discourse', *Oxford Literary Review*, 9:1–2 (1987), p. 34.

25 Laura Chrisman, 'The Imperial Unconscious? Representations of Imperial Discourse', in P. Williams and L. Chrisman, *Colonial Discourse and Post-colonial Theory: A Reader* (London, 1993), pp. 499–500.

26 N. Thomas, *Colonialism's Culture: Anthropology, Travel and Government* (Cambridge, 1994), p. 51.

27 A. McClintock, *Imperial Leather: Race, Gender and Sexuality in the Colonial Contest* (London, 1995); T. Richards, *Commodity Culture in Victorian England: Advertising and Spectacle 1851–1914* (London, 1991).

28 See R. Barthes, *Mythologies* (London, 1967); R. Barthes *Image, Music, Text* (London, 1977); J. Williamson, *Decoding Advertisements* (London, 1978); R. Goldman, *Reading Ads Socially* (London, 1992); K. T. Frith (ed.), *Undressing the Ad: Reading Culture in Advertising* (New York, 1997).

29 D. Slater, 'Marketing Mass Photography', in H. Davis and P. Walton (eds), *Language, Image, Media* (Oxford, 1983), p. 258.

30 D. Nye, *Image Worlds: Corporate Identities at General Electric 1890–1930* (Cambridge MA, 1985), pp. 52–4.

31 C. Squires, 'The Corporate Year in Pictures', in R. Bolton (ed.), *The Contest of Meaning: Critical Histories of Photography* (Cambridge MA, 1994), pp. 206–18;

S. Stein, 'The Composite Photographic Image and the Composition of Consumer Ideology', *Art Journal*, 41 (Spring 1981), pp. 39–45.

32 K. Marx and F. Engels, *The German Ideology*, quoted in G. Murdock and P. Golding, 'Capitalism, Communication and Class Relations', in J. Curran *et al.*, *Mass Communication and Society* (London, 1977), p. 39.

33 Richards, *Commodity Culture*, see introduction pp. 1–16.

34 R. Williams, 'Advertising: The Magic System', in *Problems in Materialism and Culture* (London, 1980), pp. 177–8.

35 P. Baran and P. Sweezy, *Monopoly Capital: An Essay on the American Economic and Social Order* (London, 1968), p. 122.

36 A. Briggs, *Victorian Things* (London, 1988), p. 124.

37 E. S. Turner, *The Shocking History of Advertising* (London, 1952), quoted in Baran and Sweezy, *Monopoly Capital*, p. 123.

38 J. Curran, 'Capitalism and the Control of the Press', in Curran *et al.* (eds), *Mass Communication*, pp. 213–24.

39 A. Higgins, 'Hungry Russia Feeds on Glamour of Ads', *The Guardian*, 26 August 1994, p. 10.

40 E. J. Hobsbawm, *The Age of Empire 1875–1914* (London, 1987), p. 44.

41 A. Brewer, *Marxist Theories of Imperialism: A Critical Survey* (London, 1980), p. 102.

42 See *ibid.*; V. I. Lenin, *Imperialism: The Highest Stage of Capitalism* (Peking, 1975).

43 R. Hilferding, *Finance Capital* (London, 1981), pp. 452–4, quoted in Brewer, *Marxist Theories*, p. 98.

44 P. J. Cain and A. G. Hopkins, *British Imperialism: Innovation and Expansion* (London, 1993).

45 Hilferding, *Finance Capital*, p. 454.

46 W. F. Haug, *Critique of Commodity Aesthetics: Appearance, Sexuality and Advertising in Capitalist Society* (Cambridge, 1986), p. 25.

47 *Ibid.*, p. 32.

48 K. Marx, *Capital* (London, 1954), Vol. 1, p. 76.

49 *Ibid.*, p. 77.

50 Marx distinguished between the labour time during which the worker actually earned the money which the boss gave him and the surplus labour time during which the worker worked not for himself but for the boss's profit.

51 For a discussion on essence and appearance in *Capital* see N. Geras, 'Essence and Appearance: Aspects of Fetishism in Marx's Capital', *New Left Review*, 65 (January–February 1971), pp. 69–86.

52 S. Jhally, *Codes of Advertising: Fetishism and the Political Economy of Meaning in the Consumer Society* (London, 1990), pp. 35–8.

53 Richards, *Commodity Culture*, p. 1.

54 *Ibid.*, pp. 1–3.

55 Jhally, *Codes of Advertising*, p. 50.

56 *Ibid.*, p. 51.

57 W. Leiss *et al.*, *Social Communication in Advertising: Persons, Products and Images of Well-being* (Scarborough Ontario, 1988), pp. 123–4.

CHAPTER TWO

Soap advertising, the trader as civiliser and the scramble for Africa

This chapter will explore the effect of the specific material interests of soap manufacturers, their consumers, and the general political climate of the period on the representation of black people. While soap was by no means the only product which represented Empire and black people in late nineteenth-century advertising, soap companies made the most extensive use of their image during this period. Firstly, it is clear that advertisers could find no better way to exaggerate the cleaning potential for their product than by depicting a black person – the classic symbol in Victorian England of the uncivilised and uncleansed soul – washing. Product qualities which advertisers emphasised during this period can be seen to have been racialised on many commodities. In particular, soap, boot polish, starch, grate polish, or any other commodity where the issue of black, white and cleanliness came to the fore, exploited the theme of colour. This was an age in which cleanliness was seen as next to godliness, although, as William Fraser noted, this was very much in the middle-class scheme of things. 'Godliness was not really a pursuit to which the working class devoted much attention. Cleanliness was hardly possible and not often a great concern in the working class home.'[1] Yet the consumption of soap and other cleaning products did increase throughout the century amongst all sections of society.[2] The desire for a clean home was not just one of morality, but also one of necessity. The number of ailments now affecting working-class urban families had increased dramatically because of the increased dirt and grime of industrial production, as well as the unhealthy working conditions and the new chemicals with which many were forced to work.

Soap also provides us with a classic example of a product which was simply bought by weight before the 1880s, but through increased competition developed into a branded product in the late nineteenth century. Prior to the 1880s, the industry was particularly local in nature, with companies selling their product in a small district. For example, R. C. Hudson, established in West Bromwich since 1837, only sold his dry soap powder in the Midlands, while John Knight and A. and F. Pears served the South-East.[3] William Lever changed all this with the establishment of the well-advertised, wrapped and branded Sunlight Soap, which was sold as a national product. Lever launched Sunlight in 1875, and by 1887 it was the largest single brand of soap in England.[4] In 1886 Lever was producing 3,000 tons of Sunlight Soap. The following year production had increased over three times to 9,669 tons, and in 1888 it grew again to 14,183 tons, with a further increase a couple of years later after full production had started at Port Sunlight. Through the 1890s production continued to rise between 3,000 and 5,000 tons a year.[5] Lever's encroachment on to the market of other manufacturers forced them to advertise. The change in the industry, however, must not be understood as the result of one individual. Growth in production and consumption of soap during the nineteenth century was at a rate which could not be sustained and inevitably led to conglomeration. As Wilson notes, by the turn of the century there was plenty of evidence that the period of expansion, if not entirely over, was moving to a close.[6]

The expansion in the soap industry was also linked to the commercial exploitation of Africa and other tropical countries. This is another reason why soap companies may have exploited the image of the African so heavily in their advertising. A lot of previous soap had been made of tallow, but as vegetable soaps became more popular, the demand for these oils rose rapidly. For tropical West Africa, the key ingredients in trade with the West during this period were palm oil and palm kernel oil. Trade in such goods also represented the transition from slave trading to that of 'legitimate commerce'. The kingdom of Dahomey, for instance, switched directly from slave trading with Europeans to a trade in palm oil and palm kernel oil. This shift in the primary commodity of trading relations may be one of the reasons why soap advertisers exploited the theme of trade as a civilising force so extensively during this period.

The soap advertisements under discussion all date between 1884 and 1919. Most of the images are representations of Africans, although some are more generalised. The images seem to reflect two distinct periods and attitudes, which parallel the phases of colonisation that Michael Crowder describes in *West Africa under Colonial Rule*.[7] He describes the period 1885–1900 as the 'period of conquest and occupation', since it covers the frenzied activity by European powers in their 'scramble for Africa' and the partition of the world. The period 1900–19 he describes as the 'period of pacification', when European powers tried to set up structures of control in their newly appropriated territories. This period of pacification also saw the consolidation of various commercial interests in West Africa. Although certain advertising images span both periods, we can perceive changing perceptions towards Africans by separating the two periods.

Most of the advertisements discussed in the first period were produced by Pears. Was Pears' belief in the ideology of Empire stronger, or did it simply exploit this ideology more effectively than other companies, just as it did the possibilities of the advertising medium? It is difficult to know, but in an attempt to maintain Pears' own markets from the rivalry of Lever, Knight's and others, Thomas Barratt produced an advertising campaign which has become legendary. By the mid 1880s, Thomas Barratt's advertising campaign promoted Pears' Soap not just nationally, but abroad in the USA, Australia, India and elsewhere. When Barratt joined his father-in-law's firm in the mid 1870s, the company was worth £7,000. Less than twenty years later, in 1892, Pears became a limited liability company with a capital of £810,000. It is worth noting that both Barratt and William Lever kept a particularly tight rein on the marketing side of their businesses. This highlights the crucial role of advertising during the period.

This chapter will concentrate on the racist, colonial and imperialist aspects of the identity which Pears and other soap companies constructed during this period, although we need to recognise this as part of an overall identity created for a product. It is also important to remember that the representations of black 'cleansing' and the other dehumanising images of the late Victorian era were not produced without criticism. Even amongst imperialists there were conflicting attitudes and opinions. Advertisements therefore can never be viewed as passive or simply reflective of society, but as part of a process through which ideologies are moulded and re-constructed continuously.[8]

The period of conquest and occupation

The advertisements during the period of conquest and occupation cannot be regarded as representing a coherent ideological position on colonial policy by soap companies, but highlight the shifting attitudes to Africa by merchants and traders during this period.[9]

The Berlin Conference and the white-washing of Africa
In December 1884, during the period of the Berlin Conference, which ran from November 1884 to February 1885, Pears' Soap released an advertisement in *The Graphic* depicting a black boy washing himself white (Figure 1). This was the earliest image that can be located of

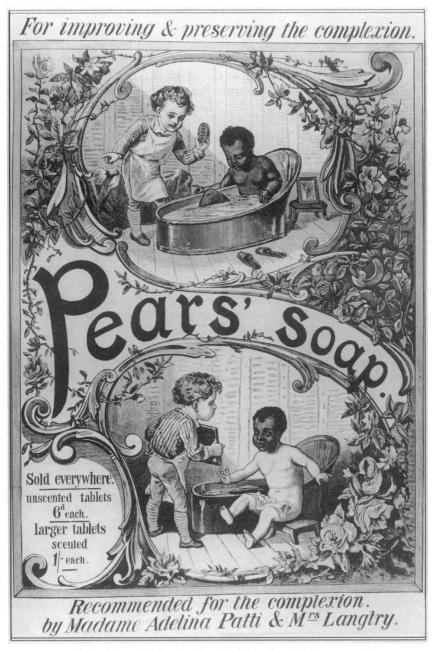

1 Pears' Soap advertisement, *The Graphic*, 18 December 1884

soap advertising which depicts the black person. The image must have been extremely popular since numerous copies of it exist in archives around the country, both in black and white and in colour. The popularity of this image also led to the whitened African boy being included in a composite advertisement on the back cover of a Pears' Christmas Annual from the first decade of this century. Other soap companies such as Dreydopel and Sunlight also later released advertisements on this theme.

The Pears image re-works the brutal European partition of Africa into one carried out with African complicity. Framed in roses and baroque decor, the black child having scrubbed himself white sits in the second frame amazed at his white body. The colour of the water in the second frame is also dirty, maintaining the notion of black skin as dirt. The advertisement does not so much relate the black boy's desire to be white and the powerful formula of Pears' Soap, as much as the white boy's desire and will to turn this child white. The white boy holds the soap in the first frame and appears to talk to the black child in an authoritative manner. The white child does not sit in the bath with the black child where they could then have appeared as equals, but remains next to the tub and fully clothed – a symbol which has frequently denoted 'civilisation' in European imagery. Interestingly, the slippers which appear next to the tub in the first frame are not worn by the black child in the second frame. In both frames the black child appears to be slightly smaller than the white one and is pictured physically below him, an obvious visual indication of the white child's importance and authority. In both frames it is the white boy who holds the commodities of soap and mirror. There seems no doubt that it is his bathroom that the black child has stepped into. It is his tub, mirror and soap that they use to carry out what is set up as a childish prank.

However, it is not just through possession that a sense of power and authority is established. This bathroom scene can also be seen as the white child's laboratory, with the black child as the object of his experiment. The white boy's apron on top of his clothes as well as being a 'familiar fetish of domestic purity' also acts as an indicator of the laboratory status of the bathroom – re-affirming Europe as the embodiment of science and rationality. Also, the black boy's face, 'for Victorians the seat of rational individuality and self-consciousness – remains stubbornly black', as McClintock has noted.[10] The exposure of this advertisement in December 1884 must have affirmed, in an accessible and popular style, the right of Europe to determine Africa's fate.

While the extended use of this advertisement over ten to fifteen years makes its general racist theme the most immediately striking, the significance of its release in the middle of the Berlin Conference should not be underestimated. By its exposure in December 1884, these two boys represent Europe and Africa. The washing and teaching act as visual metaphors for what came to be called the 'white man's burden', as well as for Europe's desire to control Africa politically and economically. As Crowder has noted:

> Britain's commercial interest in West Africa was a dual one: first the exploration of new outlets for her manufactured goods; second the securing of a commodity, palm oil, produced on the west coast that was vital to her industrial expansion. The first was undertaken through the exploration of the interior and the subsequent financing of expeditions such as those sent up the Niger in 1832, 1841 and 1854. The second, the securing of adequate supplies of palm-oil, which was essential as a lubricant for industrial machinery, for candles, and making soap, which now had become all the more necessary for a nation notoriously averse to washing because of the dirt produced by industry, was achieved by the Anti-Slavery patrol.[11]

This advertisement appears to affirm both these roles. The white boy can be seen as the symbol of the merchant-trader, selling British goods and values across Africa. The teaching metaphor also affirms Pears' role as a trader supporting the new trades in 'legitimate commerce'. It is clear from Crowder's analysis that British soap manufacturers had a direct interest in the main development in 'legitimate commerce' in West Africa and the Niger Delta in particular. Although there are no business records for Pears before 1892 to help establish if Pears did have particular investments in the area, this Pears advertisement lauds a policy of paternalism and British involvement in West African development. Despite the lack of specific knowledge on Pears, it is certainly the case that *all* soap companies in Britain had an interest in British control over the key trade in the Niger Delta – the trade in palm and palm kernel oil – since they depended on these raw materials for production. Hobsbawm mentions the soap manufacturers specifically in *The Age of Empire*, arguing that 'soap manufacturers, exploiting the market which first demonstrated to the full the capacities of the new advertising industry, looked to the vegetable oils of Africa'.[12]

British influence in the Niger region was secured through British control of trade under Goldie's newly amalgamated United Africa Company.[13] This Pears advertisement can be seen as a celebratory statement from a company whose interests were tied to this trade. The Niger Navigation Act, which secured Britain's influence over the Niger Delta, was discussed by the conference in December and accepted on 18 December 1884. This advertisement formed a full-page spread in the Christmas issue of *The Graphic*. If we consider the advertisement in the light of this history, we can view the washing of the black boy's body, but not his head, as a reference to the form of influence established by Britain – the protectorate. Whereas French and German negotiators at the conference made no distinction between annexation and protection, Britain had outlined the importance of 'the right of the aboriginal or other actual inhabitants to their own country, with no further assumption of territorial rights than is necessary to maintain the paramount authority and discharge the duties of an occupying power'.[14]

In this sense, Britain did not want total political sovereignty over the region, which it regarded as an unnecessary expense, but rather control over its trade. As Crowder noted, the British government, 'reluctant to the last to extend her hegemony over West Africa ended up by following the interests her private citizens had established for her'.[15] In their turn, the traders were happy to maintain an informal system of control, since it inevitably meant less government taxes and trading controls. In an attempt to maintain their trading interests, agents of the National African Company did obtain treaties with local rulers in which they surrendered their country 'in perpetuity' while remaining heads of state. In this sense, the naked African boy's body in the advertisement can be regarded as the body politic, with the head remaining black or African, but the body or the state coming under white or European control.

The theme of the black boy washing himself white has a history which dates back to 711 when Gibral Tariq invaded the Iberian peninsula. In the same year, a chronicler wrote about how one of the black men in the Muslim army was captured by the Goths, who had never seen a black man before and tried to scrub off his colour. Later in Elizabethan England (during early European expansion and colonisation of the Americas) there was a growing feeling of prejudice and discontent. It was at this point that the phrase 'to wash a black man is to labour in vain' began to be used across Europe.[16] The power of the Pears image rests both in its intertextuality with past representations and in its contemporary poignancy.

The fame and popularity of this Pears image constitutes what could be described as a 'cult' advertisement. Its impact on the national imagination can be found through countless references to the advertisement by journalists, song writers and others. Some of these references can be found in the cuttings volumes of the Pears archive. They could not all have been written or commissioned by Pears. An article in the *European Mail* on 1 March 1889, for example, refers to the existence of a 'white negro' in Georgia and ends with the comment that 'it may be expected that a number of Howell's countrymen will earnestly devote themselves to endeavouring to find out how it is done. Perhaps Pears Soap has something to do with it.' The ending is simply a cheap journalistic comment, but it emphasises the impact of the above advertisement on the popular culture of the period. References even found their way into song. In Harry Hunter's 'Poor Little Liza', four black girls meet their deaths in various ways (another popular theme that was played upon in this period). The fate of little Liza is recounted as follows:

> And as for 'Liz, poor little Liza,
> I regret to say,
> She got two cakes of Pears soap
> And washed herself away.[17]

These lines end the chorus, and would therefore have been repeated four or five times, with applause and participation from the crowd. There could be no more powerful apology for imperial expansion than the accepted projection in British popular culture of an image of Africans desiring to be white and in effect accepting their inferiority.

It is important to remember that it was not simply this advertisement that had a broad popularity. Pears' advertising as a whole seems to have captivated a growing body of consumers, not used to the novelties of advertising. The cuttings volumes at the Pears archive contain a number of poems and ideas for advertisements sent in by the public and illustrate the sense of identity which a body of consumers must have had with the product. These writers must have belonged to the growing group of lower-middle-class consumers who identified with the spirit of capitalism. The working classes would certainly not have had the time to indulge in such activities and the bourgeoisie would almost definitely not have bothered with such trivialities. The themes of Pears' advertising campaigns reflect the anxieties and aspirations of a growing group of consumers – the lower middle classes. As Crossick mentions, this group of consumers was central in developing a broad commercial provision, because of the size, regularity and relative security of their incomes.[18] Pears' Transparent Soap was certainly a bath soap which would have appealed to the growing group of white-collar workers in Britain obsessed with their concern for respectability. The notion of cleanliness as next to godliness was constantly evoked in Pears' advertising, along with a religiosity and morality which would have elided completely with this class's constructed codes.[19] The lower-middle-class housewife's consumption of these products could act as proof of her own civilised state against what was represented in advertisements as the vain attempts of the black child for whiteness. Finally, a sense of snobbery and superiority could so easily be encouraged by Pears' racist and nationalistic imagery. As Richard Price noted, the lower middle classes were key participants in Empire rowdyism and jingoism,[20] and this too formed part of the identity of Pears.

Through the poems and letters in the Pears cuttings volumes, it is also possible to see the broader cultural associations which consumers and journalists made with advertisements, including those of the one discussed above. A poem in *Truth* Christmas Number 1887, for example, describes a Rajah who disagrees with English society's treatment of women, believing that European women abuse their liberty. One day the Rajah sees a Pears' Soap advertisement:

> Possess'd of these views, then, the Rajah one day,
> In the course of his travels observed with dismay
> A placard which showed to his terrified sight
> A black boy who'd been by Pears soap washed quite white.

The Rajah rushes to send a telegram home as he has sent Pears' Soap along with other toiletries for his wives and fears that 'it should turn their skin white' and 'make all their action like white women's too'.[21] It is clear that the action of turning white also acts to represent the notion of turning non-Europeans into brown white men and women, i.e. men and women who would adopt the cultural values and manners of the West. As the above Pears advertisement indicates, the export of goods and commodities was read by contemporaries as representing the export of European ideas and practices – the export, in their terms, of 'civilisation'.

Pears, racist ideology and the conflict over African agency
In the same year as the poem in *Truth*, Pears released a series of advertisements which reaffirmed the relationship between Pears, Empire-building and the spread of European cultural practices. In May 1887, 'An unpacific yarn' appeared in *The Graphic*, drawing on Livingstone's tenet that 'these two pioneers of civilisation – Christianity and commerce should ever be inseparable' (Figure 2).[22] The advertisement describes how Bishop Q of Wangaloo, a black bishop, works amongst 'his native flock', but although he is white on the inside because of his Christianity, he is black to the eye and loses the support of his flock when Bishop Brown of Monkeytown – a white bishop – comes to visit. In his sorrow, he goes to Bishop Brown, who promises him that he will be able to change his colour through using Pears' Soap. Brown gives Wangaloo a couple of bars of Pears' Soap, through which he turns white and gains back the faith and support of his

AN UNPACIFIC YARN.

THE Bishop Q., of Wangaloo, in Unpacific Seas,
   A Service fair, conducted there, in dignity and ease;
   Though white within, and free from sin, it was a fact that he
Unto the eye, externally, was black as black could be.

The Bishop Q., of Wangaloo, beloved was of all,
The Unpacific residents, his people great and small,
They often said, "A Bishop bred, and born of native stock
Is fitter than another man to guide a native flock."

But Oh! Alas! a dreadful pass he came to on the day
That Bishop Brown, of Monkeytown, a visit came to pay;
Whose features fair, and silver hair, their fancy quickly gain'd,
Whose tuneful voice, and learning choice, affection soon obtained.

The natives all, both great and small, admitted with a groan,
That Bishop Brown, of Monkeytown, was better than their own;
That though they knew that Bishop Q. was pure and free from guile,
He must arrange to make a change, and leave his native isle.

Then Bishop Q., of Wangaloo, his visage wet with tears,
Repair'd to Brown, of Monkeytown, to intimate his fears
That base and rude ingratitude, and unbecoming slight,
Would bleach with care, his agéd hair, because he wasn't white.

Said Bishop Brown, of Monkeytown, "Although a grievous case,
I'll guarantee, if you'll agree, to change your nigger face,
That you'll obtain their love again, so buoy yourself with hope,
And I'll give you a cake or two of **PEARS' Transparent Soap.**"

Then Bishop Q., of Wangaloo (his present safe to hand),
With visage bright, and spirits light, as any in the land,
And grateful heart, did now depart upon his homeward path,
And arm'd with hope, and **PEARS' Soap**, repair'd unto his bath.

✳ ✳ ✳ ✳ ✳ ✳ ✳ ✳
✳ ✳ ✳ ✳ ✳ ✳ ✳

With bow polite, complexion white, and hands of lily hue,
And noble mien, he did convene that Unpacific crew:
That sable flock of native stock, who, frighten'd and amaz'd,
For pardon to the Bishop Q. their supplications raised.

And thus with hope, and **PEARS' Soap**, and bath and water plain,
The love of all, both great and small, the Bishop did regain.
And now without a care or doubt, his features wreath'd in smiles,
Lives Bishop Q., of Wangaloo, in Unpacific Isles.

MORAL.

That cleanliness and godliness go ever hand in hand;
From maxims sage, of greatest age, we're led to understand.
The former clasp within your grasp (and for the latter hope),
By getting through a cake or two of **PEARS'** Transparent **Soap.**

And when you've tried, you will decide, without a single doubt,
That such a sweet and fragrant treat you'll never be without:
That all around will ne'er be found a maker that can cope,
In purity and quality with **PEARS' Transparent Soap.**

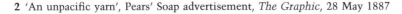

2 'An unpacific yarn', Pears' Soap advertisement, *The Graphic*, 28 May 1887

[33]

flock. In the moral at the end, Pears associates the use of the soap with achieving not simply cleanliness but also spiritual satisfaction:

> That cleanliness and godliness go ever hand in hand;
> From maxims sage, of greatest age, we're led to understand.
> The former clasp within your grasp (and for the latter hope),
> By getting through a cake or two of Pears' Transparent Soap.

The advertisement manages to condense a series of Victorian prejudices into one story. Africans are intentionally associated with monkeys, asserting the idea of them as the missing link. In the images, the Bishop of Wangaloo appears to have taken on some of the distorted features of the minstrel tradition, which Frederick Douglas had criticised earlier in the same year as 'Ethiopian singers who disfigure and distort the features of the Negro and burlesque his language and manners in a way to make him appear to thousands as more akin to apes than men'.[23] Commerce and Christianity are also both seen as white attributes since it is the white bishop who acts as a kind of saviour distributing the commodity.

Pears, however, did not simply reflect racist and colonial attitudes through this advertisement, but actually entered into contemporary debates, about (a) whether black ministers should act as bishops or not, and (b) the kind of colonial rule or 'influence' that Britain should maintain in the Niger. Pears in this way was part of a racist and imperial ideology in the making. In 1864 Samuel Ajai Crowther had been appointed as the Bishop of Niger. This marked the high point of Africans being promoted to positions of leadership in the church and reflected the Church Missionary Society (CMS) policy under the leadership of Henry Venn of establishing a 'native' church on the Niger run by African missionaries. The all-African Niger Mission was seen not simply as a means of Christian conversion, but as 'a training-ground in responsibility and organisation' for a kingdom that would eventually arise in the Niger area and 'hold a position amongst the states of Europe'.[24] The growth of racist theories in Europe after 1860 eventually undermined the idea of an imperial partnership. By the 1870s and 1880s conflicting opinions existed in the CMS and the belief that Africans were incapable of running the church gained stronger hold. Crowther and other high-ranking black pastors then came under attack. The CMS eventually sent white missionaries to 'aid' Crowther in his work, but constant criticism of his mission led to his resignation in 1890. Pears' interest in this debate was not simply ideological, but also material. Like other major soap companies, it was dependent on the palm oil trade from the Niger. The Niger Mission had been directly involved in the development of trade, with a policy of supporting British capital through African agency. However, with the formation of the United Africa Company (the forerunner of the Royal Niger Company), the senior African managers and agents of firms that joined the amalgam were dismissed. Eventually, in 1886, when the Company received its charter from the government, African traders and others were forced to obtain licences if they wished to trade on the river. These men, whom Goldie, the head of the Royal Niger Company, regarded as 'disreputable', were brothers, close relatives and friends of Crowther and others at the Mission. The Mission necessarily sided with the African traders in disputing allegations of malpractice.[25] Within the increasing climate of scientific racism, the CMS, especially Hutchinson, the new Lay Secretary, tended to support Goldie against the African missionaries and from this time onwards the position of Crowther and others was constantly undermined. With the entanglement of trade and missionary activity, Pears' support for the white missionaries (who hold access to the commodity of soap in the advertisement) also expresses support for European control of the Niger trade. In the advertisement, however, the supporters of Crowther are not alienated since the black bishop is not actually displaced, a ploy that is always important in the selling of commodities.

Wangaloo is created as the mimic of a white man, therefore obviously second rate. He also appears as a simple man smiling vapidly when happy or at the other extreme in tears. This ensures that the power of rationality and balance does not enter into his qualities even after he is washed white. The question of rationality was an issue which had been raised with regard to the capabilities of black ministers. A letter Crowther wrote towards the end of his career in 1884, when under immense pressure, indicates his own disillusionment and absorption of racist values by questioning African capabilities:

> The Europeans are better managers, their actions and report will be better confided in both out here and in England. We shall be content to work under their direction as in former years. This impediment will not be removed from the way of the extension of the mission.[26]

Pears first used this image in *The Graphic* in May 1887 and continued to use it during the period of the debate. It appeared in *The Graphic* in September 1889 and in January 1890 just before Crowther's resignation. Pears also used the advertisement in missionary magazines, although *The Banner of Faith*, published by the Church Extension Association, eventually decided that it was in bad taste, and banned the advertisement after its first appearance in the magazine in 1888.[27] It is clear from this example that Pears was not simply reflecting dominant attitudes of the day, but was at the forefront in pushing a racist and jingoistic ideology. While it may have represented the views which had been absorbed by a section of Pears' consumers, it can also be seen to reflect Pears' own interests and support for imperial expansion.

It is worth noting that Pears' Soap washes Wangaloo completely white in this advertisement, unlike the baby in the bath three years earlier. By 1887, the National Africa Company had obtained a charter over the oil rivers area, which was supposed to protect the sovereignty of native chiefs. This protection was in fact often ignored if in conflict with the commercial interests of British merchants. By the end of 1886 a number of conflicts had developed between merchants and chiefs. When the more moderate Consul Hewett left the area on sick leave at the end of 1886, his role was assumed by H. H. Johnston, who had dreams of the oil rivers area becoming a crown colony. Johnston had very particular ideas about African coast peoples, whom he described as:

> by indigenous standards barbarians, who had acquired some crude wealth as traders and middlemen by exporting the produce of the interior, but had done so by erecting a barrier between the producers and the outside world, a barrier which in the interests both of commerce and of civilisation must be speedily broken down.[28]

His racist attitudes, along with his support of British merchant interests, led him into a particularly high-profile conflict with Chief Jaja of the House of Opobo, whom Johnston and most of the British merchants regarded as a cheat. Johnston eventually tricked Jaja into deportation and then set up his own illegal scheme of administration for the City States, arguing that 'the native chiefs do not seem competent to administer the affairs of their country in a wise and just manner'.[29]

'An unpacific yarn' was first published in *The Graphic* in May 1887, six months after Johnston had taken administrative control over the area and at a time when he was negotiating with the Foreign Office for the right to take more aggressive action (such as the deportation of Jaja) to protect British interests. The story appears to engage with conflicting colonial policy, by discussing how the people of Wangaloo first thought that a bishop 'bred and born of native stock' must be the best leader for them, until Bishop Brown visits and they then decide that a white ruler would be preferable. It is only when Wangaloo, with the guidance of Brown, makes himself completely white (i.e. bows entirely to European interests) that he is welcomed back by his own people and is able to return to his 'native isle'. The name of the bishop is also worth commenting on. Wangaloo is a name which suggests that he could be a wangler, a swindler, a cheat – attributes which the merchants associated with Jaja. While it is impossible to prove that Pears is making specific reference to Jaja, in advertisements such as these, it does appear to have been actively engaged in a discussion about what effective rule in West Africa would mean.

Imperial jingoism and the commodity as coloniser

Pears certainly appears to have felt and been perceived of as part and parcel of the process of British colonial expansion. Apart from the specific political contexts of the debates, the release of this advertisement in May 1887 coincided with Victoria's Golden Jubilee celebrations. These were the first Jubilee celebrations to take place, and as Richards notes, advertising 'made an all-out effort to reclaim this moribund official figure for the greater glory of the commodity',[30] despite the rumblings of anti-monarchical feelings still present in 1887.[31] Pears entered into this spectacle by employing the figure of Victoria in its advertising through these months as well as images of Empire. Pears featured four different advertisements that represented black people during the three months of celebrations. There is no other product advertised in *The Graphic* that released so many images of black people in such a short space of time at any point before the First World War.

With the triumphant jingoism of the Jubilee, Pears even managed to turn an instance of crushing defeat in the Sudan into one of victory (Figure 3).[32] This time it was not the black person's desire for whiteness that was constructed, but the vision of the black person's potential desire for Pears' Soap, which was portrayed through a scene of potential colonisation and potential Christian conversion. Titled 'Formula of British conquest: Pears' Soap in the Sudan', the advertisement depicts a group of dervishes looking at a rock inscribed with the message 'Pears' Soap is the best'. The caption informs us that the Pears slogan has been inscribed on the furthest point of British advancement. Military and commercial interests are represented as united. While it is clear that Pears is not going to set up shop in the Sudan, it is the potential market which is important, and has been described as the 'Formula of British conquest'.

The advertisement does not simply popularise the idea of expanding markets abroad, it seems to suggest the eventual culmination of this process through religious and visual references. The dervishes do not simply glance at the statement inscribed on the rocks but stand in awe. One points and implores his companions to look, another stands but his spear touches the ground as though at the point of surrender, while a third even kneels and holds his hands up, as though to

3 'Pears' Soap in the Soudan', Pears' Soap advertisement, *The Graphic*, 30 July 1887

protect himself from the glare of whiteness. These men in the desert reflect the biblical images of shepherds surrendering to the message from Angel Gabriel, with which Victorians would have been familiar. This was the moment at which Christianity was born amongst what Victorians would have seen as the lower orders of society. Here, concepts of 'race' and class are conflated, as was often the case in Victorian society.[33] The image is all the more poignant since the battle between the dervishes and the British was viewed as a religious war between Islam and Christianity. Yet what these men surrender to is Pears' Soap. Here Pears is the Messiah and the formula for conquest is again interpreted as that of commerce and Christianity – the success of which is implicit through the knowledge of the Christ story. Printed three years after the death of General Gordon and the defeat at Khartoum, the suggestion remains that what cannot be won in warfare may be achieved through the selling of commodities.

This advertisement for Pears' Soap in the Sudan, if newspapers of the time are to be believed, represents an actual episode which took place. In May 1885, articles in the *Pall Mall Gazette, Life, Printing Times, Birmingham Daily Post, Bristol Mercury, Fireside News* and *British and Colonial Druggist* all describe how a huge advertisement for Pears' Soap could be found on a rock in the Sudan. As *The Pall Mall Gazette* described:

> At Otao, about twenty miles from Suakin, on the Suakin and Berber Railway, stands a huge bunch of rocks about one hundred feet high, of somewhat conical form. Advantage is taken of the eminence of this rock for posting sentries; hence it is known as the 'Tower Rock'. On the face of this rock a huge advertisement, two hundred and fifty [sic] square, in letters of four and a half feet high, indicates that 'Pears Soap is the Best'.[34]

Soldiers in the field apparently painted this message. The spreading of commodity culture, and the symbol of Pears as civiliser and cleanser, had moved beyond passive representation. Although Pears cannot be seen as playing an active role in the field, the fetishised product had begun to represent the ideals of British fighters to the extent that the name of Pears is used like the flag as a mark of conquest. On 22 August 1885, *Illustrated London News* even depicted an engraving of the scene (Figure 4). It is interesting that a suggestion for an advertisement on the subject was actually made at this time by a soldier named W. C. Burnett who served in Africa.[35] He sent a sketch of the scene with his letter to Pears, although he wrote on the day after the engraving appeared in the *Illustrated London News*, from which he could easily have copied it.

4 'Private enterprise in the Soudan', engraving, *Illustrated London News*, 22 August 1885

In spite of what appears like journalistic jubilation at the event, it is hard to believe that this episode actually took place. It would have taken a lot of paint and a lot of organisation on the part of a group of soldiers to carry out such an act, which is presented as entirely spontaneous. All the newspapers also borrow their description of the scene from the *Pall Mall Gazette* – in some instances word for word. Yet was the whole episode, whether mythical or actual, constructed by Pears? If so, it was a marvellous publicity stunt and must have been set up for the press coverage it would elicit. The comments in the *Illustrated London News* suggest that it was an agent of Pears who carried out the action:

> As for the Illustration, copied from a photograph, it is proof that certain departments of English private enterprise, in the ubiquitous exercise of modern advertising ingenuity, continue to make their mark on the remotest scenes of warfare, and with character perhaps more enduring than the traces of our public policy in the Soudan.

What is also important about this episode is the way in which the press discussed it. *Fireside News*, for example, exuded the possibility of Pears as 'civiliser' and coloniser further, by referring back to that 'cult' advertisement of the black child washing himself:

> It might add further publicity to this announcement, among the dark-skinned Arabs, if the picture so familiar to us in England, 'Washing the Blackamoor White' were also placarded on the 'Tower Rock' of Otao.[36]

It was not the only newspaper to suggest this; *Illustrated London News* made a similar reference at the end of its article. Some of the articles about this inscription in the Sudan also illustrate how the British population was being encouraged to view Africa with violent aggression at the time. In *Life* magazine, for example, the journalist prefaced his description of the rock by saying: 'who shall say that the slaughter of the Arabs in the Soudan has no civilising effect upon them, or that the last Suakin expedition has been without result?'[37] In statements such as these, the deaths of thousands of Sudanese are trivialised.

Pears seems to have roused the imagination of the whole nation on ways in which the commodity and the advertiser could take a leading role in the colonisation process. In popularising this idea, Pears drew on and helped to develop the growing racist attitudes of the population, which were increasingly legitimised through the new disciplines of anthropology and ethnography. Pears' Sudan incident was not an isolated one, although it appears to be the first. Colonial agents appear to have used advertisements in unusual corners of the globe to enhance a view of their own superiority. *The Ceylon Independent* of 10 September 1889 recounts details of the advertisement 'You dirty boy!' being painted in a Kandyan village by an English pharmacist outside his dispensary. In this context, Pears' Soap is given medicinal value and put in the role of instructor, carrying out the role of the 'white man's burden' as it establishes its markets abroad. By 1889, Pears' Soap had an established market in many areas of the world, including the South Asian subcontinent, since there are details of imitation Pears' Soap being sold in India in March of the same year.[38] There are also details of Pears' message being planted by missionaries and soldiers in China,[39] British Guinea[40] and West Africa.[41] The theme of Pears as saviour and civiliser in remote corners of the earth was adopted by Pears in later advertisements. One such advertisement, titled 'How we were saved' (1893), uses the style of travel writing to suggest how some explorers saved themselves from a savage cannibalistic tribe in New Guinea by offering them Pears' Soap. The tribesmen find the use of Pears' Soap so exceptional that they implore the explorers at the end of the anecdote to return with more.

The place of advertising in the colonisation process should not be underestimated. An anecdote from Emil Torday's writings on his trip

[41]

to the Congo in 1905–6 provides us with an example of an advertisement being used by another type of colonial agent – the anthropologist:

> The villagers' confidence was not yet completely won, and I saw women and children peeping from behind houses, so I had recourse to a sovereign remedy in such cases – curiosity. Sitting down I took out an old number of *The Graphic* and began to inspect the pictures with much deliberation. Holding it so that they were visible to others too, I noticed that the crowd gradually crept nearer and nearer . . .
>
> Singularly enough, they did not seem to take in the picture as a whole, but recognised first a face, then a hat, then a stick, till at last they exclaimed: 'Why it's a man.' Undoubtedly the great success of the exhibition was the advertisement of Monkey Brand Soap; the monkey was instantly recognised, and when we went on to other pictures they continually begged me to turn back to that funny monkey, upon all the features of which they commented with the utmost appreciation.[42]

Torday, as an anthropologist-cum-trader employed by the Kasai Company, epitomises in his career the relationship between scholarly/cultural and commercial interests. His use of the Monkey Brand advertisement also provides a place for the advertisement in the process of conquest. Just like the Pears image, where the text below suggests puzzlement on the part of the dervishes with a visual representation of surrender, so Torday's anecdote suggests curiosity on the part of the villagers, with a metaphoric surrender through humour. The anecdote also highlights commodity culture as a measure of cultural superiority, which is also implied in the Pears image. Torday's use of images and advertisements as an anthropologist was not particular to him; in fact he mentions further on in his notes how he got the idea from Harry Johnston. At other points in his journals Torday noted how he used mechanical toys to break the ice and edge his way out of tense situations.[43] These act as classic examples of 'machines as the measure of man', as Michael Adas describes.[44] Here, Torday's use of the advertisement – also the product of machine production – represents not only technology as a measure but also Western capitalism.

If advertisements and advertisers were actually contributing to altering activity in the field, their involvement in colonisation was not simply ideological but to some degree actual. It is imperative for us to view these images as not just reflecting the ideology of the moment but also playing an active part in its creation, in this brutal phase of 'high imperialism'. Raymond Williams has commented on the violence of advertising and marketing language, with the use of militaristic vocabulary within the industry. People talk about 'campaigns', about 'cornering the market', about advertising as a 'weapon' in the 'hunt' and 'battle' for markets. These comments are particularly pertinent in this early context, where the military invasion of Africa coincided with the burgeoning of advertising's propaganda, and capitalism (as Hilferding noted) ceased to have even the illusion of being 'pacific and humanitarian', as the 'ideal of the grandeur and power of the state' rose.

The metaphoric relationship between military and commercial violence, which Williams describes, is captivated in an advertisement for Izal disinfectant in which Lord Kitchener with Izal as his armour is represented destroying the Sudanese. For Izal, the Sudanese are turned into no more than a bug that has to be exterminated. At the bottom a jingoistic caption reads: 'The dervish, like the microbe, is a nasty beast that tries to spread disease and death'. In classic colonial style, the victim of an atrocity is presented as the enemy. The picture reinforces the dervish as an undesirable monster, almost amoebic in shape, with human bones around him to enforce the idea of his savagery. The cleaning product uses the ultimate allusion: it expresses a desire not simply to clean or assimilate black people, but to ethnically cleanse the world.

Imperial exhibitions and the commodity as civiliser

Along with the violent images of aggression and conquest which Pears used during 'the scramble', there were also a number of simple, exotic images which served to sanitise Empire. These were also used during the Jubilee month, as well as on imperial catalogues that wished to present the Empire in cordial terms. Most of these images chose to represent black women, rather than men, since it was presumably easier to position women in exotic and subservient positions which suggested no threat and also naturalised hierarchies. In many of these images, women's sexuality is employed to deflect the aggression of Empire.

One of the Pears advertisements which appeared in *The Graphic* during the months of the Jubilee celebrations depicted a white and a black woman together in the clouds. The white woman reclines in a bed of flowers, while the black woman leans forward to fan her. The image of black servitude is naturalised and harmonised by its representation in a heaven-like scene, with four cherubs holding a bar of soap above the two women, almost like a halo. The two women are also distinguished in a variety of ways. The white woman's hair is loose, her left arm cradles her head and her body is turned towards the viewer suggesting availability, in a similar way to that of countless European paintings of the female nude. This woman, however, is covered by a white sheet and her eyes are closed as though in sleep, which suggests a purity which is enhanced by the heaven-like setting. The black woman by contrast is not positioned to suggest availability to the male viewer. Her position is entirely devoted to serving the white woman. This is not to suggest that she is not sexually objectified like the white woman, but that they are differentiated in terms of desirability. The black woman, for example, is denied the possibility of modesty by the drapery which only covers half her body, and her heavy jewellery carries associations of exoticism and savage sensuality within European imperial culture.

On imperial exhibition catalogues, Pears frequently lent an exotic and imperialised tone to advertisements which appeared English and domestic in flavour. For example, on the back cover of the brochure for the Adelaide Jubilee International Exhibition of 1887, Pears used a colour version of its famous advertisement of a mother scrubbing a young boy behind the ears, with the slogan 'You dirty boy!' (Figure 5). It appears that Pears, in paying for the back cover advertisement, must also have been able to negotiate certain demands for the front cover too, a position which advertisers today would certainly find enviable. In form, the front cover parallels the Pears advertisement. The mother on the back cover is dressed in a blue apron, reddish shawl and a white bonnet, and these become symbols of Britain and Empire when paralleled with the image of white Australia on the front cover. The young aboriginal boy on the front, draped paternalistically in the union jack, mirrors the boy whom the mother washes in the advertisement on the back (Figure 6). Finally, the oval picture of Queen Victoria with its yellow and red frame on the front matches the reddish bowl of Pears' Soap with its yellowish rim in the advertisement on the back cover. The relationship asserted between the two images affirms the notion of the imperial family and the act of washing becomes a symbol of imperial superiority. Pears' control over the whole cover design can be seen through the parcels to Australia's right on the front cover – the most prominent one, and the only one which is crated, is stamped with the name of Pears.

Pears certainly seemed to bask in the image of itself as an imperial producer, promoting 'civilisation' through the spread of commerce. It repeatedly exploited the possibilities of collapsing its identity with that of imperial exhibitions. Two other colonial exhibition catalogues in the John Johnston collection, the Orient at Olympia (1894) and Constantinople at Olympia (no date), enhance the image of Pears' Soap as an exotic and imperial product through formal and colour relationships that were made between the Pears advertisements on the back covers of the brochures and the front cover designs of these catalogues. In fact Pears appears to have gone to great lengths to ensure that it obtained the back cover of many of these catalogues. In 1900, it paid the largest amount for the insertion of an advertisement into a single issue of a publication for the period, when it agreed the fee of £2,500 to have a Pears advertisement on the back cover of all eighteen volumes of the Paris International Exhibition catalogue.[45]

It is significant that Pears never seemed to miss an opportunity to mark out its product as imperial and comment on the ideological debates of the day. In 1890 Pears launched itself into another expression of Empire jingoism. Stanley's return to England in the year after the Emin Pasha relief expedition released a wave of advertising and literature that exalted the spread of commodity culture. Absorbing the ideology of the moment like a parasite, Pears abandoned the Christianising images identifiable during the Jubilee season three years before, for the bare promotion of commodity culture. Stanley, unlike other imperialists, believed implicitly that the Empire would only be 'won' through the expansion of commodity culture.[46]

Between 1887 and 1890, Pears did not issue any new images representing black people in *The Graphic* until *The Graphic Stanley* commemoration magazine. Pears' full-paged colour advertisement on the back cover of this issue depicted an African man wearing a loin cloth and standing on a beach where a crate of Pears' Soap has been washed up on to the shore (Figure 7). The man holds a bar of soap, uncertain and curious as to what it is. He stands erect, the epitome of the 'noble savage' – a Man Friday. In the background there is a shipwreck, which must have carried the goods. Titled 'The birth of civilisation – a message from the sea', commodity culture appears as the only arena through which 'civilisation' is seen to be achievable in the image. Thomas Richards notes how the scene represented depicts the product in a transitory state – in a rite of passage. 'The clear indication', he notes, 'is that the bar of soap will not remain in its liminal limbo forever, and that before long, Africans like this one will learn just what exchange value means.'[47]

Apart from the representation of the commodity – and soap in particular – as civiliser, the image of the African as has been mentioned is the epitome of the 'noble savage', a representation of Africans that was frequently promoted by anti-slavery and missionary groups. In 1889 the Brussels Anti-Slavery Conference opened to discuss the obligations of European powers in the suppression of slavery within African society, an issue for which Henry Morton Stanley himself appears to have declared support before he left on his travels.[48] While the Brussels Act supposedly advocated Europe's moral obligations to Africa, it also provided ample justification for the imposition of direct European political control on all acquisitions including protectorates.

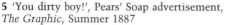

5 'You dirty boy!', Pears' Soap advertisement, *The Graphic*, Summer 1887

6 Front cover, Adelaide Jubilee International Exhibition brochure, 1887

I would like to consider, for a moment, not just the production of meaning by Pears but an oppositional understanding in order to explore the ideology of imperialist expansion further. Pears represents the soap in a rite of passage from pre-capitalist to capitalist modes of exchange. In doing so it ignores the history of trade, which has already taken place in Africa for centuries. Mercantile-capitalist relations were well established along various parts of the African coastline by the beginning of the nineteenth century, and the trade in palm oil increased steadily from 1,000 tons in 1810 to over 40,000 by 1855, with the trade stabilising at about 50,000 tons between the years 1860 and 1890.[49] Yet Pears, along with every other trader and explorer, was here perpetuating and creating an image of total African underdevelopment, which could only be broken by 'exchange' with the West. If commodities also hide the modes of production and the social relations they produce, as Marx discusses in his short section on the fetishism of commodities,[50] this advertisement enhances the fetishism further.

7 Pears' Soap advertisement, *The Graphic Stanley*,
30 April 1890

The bars of soap on the sand appear strewn like pebbles on a beach as
though emerging organically and devoid of labour.[51] In fact the title
enhances this idea. The birth of civilisation is suggested as coming out
of the sea, like a mythical and magical figure from Greek mythology.
In this way the concept of civilisation is mystified and naturalised.
Finally the advertisement only suggests African involvement in commodity consumption. The palm oil and African labour used in its
production are doubly negated in the image where the foreign soap
is expunged of any associations of labour at all. The extraction of
African material wealth is overturned into an image of Europe providing for Africa, in a similar way to the 1884 image of a black boy being
washed white. When we consider economic relations between West
Africa and Europe during this period, the Pears image is also significant for its total interest in mercantile-capitalist relations, which operated to the benefit of Europe and perpetuated underdevelopment in
Africa.[52] This ideology, of the 'white man's burden', of Africa's 'need'

for European charity and the naturalisation of 'racial' hierarchy as though ordained, continued into the period of pacification and consolidation. The jingoism of the early advertisements, however, was not maintained.

The period of pacification and consolidation

While Crowder has called these decades the period of 'pacification and elaboration of systems of administration', it is important also to understand this period as one in which the major capitalist enterprises with interests in Africa consolidated their hold over markets and raw materials. It is during this period that conglomeration began to affect the soap trade, with Lever Brothers in particular acquiring a number of smaller firms. In 1899, Lever acquired Benjamin Brooke and Co., who produced Monkey Brand. This was followed by the acquisition of Hodgson and Simpson Ltd and Vinolia Co. Ltd in 1906, and the purchase of R. S. Hudson Ltd in 1908.

The imaging of African dependency

How can we understand this process of pacification and consolidation as affecting representations? To begin with, from around the turn of the century, the more violent images of conquest disappeared from

GOOD MORNING! Have you used PEARS' SOAP?

8 Pears' Soap advertisement, 1893

soap advertising. Scenes of brutal colonial aggression were no longer used, although certain 'softer' images such as Pears' advertisement of a white woman and a black woman in the clouds continued to appear. During this period images of Africa seemed to recede, to be overtaken by images of the black person – mainly child – in Europe. By the mid 1890s other soap companies had also started to use black people in their advertisements. These images, along with those from Pears, were much more domestic in their setting, although they continued to evoke the same themes of the 'white man's burden' and African underdevelopment.

We can view the increasing domestication of imagery through two advertisements from 1893 (Figures 8 and 9). Although these images are slightly earlier than the periodisation indicated, they reflect tendencies which took place in this period, and by 1890 the Brussels Act had indicated a nominal concern with African welfare. The two advertisements, one from Pears and the other from Vinolia, both depict scenes on the seashore, echoing Pears' advertisement from *The Graphic Stanley*. Both advertisements still suggest the black person as entering commodity consumption and, by inference, civilisation through the help of Europe, and the setting of these images by the sea also encourages the notion of first contact.

9 Vinolia Soap advertisement, 1893

Yet the shore in the 1893 images, although not specific, could just as easily be seen as the English seaside as the coast of Africa. In the Pears image, a mermaid appears to drive the by now well-known slogan 'Have you used Pears' soap?' into the ears of a surprised black child; while in the Vinolia image a little middle-class white girl complete with pinafore and bonnet holds a bar of soap and reprimands the black boy in the picture with: 'You dirty boy!'. The black man of the 1890 Pears advertisement has been transmuted into a dependent and infantile-looking boy in both of these later advertisements. In the Vinolia image he even wears what appear to be babies' underclothes. The period of pacification in this sense was also brutal. For the Victorians, with their rigid familial hierarchies, the positioning of a white girl as his teacher must have indicated his diminished status. Of course there is no doubt that these images also acted to provide a sexual frisson by depicting the taboo of the white woman and black man together – albeit as children. The sexual innuendoes of these images are also indicated by their situation on the seaside – a place which permitted a much greater degree of sexual freedom than was normally accepted in Victorian society.[53] As Richards notes, 'the seaside resort was a site of fantasy and a primary locus of Victorian sexual politics', where men and women were able to swim together in what was known as 'mixed bathing'. The conflation of gender and 'racial' relationships is directly played upon in a 1907 advertisement for Coal Tar Soap published in *The Graphic Summer Number*. Using the title 'mixed bathing', the image depicts a young girl washing dolls of various ethnicities. The image appears entirely innocent yet it inevitably carries sexual undercurrents. Interestingly, the African and Chinese dolls appear to be boys, while the white doll separated from them by the bowl is a girl. This relationship seems to have been played upon constantly by advertisers, in contrast to the relationship of a white man/boy and black woman/girl, who are rarely represented together during this period and then only in a master/servant relationship.

The image of the black man was diminished to that of a child and in some instances almost a baby in many soap advertisements of this period. After 1900 there appear to be no images which represent grown black men in soap advertisements. One reason may be that while nakedness and savagery could be used to ensure a subordinated image in Africa, the setting of scenes in Europe demanded a different form of diminution. As children they could pose no threat to the white woman consumer and also appeared 'naturally' dependent. This image of the African as child-like was generally predominant in the popular culture of the period, with the rising use of the golliwog and the emergence of figures such as 'Little Black Sambo'[54] in children's literature.

The image of the child/baby evoked the notion of African dependency so simply.

Hudson's Soap also brought out a series of advertisements which employed the image of black and white children in the first decade of the twentieth century. One advertisement represented three little black boys asleep in bed, with a sister advertisement depicting three white girls asleep. In the same campaign there was also an advertisement of a single black boy and another of a single white child. Although the images suggest a superficial equality by their equal use, the text under the face of the black baby reads 'MERCIFULNESS Hudson's soap is merciful to the clothes; it only removes the dirt, grease, stains, leaving the linen behind – spotlessly white, wholesome and pure'. In contrast, under the face of the white child the text reads 'MAKE BABY SMILE In her nice clean clothes so sweet and white when washed with Hudson's soap'. There is a sharp distinction between the ways in which these two children are regarded. The text with the white child shows human concern for the baby and her comfort. The text under the black baby shows no concern for him, but rather identifies with the person who is doing the washing. The black baby is simply reduced to the symbol of dirt. If any emotion towards the black baby is suggested by the text, it is within the abolitionist and missionary context of pity, evoked by the title word 'Mercifulness'. The concept of the 'white man's burden' and African underdevelopment is again highlighted and 'naturalised'.

Hudson's was not the only company to produce this kind of image: the Gold Dust twins provides us with an example of a product whose identity was completely tied to this diminishing status of the black person. The Gold Dust packet depicts two little black boys wearing nothing but an emasculating grass skirt around their waists. The grass skirt is an object that seems to have taken on an iconic significance in the representation of the 'savage'. While the twins act as trademark and logo on the packet, they are animated in print advertising. These children are less consumers of the product than representations of the product itself. The print advertisements depict scenes which represent them scampering about attempting to wash floors and dishes, but always creating mini disasters (Figure 10). The scenes ensure that we position these children as inept and in need of guidance, again upholding the belief in African dependency.

Lever Brothers, racist theory and the attempt to
consolidate control over raw materials
While the image of the black child as a general cultural representation of the diminution of black people within the early twentieth

10 Gold Dust Soap advertisement, n.d.

century has been discussed, the economic concerns of the soap companies for consolidation of control over raw materials may also be another reason behind such images. By the turn of the century, it was clear that control over raw materials was crucial to any soap company's success. A few years later, Joseph Meek wrote to Lever declaring this explicitly:

> The large soap maker in ten or twenty years from today who has not behind him a raw material scheme must go under no matter what be his advertising. Advertising will I believe be a dead letter in soap by then. Mere investments in planting schemes will be no use: the soap maker must own the raw material scheme and have it as a background to his business.[55]

Meek's comments must have come in response to what was clearly Lever's preoccupation during the first two decades of the twentieth century. In 1901 Lever had visited Sydney and the South Sea Islands, eventually buying plantations of copra in 1902. In 1902 Lever had also sent an investigator to West Africa, where he reported 'an inexhaustible supply of Palm Oil and Palm Kernels in the hinterland there only awaiting development and the opening up of markets'.[56] Lever was keen to buy and run plantations in West Africa and tried to do so on more than one occasion during the 1910s, although he was constantly hindered by the government's policy of first trusteeship and then indirect rule, which maintained that Africans should continue to own and cultivate their own land, with colonial rule maintained through the support of traditional chiefs. This was not a policy based on a moral belief in African independence but rather one which developed as a result of a lack of labour supply to build roads and railways in the conquest of West Africa. Although the importing of Indian and Chinese labour was considered, no plans ever came to fruition and both British government and traders were dependent upon African chiefs as their main labour recruiting agents. This dependence led to a commitment to communal land tenure in order for conflict and unrest not to be unleashed. In the 1890s and 1900s, this policy of communal land tenure was not fixed, but in the process of negotiation. In 1897, for example, the Public Land Holding Ordinance decreed that all land belonging to conquered or deposed rulers and not yet owned by individuals should come under government control. Occupants of public land had to obtain a certificate, but the resulting opposition to this system meant that the certificate had to be dropped. Conflict with labourers, it was felt, was best dealt with by native rulers.

The policy of native land tenure, although still geared towards African exploitation, did not suit the interests of Lever. He wanted to try to refine both palm and palm kernel oil in Africa in order to reduce his transport costs. Without ownership of plantations, which would enable him to control the supply of raw materials, Lever felt vulnerable. His attempts at plantation ownership, however, failed. He tried to obtain monopolistic concessions including vast tracts of land in return for capital investment, but the government, faced with conflicting demands from various firms and financial institutions, was unable and unwilling to decide in his favour.

Palm oil was supplied by peasant production, as was cocoa. This system was one in which native producers brought their raw materials to the open market to be sold. While the system suited the cocoa manufactures, it did not suit the soap firms. Lever simply translated what he saw as his economic loss into racist ideology. In a speech that he gave in 1924 he noted:

> I am certain that the West African races have to be treated very much as one would treat children when they are immature and under-developed . . . Now the organising ability is the particular trait and characteristic of the white man . . . I say this with my little experience, that the African native will be happier, produce the best, and live under conditions of prosperity when his labour is directed and organised by his white brother who has all these million years start ahead of him.[57]

This short extract clearly indicates Lever's belief both in European cultural and intellectual superiority and in racist evolutionary theories. On another occasion Lever wrote:

> A native cannot organise. He cannot even run a wooding post on the river satisfactorily. You have only to compare one run by a native with one run by a European to prove that.[58]

Lever believed quite categorically that Europeans were well adapted to organise and control capital, and Africans were adapted to labour.[59] How did these developing beliefs surface in his advertisements post-1901, when he was searching for control over raw materials in various parts of the globe? In the first instance, the diminution of the black boy to that of a baby is particularly characteristic of soap advertisements of the period and contrasts with that of cocoa advertisements (as will be discussed in the next chapter), where they are at least represented as young boys. The only Sunlight Soap image in *The Graphic* to depict black boys, rather than babies, in this period is one which presents them as simple 'junglees'.

The relationship between Lever's commercial interests and racist representation on Lever Brothers advertising can also be seen through the image of a black woman on Plantol Soap advertising from 1903 (Figure 11). This was a brand developed by Lever Brothers at the turn of the century in an attempt to compete in the bath soap market with Vinolia (which he later purchased in 1906) and Pears (which he purchased in 1914). Visually, the advertisement poses the black woman in the position of a servant offering the commodity to the viewer. Her beauty and sexuality are also mocked with her hair dishevelled and her clothes falling off her shoulder, not to suggest her body as one to evoke desire, but rather to assert her savagery. The advertisement was paired with that of a traditional image of a white woman bathing (Figure 12). Although she also offers the soap up for the viewer to use, it is positioned to suggest her own consumption too. Her stereotypical image signifying purity, femininity and availability is a format mocked in the image of the black woman, not to question the codes with which women are represented but in order to degrade the black woman.

1, 12 Plantol Soap advertisements, *The Graphic, Summer Number*, 1903 and 21 November 1903

If we recall Lever's commercial interests at the time, we can read this image on another level. Lever was investigating the West African palm oil trade as early as 1902, with quite clear monopolistic interests. Within the system of peasant production, it was in fact women who gathered much of these extra subsistence products.[60] Here this woman literally offers up the produce of her labour, which has already been transmuted into a bar of soap. Structured around notions of consumption, through its pastiche of other toiletry advertisements, the image derides and denies not only this woman's beauty but also her labour. She appears ignorant and unproductive, since the product of her labour is not actually shown. It is only the bar of soap that is shown, which was so strongly associated with Europe and European industrial production by this time. The denigration of this woman seems to represent Lever's discontent with the emerging Colonial Office support for peasant control over production. This image, however, is conflated with a symbolic act of servitude – she offers up the product. In this way it also suggests Lever's desire to transform her into a labourer in order to maintain vertical control over production. 'The vision of British West Africa as a world of small peasants became possible in the twentieth century, but was not yet determined in the years of colonial conflict',[61] as Ann Phillips has indicated. Lever's soap advertisements, along with those of others, can be seen to be part of a negotiation between conflicting colonial ideologies.

In the post-1900 period, other soap companies also represented the black woman within their advertisements. All depicted them as slaves to white women. Swan Soap, owned by Lever Brothers, represented a classical bathing scene in 1902 (Figure 13), as did Pears in 1905. In both, the slave woman represented is black. While soap companies were certainly influenced by paintings such as Gerome's *Moorish Bath* (1870), in which a black woman slave serves her white mistress, were not soap companies also affirming the idea of black slavery or servitude as desirable and acceptable? Lever clearly wished to be able to use indentured labour on plantations in West Africa, and had in fact already used such labour in his Pacific plantations. He must have been aware of the use of forced labour by African chiefs in their plantations and the use of forced labour by the government in developing railways and roads etc., since it was the source of much debate during this period. In 1890, for example, the most popular of the four sections in the Stanley and Africa Exhibition was the one devoted to domestic slavery in Africa. These soap advertisements appear to affirm the desire of companies to have access to the same kind of labour relations as both the government and African chiefs. As Phillips has discussed, slavery was not outlawed in the Gold Coast and Nigeria in 1900. Only slave raids were declared illegal and many Europeans in West Africa, as a resident of Bida commented, could not envisage African society in the near future as operating without slavery: 'If slavery . . . be abolished, with what are we to replace it? It will take years – generations – to teach the pagans who form the slave population the meaning of hired labour.'[62]

If the notion of these images as affirming slave relations seems ridiculous, why was an image used by Pears as early as 1887, of a black slave and white child, printed again on 26 January 1907 with the caption 'Look how the black slave smiles' (Figure 14). Such a reference appears to naturalise slave relations and suggest that these women are happier and better off in their servitude. Lever also produced a series of inset cards depicting a black 'mammy' for Sunlight Soap about 1906. The representation of black people as servile and racially different is repeatedly advocated. An advertisement for Sunlight Soap

13 Swan Soap advertisement, *Punch*, 27 August 1902

14 Pears' Soap advertisement, *The Graphic*, 26 January 1907

in the *Illustrated London News* in the same year also depicted a desexualised, rolling-eyed black 'mammy' (Figure 15). In 1907 Vinolia Soap, bought by Lever the previous year, also adopted the image of the slave 'mammy' for its advertisements (Figure 16). The general subordination of women within Victorian and Edwardian society must have made it easier to represent black women's servitude without an outcry from the morally righteous. The use of images of women to legitimise slave relations may also have come about because of the Anti-Slavery Society's own patriarchy and continuous use of the black male as freed slave in its images. In terms of inter-textual references within advertising, these women contrast with the cocoa manufacturers' 'free' male peasant producer in their post-1900 advertising. The images of the black slave affirm a desire for total control over resources in contrast to the images by cocoa manufacturers that promote 'native' control over production, which will be discussed in the next chapter. 'West Africa in the 1890s', as Phillips notes, 'still offered scope for contrasting notions of development. It contained its centralised states and empires with their history of slave production and their evidence of social differentiation, but at the

15 Sunlight Soap advertisement, *Illustrated London News*, 31 March 1906

same time it contained the basis for a future peasantry.'[63] The conflict of image, emphasised through a gender contrast, represents the conflict of interests in developing colonial policy. 'The formulation of . . . West African Policy took place in discussions of land policy, [although] . . . the ultimate difficulty lay in the absence of free labour.'[64]

Soap companies were one of the key groups to exploit the image of Africans in their advertising during the late nineteenth century. Their expanding industry was dependent on the newly exported vegetable oils from West Africa. Pears, the first soap company to employ an image of an African boy, did so at the very moment when the European powers met at the Berlin Conference to carve up the continent of Africa between themselves. Apart from reflecting the general political climate of the period, soap advertisements from the first decade of the twentieth century reveal support by soap barons such as Lord Lever

16 Vinolia Soap advertisement, *The Graphic*, 20 August 1904

for specific forms of government through their projected image of Africans. Lever's frustration with his lack of control over the palm oil trade and its affect on his profits led him to support the view that Africans were incapable of organising anything without European supervision. In company advertisements, African men were depicted as helpless babies and African women were represented as happy in slave servitude. They were perceived as unable to order and develop their world by themselves. These representations legitimised the right for Europeans to have direct control over the lands and labour of Africa. The political position of soap barons such as Lord Lever was to bring them in conflict with companies in the cocoa and cotton trade, as we will see in the next chapter.

Notes

1 W. H. Fraser, *The Coming of the Mass Market 1850–1914* (London, 1981), p. 53.
2 For statistics see Fraser, *Mass Market*, p. 53.
3 *Ibid.*, p. 205.
4 W. H. Leverhulme, *Viscount Leverhulme, by his Son* (London, 1927), pp. 38–9.
5 C. Wilson, *The History of Unilever*, Vol. 1 (London, 1954), p. 37.
6 *Ibid.*, p. 9.
7 M. Crowder, *West Africa Under Colonial Rule* (London, 1968), p. 19.
8 S. Hall, 'Encoding, Decoding', in S. Durring (ed.), *The Cultural Studies Reader* (London, 1993).

9   Flint notes the incoherence in British policy to West Africa in 'Nigeria: The Colonial Experience from 1880 to 1914', in L. H. Gann and P. Duignan (eds), *Colonialism in Africa 1870–1960* (Cambridge, 1969).

10 A. McClintock, *Imperial Leather: Race, Gender and Sexuality in the Colonial Contest* (London, 1995), p. 214.

11 Crowder, *West Africa under Colonial Rule*, p. 27.

12 E. J. Hobsbawm, *The Age of Empire 1875–1914* (London, 1987), p. 65.

13 J. Flint, *Sir George Goldie and the Making of Nigeria* (London, 1960).

14 Quoted in J. C. Anene, *Southern Nigeria in Transition: Theory and Practice in a Colonial Protectorate* (Cambridge, 1966), p. 65 (PRO, FO 84/1819 Report of the Law Officers, 7 January 1885, and Lord Chancellor's comment on the Law Officers Report, n.d.).

15 Crowder, *West Africa under Colonial Rule*, p. 51.

16 J. N. Pieterse, *White on Black: Images of Africa and Blacks in Western Popular Culture* (New Haven, 1992), p. 195. An example of the perpetuation of this theme is 'The Labour in Vain' pub in Yarnfield, Stone. In the 1990s, the pub sign, which depicted a black boy being washed white, was removed after two schoolgirls complained of its racism. It was reinstated after villagers protested.

17 Song from *The Mohawk Minstrels' Magazine of Music*, No. 108, see M. Pickering, 'Mock Blacks and Racial Mockery', in J. S. Bratton *et al.* (eds), *Acts of Supremacy: British Empire and the Stage 1790–1930* (Manchester, 1991), p. 198.

18 G. Crossick, 'The Emergence of the Lower Middle Class in Britain: A Discussion', in Crossick (ed.), *The Lower Middle Class in Britain* (London, 1977), pp. 34–5.

19 H. McLeod, 'White Collar Values and the Role of Religion', in Crossick (ed.), *ibid.*

20 R. Price, 'Society, Status and Jingoism: The Social Roots of Lower Middle Class Patriotism 1870–1900', in Crossick, *ibid.*, pp. 89–112.

21 Pears Archive, Unilever Archives, Port Sunlight, reference AFP 10/1/2.

22 Quoted in Pieterse, *White on Black*, p. 64.

23 P. Foner, *Frederick Douglas: A Biography* (New York, 1964), pp. 343–4.

24 Flint, 'Nigeria: The Colonial Experience', p. 220.

25 J. F. A. Ajayi, *Christian Missions in Nigeria 1841–1891: The Making of a New Elite* (London, 1965), p. 243.

26 J. Page, *The Black Bishop: Samuel Ajai Crowther* (London, 1908), p. 369.

27 Pears Archive, reference AFP 10/1/2, *Evening Post* (12 July 1888).

28 Quoted in Anene, *Southern Nigeria*, pp. 81–2 (PRO, FO 84/1762 Johnston to Salisbury, 15 January 1886, and Johnston to Rosebury, 17 June 1886).

29 Quoted in *ibid.*, p. 92 (PRO, FO 84/1828 no. 18, Johnston to FO, 24 September 1887).

30 T. Richards, *Commodity Culture in Victorian England: Advertising and Spectacle 1851–1914* (London, 1991), p. 74.

31 J. MacKenzie, *Propaganda and Empire: The Manipulation of British Public Opinion 1880–1960* (Manchester, 1984), p. 4.

32 In reworking historical facts the company was not on its own. The colonial melodrama *Khartoum!* of March 1885 had already reworked this episode of history to maintain an image of unquestioning British supremacy.

33 D. Lorimer, *Colour, Class and the Victorians: English Attitudes to the Negro in the Mid-Nineteenth Century* (Leicester, 1978).

34 Pears Archive, AFP 10/1/2, *Pall Mall Gazette* (21 May 1885).

35 Pears Archive, AFP 10/1/2, letter dated 23 August 1885.

36 Pears Archive, AFP 10/1/2, *Fireside News* (5 June 1885).

37 Pears Archive, AFP 10/1/2, *Life* (28 May 1885).

38 Pears Archive, AFP 10/1/2, *Hospital Gazette* (16 March 1889).

39 Pears Archive, AFP 10/1/2, *Modern Church* (20 August 1891).

40 Pears Archive, AFP 10/1/2, *Nottinghamshire Gazette* (1891?).

41 Pears Archive, AFP 10/1/2, *Liverpool Mercury* (1 May 1891).

42 E. Torday, *Camp and Tramp in the African Wilds* (London, 1913), pp. 164–5.

43 J. Mack, *Emil Torday and the Art of the Congo 1900–1909* (London, 1990), p. 37.
44 M. Adas, *Machines as the Measure of Man: Science, Technology and Ideologies of Western Dominance* (New York, 1989).
45 Pears Archive, AFP 10/1/6, *Publicity* (January 1900).
46 Richards, *Commodity Culture*, p. 125.
47 *Ibid.*, pp.139–40.
48 The Anti-Slavery Society supported Stanley's expedition because of his purported anti-slavery position, and covered the progress of his expedition in almost every edition of the reporter. See A. Coombes, *Reinventing Africa: Museums, Material Culture and Popular Imagination* (New Haven, 1994), p. 68.
49 A. G. Hopkins, *An Economic History of West Africa* (London, 1975), p. 152. For a general discussion see also W. Rodney, *How Europe Underdeveloped Africa* (London, 1972), Chapter 5.
50 K. Marx, *Capital* (London, 1954), Vol. 1, pp. 76–87.
51 Judith Williamson discusses the denial of labour in *Decoding Advertisements* (London, 1978), pp. 122–37 and in 'Great History that Photographs Mislaid', in P. Holland *et al.* (eds), *Photography/Politics One* (London, 1986).
52 See, for example, A. B. Zack-Williams, 'Merchant Capital and Underdevelopment: The Process Whereby the Sierra Leone Social Formation Became Dominated by Merchant Capital 1896–1961', *African Review*, 10:1 (1983), pp. 54–73.
53 Richards, *Commodity Culture*, pp. 226–7.
54 *Little Black Sambo* was first published in 1899, and was the first of a series of children's books by Helen Bannerman.
55 Wilson, *History of Unilever*, p. 159.
56 *Ibid.*, p. 165.
57 Crowder, *West Africa Under Colonial Rule*, p. 5.
58 Leverhulme, *Viscount Leverhulme*, p. 312.
59 *Ibid.*, p. 312.
60 Zack-Williams, 'Merchant Capital', p. 60.
61 A. Phillips, *The Enigma of Colonialism: British Policy in West Africa* (London, 1989), p. 22.
62 *Ibid.*, p. 30.
63 *Ibid.*, p. 22.
64 *Ibid.*, p. 50.

CHAPTER THREE

Cocoa advertising, the ideology of indirect rule and the promotion of the peasant producer

For cocoa manufacturers the period of pacification and consolidation was marked by support for what became known as indirect rule in West Africa. This support is apparent both from the kind of images of Africans depicted in cocoa advertising during the first decade of the twentieth century and from the frequency with which such images were used. As we have seen, soap firms repeatedly used an image of a black child, which diminished the African to the figure of a helpless baby or contented slave from the period of 'the scramble' in 1884, and appear to have supported the dominant conservative racist creed which maintained that Europeans were inherently superior to Africans and others. By contrast the cocoa companies (mostly owned by Quakers) were to develop an image of an African peasant producer – albeit as a child – but with an appearance of potential development. The cocoa images supported the ideological position of the Third Party, whose members were close to businessmen such as William Cadbury. The Third Party was 'a school of thought which saw itself as the keeper of the true colonial conscience in Britain'. Originally conceived by Mary Kingsley as a commercial lobby, it was mainly sustained by the humanitarian idealism of John Holt and E. D. Morel. It condemned both the predominant racist creed and the patronising condescension of traditional philanthropy, believing that the interests of Africans would be best served by allowing them control over their own resources, so as to encourage development through 'free trade'.[1]

The conflict between business interests that is apparent from a comparison between cocoa and soap advertising affirms the analysis by Hopkins that official colonial policy evolved during the initial phase of colonial rule and was not a fixed policy to which business-men were forced to bend: 'The controversy was not simply between enlightened, liberal civil servants on the one hand, and the "soap boilers of the world", (as Hancock called them), on the other, but between combinations of various interests with officials and businessmen represented on both sides'.[2]

In order to appreciate the ideological intent of the post-1900s cocoa advertising, it is essential to look back over the representations of black people in cocoa advertising prior to this period. Analysing some of the previous advertisements enables us to appreciate what appears to be a break within the intertextuality of cocoa images after 1900.

Early cocoa advertising

Cocoa was originally grown in Central America and was first brought to Europe by Christopher Columbus. It did not become familiar in England until the mid seventeenth century and in 1657 a Frenchman opened the first chocolate house in England.[3] During this period, illustrations and engravings always represented its Central American origins. They depicted native Americans with traditional objects for mixing and drinking cocoa, as can be seen on the fronticepiece of *Traitez nouveau et curieux du café, du thé et du chocolat*, published in 1693. It depicts three non-Europeans, each one representing one of the tropical products under discussion. The Chinese man represents tea, the Turk represents coffee, and the Native American represents cocoa.[4]

As a tropical product, cocoa retained its exoticism in consumption, unlike soap, although its identity appears to have shifted from a native American identity to an African one during the period of the European-Atlantic slave trade. William Hogarth, for example, depicts a black boy serving chocolate to a white lady in one of the images for *Marriage à la Mode*. The boy acts as a symbol of the colonial trade and slave labour upon which English aristocratic culture was dependent.[5] While Hogarth often inserted the figure of a black boy to critique the decadent and exploitative society of eighteenth-century high culture, other artists of the period inserted the black boy as a symbol of exoticism and of the wealth of the painting's commissioner. These eighteenth-century images were certainly familiar to the dominant cocoa firms of the late nineteenth and early twentieth centuries. A painting which depicts a black boy as exotic plaything adorned the Girls' Dining Room at the Cadbury's factory in Bournville. The painting by H. W. Smith depicts *White's Chocolate House, Saint James's, London, in the Time of Queen Anne, 1708* (Figure 17). It illustrates high society conversing and drinking cocoa. On the floor, towards the right-hand side of the painting, an exotically dressed black boy sits and plays, enhancing the exoticism of the chocolate house and its produce. The colour of Africans and chocolate was frequently associated

H. W. Smith, *White's Chocolate House, Saint James's, London*, 1708

from the eighteenth century onwards. Even in the twentieth century black people have been equated with chocolates. For example, in Germany, a chocolate cake is referred to as 'the edible Negro', and during the inter-war period the term 'petite chocolatière' or 'little chocolate bon-bon' became a term of endearment for black women.[6] Such references diminished the black person to the status of exotic plaything or inept child and also existed in British popular culture.[7]

By the late nineteenth century, it was not just the exoticism of black people and their skin which was depicted in cocoa advertisements and images. A dominant image of Africans on cocoa and other advertising during this period was of labourers working tropical plantations, producing raw materials for European consumption. An advertisement for Baron Liebig's Cocoa and Chocolate depicts such a scene (Figure 18). The image recalls the countless images of black slaves used on tobacco advertisements during the eighteenth and nineteenth centuries, where Africans carried the raw produce and became representative of the raw material. The image of a refined, well-dressed European woman carrying a cup of the final product dominates the centre of the advertisement. Her image is framed like a portrait by the capital 'C' of cocoa. This immediately adds a sense of individuality to her in contrast to the African labourer. She stands above both African workers in the advertisement, who structurally are coming forward to present her – as Europe – with the raw produce. Significantly, she is also not situated in Europe, since the vegetation in her portrait suggests that of the plantation, although hers is a life of leisure, which is distanced from the African workers through framing. The representation of Africans as producers of raw material for European consumption

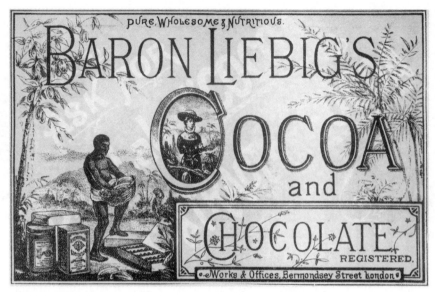

18 Baron Liebig's Cocoa advertisement, n.d.

is one which was to dominate the whole period of Empire. In the late nineteenth century, these images almost always represented Africans working as labourers on European-run plantations.

A Taylor Brothers advertisement from 1868 and a Cadbury's advertisement from the 1880s also represent plantation production (Figure 19). They both emphasise the notion of Europe's technological development and supremacy through the depiction of scenes from metropolitan factories that contrast with the rural scenes of the colonies. These advertisements, like the previous one, depict the material reality of the period, with European firms manufacturing cocoa and chocolate at their British factories and controlling the production of cocoa on estates in the Caribbean. In focusing on the plantations which they owned as a way of depicting the raw material, as opposed to the cocoa that they bought on the open market, Taylor's and Cadbury's were also emphasising the ideologically desired method of production for the period, with a belief in total vertical control over production by European companies. These images also assert a false idealism. The plantation scenes suggest areas of 'natural' abundance and the scenes of rural toil are picturesque and harmonious, representing the labourers as working in a contented world.

By 1900, however, these images ceased to be the dominant representation of Africans on cocoa advertising. Instead, cocoa advertisements began to represent what could be seen as a romanticised image

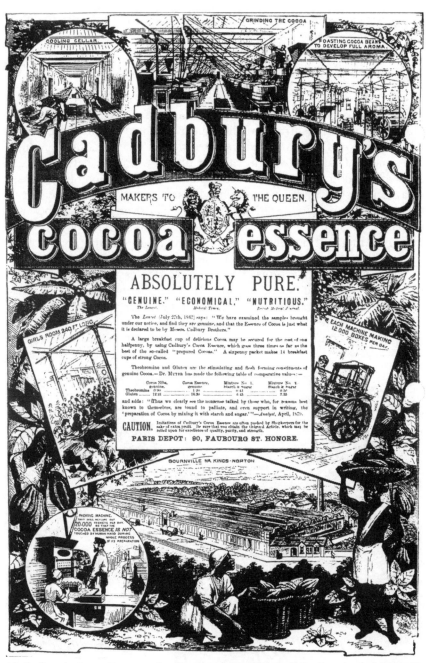

19 Cadbury's Cocoa Essence advertisement, *The Whitehall Review Annual*, 1881–82

of the African peasant producer, a figure who was eventually to define the cornerstone of West African colonial policy.

Cocoa advertising in the period of pacification and consolidation

The most striking transformation of imagery in cocoa advertisements after 1900 was the shift from the image of a black plantation worker to the image of a domesticated, yet 'freely' subservient 'sambo' producer and server of chocolate. The earliest of these images dates between 1899 and 1900 for Fry's Cocoa. It depicts a young African boy dressed in a striped shirt and white apron who smiles broadly as he carries a tray declaring 'Cocoa, Sah!' (Figure 20). The image of 'sambo' was probably the most popular and ubiquitous stereotype of the black man in American popular culture. He represented the 'prototype of the contented slave', 'the eternal child, the eternal dependent, happy though given to unaccountable moods of depression, lazy, enjoying the banjo and the dance, passionately religious, but passive in most other things – a rather spirited but lazy, over grown child'.[8] He was the antidote to the image of the rebellious slave. As George Frederickson comments in *The Black Image in the White Mind*, the

20 'Cocoa, Sah!', Fry's Cocoa advertisement, 1899–1900

two images of 'sambo' and 'savage' represented white inventiveness in forestalling an egalitarian bi-racial society. Apart from representing the eternal, happy child, 'over a period of time sambo became an integral part of the colonial family, particularly as worker but as entertainer too'.[9] As Boskin comments, 'sambo' was 'worker and entertainer, producer and performer'.[10]

Following the military conquests of Africa, the aim of both British companies and the government was to find a system of administration which would allow for the material exploitation of Africa whilst suppressing any African conflict. 'Sambo', as a figure of servile and contented obedience, was the coloniser's dream. He transformed the male labourers of the early advertisements into unthreatening boys. The cocoa advertisements from Quaker firms after about 1906, however, did not simply exploit the 'sambo' figure in order to image the African as servile and contented, since the earlier images also represented contented labourers. 'Sambo' was also employed to represent an unsophisticated peasant producer serving Europe with his product. Such an image affirmed the developing policy of indirect rule, which took the cocoa manufacturers into debates and conflicts surrounding British colonial policy in West Africa.

The establishment of West Africa as a Crown territory in 1900 could easily have led to the granting of concessions to major traders and capitalists for the development of a European-owned plantation economy.[11] The early colonial period saw conflicting interests on the part of British traders and capitalists. While men such as Lever were searching for concessions, some traders feared that such actions would jeopardise their interests because of their own lack of involvement in production. Others, however, were sceptical about the value of their direct involvement in production. Plantation production was not a success in many instances in West Africa. The British Cotton Growing Association, for example, established in 1902, did not believe it was economically worthwhile to have a direct hand in production, as the Association Manager commented in 1913: 'My experience of the African is that he will take on risks that people in civilised countries will not'.[12] It was the conflicting interest of British traders, the impact of successful African enterprise versus the failure of European-owned plantations, that led to the securing of a West African land and labour policy that encouraged African enterprise. African-controlled cocoa production was a key success story that impacted on policy development. As Gareth Austin notes:

> The story of African enterprise in Ghanaian cocoa farming is often seen as the epitome of the British 'West African Lands Policy' of leaving the

land in West African colonies under indigenous ownership, and therefore looking to African farmers rather than European settlers or planters to produce export crops. But the establishment of the West African Lands Policy did not precede, but rather accompanied and even, to some extent, followed the emergence of Ghana as the world's leading cocoa producer, with the overwhelming majority of output coming from African-owned farms.[13]

Exports of cocoa rose from nil in 1892 to 13 tons in 1895 with an export value of £500. It rose to 536 tons in 1905 with an export value of £187,000, and to 22,629 tons in 1910 with an export value of £867,000. By 1911 the Gold Coast became the world's largest cocoa producer, exporting £1,613,000 worth of cocoa.[14] Colonial policy and the support of the major cocoa firms such as Cadbury's and Fry's, while not necessarily instrumental in the development of the cocoa industry, did affect the magnitude of this production.[15]

The cocoa advertisements under discussion can be seen as evidence of the cocoa companies' ideological support for peasant production and indirect rule at the crucial moment when such policy was being defined. As we shall see, there were other reasons too, such as the maintenance of the Quaker companies' philanthropic image after news was released of their purchase of slave-grown cocoa. Cadbury's relationship to the 'Third Party' will be discussed first, before considering the Quaker companies' response to the issue of slave-grown cocoa.

William Cadbury and the Third Party

The cocoa companies, Cadbury's in particular, appear to have been at one with the ideas disseminated by the Third Party. The advertisements under discussion can be seen as part of the political lobbying with which Morel's 'Third Party' was involved. William Cadbury saw Morel as a political exponent of his beliefs, and supported Morel financially in his attempts to become an MP. In 1910 Cadbury agreed to give Morel £800 a year when he tried to enter parliament, another £400 'for each election he had to fight before he entered parliament', and to support Morel's wife and family in the event of Morel's death, by paying £500 to his widow until their youngest son was of age, at which point the amount would be reduced to £300.[16] Their political closeness makes it essential to outline the Third Party's ideas on African development. As Morel outlined, the Third Party

was a school of thought, which saw in the preservation of the West African Land for him and his descendants; in a system of education which shall not anglicise; in technical instruction; in assisting and encouraging agriculture, local industries and scientific forestry; in introducing labour-saving appliances, and in strengthening all that is best, materially and spiritually in aboriginal institutions, the highest duties of our Imperial Rule.[17]

This position, while championing the issue of African rights, clearly affirmed the right of a European presence in Africa. Morel never contested the basis of the relationship between Europe as manufacturer and Africa as provider of raw materials. To him Europeans and Africans were in a 'partnership', which if properly administered would be beneficial for both parties. In administering Africa, Morel and his supporters believed Europe had what Lugard would later describe as a 'dual mandate'. Firstly, there were 'moral obligations', which included

the training of native rulers; the delegation to them *of such responsibility as they are fit to exercise*; the constitution of Courts of Justice free from corruption and accessible to all; the adoption of a system of education which will assist progress without creating false ideals; the institution of free labour and of a just system of taxation; the protection of the peasantry from oppression and the preservation of their rights in land &c. (my emphasis)

Secondly, there were 'material obligations', which involved the 'development of natural resources for the benefit of the people and of mankind in general'.[18] The entwining of material with 'moral obligations' gave an almost moral value to Britain's rule. Progress, interpreted in material rather than social terms, could be used to justify almost any position. It is clear that despite believing in the importance of African agency, Morel, Holt and Kingsley, like Lugard, did not believe Africans were equal to Europeans and believed that Europeans were the best qualified to rule by virtue of experience, justice and humanity. They believed that the evolution of the African should be encouraged, but was certainly not at the same stage as the European. As Mary Kingsley put it: 'we are apt to forget in England that it has taken us nearly two thousand years to raise ourselves from the wood and fur-skin clothing ante-Roman period to the silk hat and frock coat' and 'we have not made a better man of the Native in West Africa by enabling him in less than one generation to jump to the silk hat and frock coat period. We have made him a worse man in my opinion.'[19] It was the attempt by philanthropic and missionary groups to 'develop' Africans in one generation to which the Third Party objected. As Morel put it, 'patience, more patience, and again patience ought to be the cornerstone of British policy in West Africa'.[20] For the Third Party the key road to development was the encouragement of free trade. Morel, like imperialists of other hues, believed that 'Commerce is the greatest civilising agent'.[21] However, Morel believed that the practise of free trade could only be satisfied by native ownership and development of land:

> Native ownership in land must needs be the foundation-stone of all normal European rule in the African tropics, because the economic objects of normal European rule is the development of commercial relations and any between the European and the native is impossible, unless the native has articles to sell with which to purchase manufactured goods. . . . In other words, as long as the native has free access to the soil, he will develop his land, he will put forth every effort to increase its productive value, he will exchange its produce with manufactured goods, sent from Europe, a normal commercial relationship will be set up, imports and exports will expand, the prosperity of the whole country will increase, and incidentally, the workers of Britain, or France or Belgium will benefit, first by the employment created by the manufacture of the goods exported to West Africa, secondly by the increased supply of valuable foodstuffs and raw materials.[22]

The cocoa advertisements from the first decade of the twentieth century appear to advocate support for the notion of 'partnership' as well as the value of promoting African peasant production.

One of the most famous Cadbury's images of the period depicts a young African boy and a young English girl sitting on a rug in the open air (Figure 21). The vegetation behind them suggests a tropical location. The boy holds a cup of cocoa, offering it to the young girl. He, as Africa and producer of raw materials, offers the cocoa to Europe for consumption in a manner which suggests 'partnership'. The notion of partnership is increased by the fact that they both sit on the same rug. Symbolically they are part of the same economic system.

Yet while the two children sit together on the mat, this partnership is based on the notion of difference. The colour difference of Africans and Europeans is deliberately accentuated; the boy's skin is almost black, while the girl is blonde. There is no doubt that the African boy is a worker serving the European girl who is part of the leisured class. The boy wears a plain checked shirt with a large hat, while the girl's clothes are more elaborate, with lace and frills. She wears shoes in contrast to the naked feet of the black boy. The black boy looks towards the white girl as though in search of approval. The girl, however, does not reciprocate, but looks confidently ahead. She reclines in contrast to the black boy's more upright position and in consequence takes up more room, affirming her superiority. The scene, in spite of its surface equality, asserts the colonial concept of Africa in need of 'European supervision' and represents Africans, as Lugard was to describe, as 'attractive children, whose confidence when once it has been won is given ungrudgingly as to an older and wiser superior, without question and without envy'.[23] The scene seems to reflect and endorse an imperial relationship which was not brutally oppressive nor patronisingly philanthropic – the African boy is not represented as brutal savage, nor is he totally helpless – yet the belief in Europeans and Africans as culturally and racially different is affirmed. The advertisement asserts the concept that 'the Africans are Africans, and not immature Europeans, and that they are capable of social progress, economic improvement and political advancement *under European supervision*' (my emphasis).[24] It should be noted that this belief of African need for European guidance and supervision allowed the colonial government to modify anything they found repugnant or did not suit British interests.

While Cadbury's image concentrates on the colonial relationship, which affirms difference as a crucial way to define national roles, a Fry's advertisement from *The Graphic* in 1906 emphasises, exalts and romanticises the image of the 'free' peasant producer bringing his goods to the open market (Figure 22). In the Fry's advertisement, a

Cadbury's Cocoa advertisement, n.d.

22 Fry's Cocoa and Milk Chocolate advertisement, *The Graphic*, 3 November 1906

young African boy is represented with 'sambo'-like characteristics of worker and entertainer, easily contented in child-like happiness. He stands on the map of Africa and holds an enormous pod of cocoa, from which he pours cocoa powder into cups that spread across the Western world. The cups are decorated with shields and crests of various European powers. The first cup is, of course, that of Britain, but there are no worries about the quantity of cocoa, which seems never-endingly abundant by the row of filled cups and the almost jubilant abandon with which the boy fills them. The boy's image visually asserts Morel's stereotypical description of 'the tropical African' as a carefree 'sambo', but one who is productive when working under his own steam. The tropical African, Morel wrote, is

> essentially a creature of moods; a child of joy and a child of sorrow; a being of strong emotions which must find an outlet. He likes a dance, to linger chatting over camp fires, to vary his life according to the seasons. In his natural state the twin emotions of joy and sorrow merge into one another ... The tropical African is a bad labourer when he is working for the white man; an excellent labourer when he is working for himself, a free man.[25]

The abundance of cocoa pouring from the pod which is carried by a happy and smiling African boy, with no symbolic representation of a white overseer or Western 'scientific' cultivation techniques, affirms the authority of the Third Party's position on the possibilities of African productivity if native control over production and by necessity land ownership was maintained. For Morel, the Gold Coast cocoa industry was a monument to his beliefs:

> How many Englishmen are acquainted with the romance of the free grown cocoa in one of their own West African dependencies? ... [T]he story should go far to convince even the most obstinate sceptic of the Negro's capabilities that (in a natural setting of circumstances and conditions) this maligned race can accomplish wonders, provided it is given a chance.[26]

The representation of over-abundant produce, carried by a figure who historically represented a happy-go-lucky existence as opposed to that of a hard worker, is also significant in terms of the contemporary analysis of African success in cocoa production during this period. Lugard, for example, qualified the success of the Gold Coast industry: 'While giving healthy praise to the initiative of the Gold Coast native, and to the methods which produced such results, it is misleading to cite them as evidence of astonishing industry, due to a policy however excellent, when they are due primarily to an exceptionally favourable soil, climate, and rainfall'.[27]

In similar fashion, the Governor of the Gold Coast, Sir H. Clifford, remarked: 'cocoa is notoriously one of the least exacting forms of permanent cultivation known to mankind'. The natives would probably not have undertaken it otherwise, 'or any task of the sort that made a more severe demand on their physical energies'.[28] The initiative of African planters was also questioned by some. While Governor John Rodger of the Gold Coast admitted a European lack of involvement in the development of the cocoa industry in 1909, commenting that 'this remarkable development has been carried out with only slight assistance from the Government agricultural staff, and entirely by Native, not by European planters', Alan McPhee, writing in 1929, describes it as the 'foster child of the Government'.[29] The impact of racist ideologies which questioned Africans' organisational ability must have influenced McPhee's perception of the industry twenty years later. If we bear in mind that much of the success of cocoa production was due to the establishment of farms by migrants within West Africa, who were involved in planting and caring for trees that were not indigenous to West Africa, and caring for them for at least four years before seeing any financial results, we can see the extent to which African labour and agricultural knowledge were diminished by scholars and image-makers. As Polly Hill has noted, the involvement of the colonial government in both the establishment of the industry and its development was negligible. The industry developed through the migration of workers by their own initiative, from the Akwapim ridge to the virgin land near Akim Abwakwa in the 1890s.[30] In the nineteenth-century scenes of European plantations there were images of organised labour, which indicated effort, but in these later images it is the idea of tropical abundance that is emphasised. The Fry's image, while drawing attention to the production of cocoa, falsifies and fetishises it. In fact, it is not only African labour which is denied in this image, but also the labour of British workers – the processed cocoa is simply poured abundantly from the pod.

The image of natural abundance and the happy-go-lucky 'sambo' was followed through in a series of Fry's advertisements of which the above one was the first.[31] In the next Fry's advertisement of the series, published in *The Graphic* on 2 November 1907, Africa's raw material and the African himself become almost one (Figure 23). The key concern with the exploitability of Africa's raw material is made manifest. The young boy from the previous advertisement wears a cocoa pod. Simply his bare feet and smiling face, two key attributes that assert his role as uncivilised and immature, protrude from the pod. The equation of Africans with natural produce is one that was often used in American popular culture too, with, for example, black Americans

23 Fry's Cocoa and Milk Chocolate advertisement,
The Graphic, 2 November 1907

represented in smiling contentment eating watermelons. Other cocoa companies also represented black Africans with abundant natural produce, but always in images that diminished their actual initiative and labour. An advertisement for Clarnico Cocoa in the Robert Opie Collection (n.d.) shows a young smiling boy canoeing in an empty pod. He sails in the product of his labour yet is represented with it, at leisure. A Cadbury's composite advertisement in the archive at Bournville also includes one image of another grinning 'sambo' character almost weighed down by the pods in his arms.

The diminishing of African capabilities is all the more apparent when we remember that European attempts at plantation production for cocoa under 'scientific conditions' were in fact a failure in West Africa. Europeans, as Austin has noted, were unable to admit that their technologies and systems of labour-intensive cultivation might not actually produce better quality and more abundant cocoa. Austin cites their racist and colonial attitudes, which demanded the preservation of the image of European science and rationalism as superior, as one reason why a 'hands off' colonial policy may have developed.[32] Through their advertisements, cocoa companies, while affirming general racial and colonial hierarchies, also aligned themselves with supporters of indirect rule, in which a system of peasant production of raw materials was privileged. These companies were therefore involved in the production and propagation of particular colonial ideologies through advertisements that were able to communicate specific policies to a general audience.

Yet, why was this picture of peasant production the key image which cocoa manufacturers propagated during this period? Cadbury's, for example, obtained most of its cocoa through plantation estates and even owned two estates in Trinidad, which employed waged labour. Only one advertisement from 1906 can be found that depicts a scene on the Maracas Valley estate.[33] This advertisement is the only one that represents women collecting the ripened cocoa. It is important to note that this advertisement represents a rare image of adult labourers in post-1900 cocoa advertising. It does not appear accidental that they are women. Although they are represented as physically strong and are de-sexualised, they do not represent the threat with which the black male (through myths relating to his sexuality and savagery)[34] would have been viewed. Perhaps it is for this reason that no white overseer is represented to assert a hierarchical authority, in contrast, for example, to the Lipton's cocoa planter label where a white man is pictured overseeing black male workers (Figure 24).

The Quaker firms and the controversy over slave-grown cocoa

One reason why Cadbury's and the other cocoa firms would have been keen to represent their approval of a system of peasant production was the rising concern amongst philanthropic groups by 1900 about slave-labour conditions on the cocoa estates of two Portuguese controlled islands, Sao Thomé and Principe, off the coast of West Africa.

Sao Thomé cocoa was known to be of good quality and although Cadbury's and other cocoa manufacturers did not buy cocoa direct from the islands, a third of the cocoa from Sao Thomé was imported

24 Lipton's Cocoa advertisement, n.d.

into England in the 1900s and Cadbury's, along with other manufacturers, bought Sao Thomé and Principe cocoa from the London
markets.[35] Cadbury's was heavily reliant on this source, drawing
50 per cent of its supply of raw cocoa from there in 1900 because of
its relatively even quality and consistency. As a Quaker firm which
adopted a philanthropic attitude towards its British workforce, it was
difficult for Cadbury's to ignore the rising criticisms. These criticisms
seem to have been as much a result of inter-colonial rivalry as out of
philanthropic concern, as editorial commentary in *The Reporter*, the
journal of the Anti-Slavery Society, makes clear:

> The Administration of Portugal in her African territories has ever been
> known to be inefficient and corrupt. It has been said that the slave-trade
> is the only trade for which the Portuguese have shown a marked
> aptitude . . . and the traffic in labourers to the islands of Sao Thomé and
> Principe under the so-called engage system is practically slave trading.[36]

The Portuguese colonies had been a source of criticism by the
Anti-Slavery Society in the 1880s, but criticism had died down in
the 1890s with the increased concern over abuses in the Congo. The
1900s saw the rise of another humanitarian outcry against Portuguese
slavery. Although histories of Cadbury's suggest that William Cadbury
first heard a rumour of slaving conditions on the islands when on a
visit to Trinidad in 1901,[37] as a member of the Anti-Slavery Society,
he must have been aware of the conditions at least a year earlier and
was most probably aware of them as early as the 1880s. In 1900 the

Anti-Slavery Society launched a programme of education for its members on labour migration to the two islands. Almost every issue of *The Reporter* appeared with extensive extracts from the English and European press or with letters from missionaries in Central Africa, exposing the abuses. The society kept its members informed of every detail of the trade that it came upon between 1900 and 1903. In 1901 Cadbury's received incontrovertible evidence of slavery when an offer for sale of a cocoa plantation on Sao Thomé was made, including as an asset '200 black labourers' valued at £3,355. For a firm that had a reputation for philanthropy this evidence raised a major problem. The loss of Sao Thomé cocoa in 1901 would have meant 'considerable financial loss . . . and a possible retrenchment of some 500 hands'.[38] It would undoubtedly have affected the success of Cadbury's social experiment at Bournville.

The Board's approach was therefore cautious. It did not stop purchasing Sao Thomé cocoa immediately, but left William Cadbury to investigate the issue. He did not make any enquiries into the issue for two years. This stalling of the issue indicates the financial implications of withdrawing purchase of Sao Thomé cocoa for Cadbury's. In 1902 it had introduced the popular line of Cadbury's Milk Chocolate on to the market. In 1906 it was to launch Bournville Cocoa. All this expansion demanded a steady supply of good quality cocoa. Yet the firm's philanthropic reputation, along with pressure from the Anti-Slavery Society, must have forced Cadbury into making enquiries about the plight of the 'serviçaes' in Sao Thomé when he visited Lisbon in 1903 and met the colonial Minister, Gorjao, with Reverend Stober, another member of the Anti-Slavery Society. The British Minister in Lisbon, Gosselin, also spoke of the Anti-Slavery Society and Cadbury together, as being 'in on the thing' in correspondence to the Foreign Office in May 1903.[39] While in Lisbon, out of both public pressure and philanthropic concern, William Cadbury had asserted that if no change were made to the conditions of the 'serviçaes', he would recommend that the English chocolate manufacturers buy their cocoa elsewhere. Before engaging in a boycott Cadbury's obtained the support of two other English chocolate manufacturers, Fry's and Rowntree's, as well as Stollwerk's of Cologne, to carry out an investigation. This was eventually undertaken in 1904–6 by a researcher called Joseph Burtt. The British government, however, simply stalled any actions of its own, since in 1901 it had drawn up an agreement with Portugal facilitating the recruitment of labourers from Mozambique for South African mines. The cocoa companies were apparently unaware of this arrangement and simply waited for government advice and support. While Burtt was carrying out his investigation, William

Cadbury tried to restrain the Aborigine Protection Society and the Anti-Slavery Society from giving the slavery issue too much publicity, ostensibly so that Burtt's mission would not be prejudiced in the eyes of the Portuguese planters. He must also have been concerned about the attacks on his firm, since the Tory press was eager for an excuse to attack him after his purchase of the *Daily News* in 1900 and its anti-Boer War propaganda.

By 1905, however, 'English commentary [had] gradually worked its way up to a hysterical pitch',[40] especially after the renowned journalist Henry Nevinson visited the islands for *Harper's* magazine. His articles on 'The New Slave Trade' appeared in the magazine in monthly instalments from August 1905 to February 1906. Nevinson revealed to the general public the way in which Angolans were being dragged into service as indentured labourers under conditions in which they would never be able to return to their homes. He described the brutality with which slaves were treated, calling Sao Thomé and Principe 'islands of doom'. Nevinson wrote emotively in his articles about the attitude of whites towards blacks, as well as the impossibility of discussing slavery in any kind of humanitarian way: 'The only motive for slavery is money making, and the only argument in its favour is that it pays. That is the root of the matter, and as long as we stick to that we shall, at least, be saved from humbug.'[41]

Nevinson's powerful and dramatic articles, along with his book *A Modern Slavery* published in 1906, increased pressure on the cocoa manufacturers to boycott Sao Thomé cocoa. This increasing pressure must have encouraged William Cadbury to write to the Foreign Office later that year asking for an interview, expressing the concerns of the cocoa manufacturers and the fact that they were 'prepared to make some sacrifice in the interest of the natives'.[42] He also noted their desire to work in harmony with the British government. Whatever Cadbury's purported philanthropy, the maintenance of Britain's colonial authority was never questioned. The result of the interview left William Cadbury and the cocoa manufacturers agreeing to wait further until the report by Burtt, which the manufacturers themselves had commissioned, was completed.

By March 1907, however, the Foreign Office had an advance copy of Burtt's report, which began unreservedly: 'The law is a dead letter and the contract a farce. The native is taken from his home against his will, is forced into a contract he does not understand, and never returns to Angola. The legal formalities are but a cloak to hide slavery.'[43] Cadbury's still agreed, however, to remain silent while the British government tried to encourage the Portuguese to change the conditions. By this stage, however, there were a number of organisations, not all philanthropic, which were encouraging cocoa firms to boycott the cocoa. In September 1907, even the African trade section of the Liverpool Chamber of Commerce asked the firms to cease purchasing it. The interests of the Liverpool Chamber of Commerce could not be described as philanthropic. In the same year the Chamber was protesting about monopolistic concessions which Lever Brothers was trying to procure from the government for investment in West Africa.[44] With the rising importance of the Gold Coast cocoa industry, the Chamber must have been aware that in supporting a boycott of Sao Thomé cocoa it would be encouraging the Gold Coast cocoa trade, which would inevitably boost support for maintaining looser systems of governmental control in the region. The Chamber had direct interest in the West Coast trade through the African Association. When Cadbury's explained the diplomatic efforts of the cocoa companies, a more mild resolution was passed by the Chamber a month later.

In September 1908 Cadbury and Burtt decided to make one more trip to the Portuguese-controlled islands to see if any reforms had been implemented. With the crescendo of interest in the press and elsewhere, the *Evening Standard* launched into an attack on the cocoa companies for buying slave-grown cocoa. It refused to issue an apology and Cadbury's eventually sued the paper and won in 1910. However, with the venom of attack increasing at such a pace the cocoa companies could not wait any longer and finally called a boycott of Sao Thomé and Principe cocoa in March 1909.

The humanitarian outcry against slave-grown cocoa obviously concerned the cocoa manufacturers, who fostered an image of Quaker philanthropy with the British public. This must have influenced them in creating an image through their advertising which suggested support for 'free' labour and fair treatment for African workers. The 'sambo' image of the contented and happy African, together with the notion of the peasant producer, can be seen as an attempt by the Quaker firms to 'clean up' their image in the face of a growing storm of protest, which had begun over twenty years before the eventual boycott.

It is interesting that Fry's images in *The Graphic* start in 1906, at the time when criticism was rising fiercely, after the publication of Nevinson's articles. In fact all the images which can be dated were published after 1906. Did 1905–6 mark the crucial point of both change in images and an increased use of the black figure because of the rising interest in these debates? It is worth noting that in 1905 Cadbury's returned to advertising in-house, whereas it had previously been franchised to another company.[45] It is also important to note, however, that all the images from 1906–7 are Fry's and not Cadbury's images, despite Cadbury's centrality to the whole affair. In fact William Cadbury is reported to have told the West African Lands Committee that the firm was reluctant to advertise the fact that it was using Gold Coast cocoa for a few years because of the cocoa's uneven quality. The company feared that this intelligence might damage its reputation within the trade.[46] Fry's, however, appears not to have been afraid to align itself with this new source. Perhaps this was an attempt to distance itself from the controversy which was centred on Cadbury's. Fry's used the image despite the fact that it must have used very little Gold Coast cocoa in 1906, since the bulk of the crop was of poor quality, could not be sold in England and was shipped to Hamburg, the centre of the continental cocoa trade at that time.

Quaker cocoa interests on the Gold Coast

By 1906 the cocoa companies were keeping a watchful eye on the Gold Coast industry and Cadbury's bought its first 'small parcel' in that year.[47] Although Gold Coast cocoa had only been worth £27,300 in 1900, by 1906 it was worth £336,000.[48] This was an increase of 1,900 per cent in just six years! A year later, in 1907, Cadbury's sent out its first representative to the Gold Coast to lay the foundations of its business in that country.

Apart from knowledge of the rising size of the Gold Coast industry, the cocoa companies must have been aware of the economic incentives for maintaining systems of peasant production in West Africa. In a paper to the Royal Colonial Institute in 1907, a member of the British Cotton Growing Association outlined the extent of the financial benefit. He noted how, while self-employed Africans were content with 2d a day return for their labour, wage workers expected 1s 6d:

> There are hundreds of thousands of the best type of native who would not go out and serve under a white overseer for a daily wage, but who working in their own way, and in their own time, would accomplish far more than the average paid labourer, and would in my opinion, be content with the proceeds which give them even less than the equivalence of 6d a day.[49]

Africans were clearly ready to lose some financial gain in order to maintain a degree of distance from the coloniser.

Cadbury's and the other cocoa firms were not against waged-labour or plantations. In fact, upon buying Gold Coast cocoa on any scale in 1910, the Gold Coast government encouraged Cadbury's to establish two 'model estates'. Despite the obvious success of the African producers, the racist perceptions of government officials made it impossible for them to perceive anything but plantation production under European control as the ideal. In 1905 W. T. D. Tudhope, the new Director of Agriculture on the Gold Coast, continued to believe that the careful, cautious and intensive methods of cocoa planters in Ceylon were superior to the local methods of cultivation by African farmers on the Gold Coast. Cocoa planters such as Lipton's in Ceylon maintained an image of plantation production in their advertisements. Such a system of production was supported by the planters and the colonial administration in Ceylon, as we shall see in the following chapter. The image of the peasant producer, however, was the most effective rebuttal to criticisms of the Quaker cocoa firms. The later failure of Cadbury's plantations also affirmed the firm's position of leaving production to African producers. In correspondence to the West African Lands Committee in 1916, William Cadbury wrote: 'We would very much rather not have the responsibility. Let the natives bring it to the open market.'[50] There was, of course, no 'open market'. This cash crop had to be sold abroad and most European buyers agreed prices with each other in advance, in order to obtain the raw materials at exceptionally low prices.

Apart from a general affirmation and propagation of the policy of 'indirect rule' and support for 'peasant' production, some advertisements even seem to engage in quite specific concerns which the cocoa manufacturers had about Gold Coast cocoa. The last Fry's advertisement from the series of four in *The Graphic* deals specifically with the issue of quality. It depicts the smiling 'sambo' with a John Bull type figure who is named as Mr Fry. The young African points to an enormous pod of cocoa, declaring 'Dat's for Massa Fry 'cos its de best' (Figure 25). Released in *The Graphic* on 26 December 1908, three months before the boycott, Fry's was concerned to dispel concern over the varying quality of beans from West Africa, in contrast to the uniformity of quality from Sao Thomé. Cadbury's, which acted as buying agents for both itself and Fry's on the Gold Coast,[51] had complained about the difficulty of acquiring a good quality bean. Part of the reason was that the Gold Coast bean was a different type and shape from that of Jamaica and Sao Thomé, but it was also the result of the refusal by many of the buying firms to offer higher prices for better quality cocoa.[52] Cadbury's was concerned about the quality of the produce and was prepared to pay more for a better quality crop. During the 1909/10 season it was reported to have paid 17s per 60 lb in comparison to its rivals, 12s 6d, as long as the beans were properly fermented. Although Cadbury's did pay more for its cocoa initially, the differential between its payments and that of others decreased through the years until some farmers did not believe it worth the

25 'Dat's for Massa Fry 'cos its de best', Fry's Cocoa advertisement, *The Graphic*, 26 December 1908

effort to produce a better quality crop. Later in the 1930s low price fixing by Europeans was to lead to cocoa boycotts, with African producers collectively refusing to sell their produce for the criminally low prices which were then offered.

Apart from dealing with a specific fear associated with the transference of trade, the representation of Master Fry as John Bull is significant. Miles Taylor has noted how by the mid nineteenth century John Bull had begun to represent support for free trade imperialism.

Between 1906 and 1909, both the Conservative and Liberal parties used the image of John Bull to represent 'business government'. In fact, as Taylor outlines, 'by the early twentieth century John Bull was the very embodiment of free-trade orthodoxy'.[53] The use of John Bull, therefore, further affirmed the Third Party ideology and in this context he appeared as a figure who was actively spreading such a system to the corners of Africa.

There is one other myth which these Fry's advertisements also helped to maintain – the notion of the smallholder and family producer. The size of the African boy and the size of Master Fry establish without doubt a sense of importance and scale for each. While the proportion of small-scale production in Ghana compared to other cocoa-growing regions was much more substantial, the size and shape of farms varied considerably, with many of the larger farmers hiring labour. The cocoa manufacturers, however, continued to maintain that the majority of holdings were 'very small', as W. A. Cadbury commented to the West African Lands Committee in February 1913.[54] The image of the small boy in comparison to the larger-than-life John Bull figure assures the image of a paternal relationship, which benefited from the belief in the existence of the inexperienced African producer.

Finally the image of John Bull with boy 'sambo' also asserts the image of the Empire as a family. In transferring from Portuguese to British colonial cocoa, the manufacturers were maintaining support for British imperial interests. The transfer of trade established the Gold Coast as the largest cocoa-producing area in the world. A Cadbury's image from 1910 also reaffirms this notion of the Empire's family (Figure 26). It depicts a white boy and a black boy sitting together in an image which, like the previous Cadbury's advertisement discussed, denotes 'partnership'. Interestingly this is the only image which represents both black and white children holding the product together. Yet the 'partnership' is still uneven, since the boys are not dressed in the same way. The white boy wears shoes in contrast to the black boy. It is also the white boy who has his arm around the black boy, causing him to lean in support on the white child. There could be no simpler image of paternalism and the so-called mutual dependency of Empire. The rapid expansion of cocoa production in West Africa undoubtedly shifted commitment towards a policy of preserving native land rights and 'destroyed the case for the English land law as a pre-condition for permanent cultivation of cash crops'[55] in line with Morel's approach. In 1910, the year following the declaration of a boycott, the Land and Native Rights Proclamation for Northern Nigeria was passed. It declared all land public land. By 1911

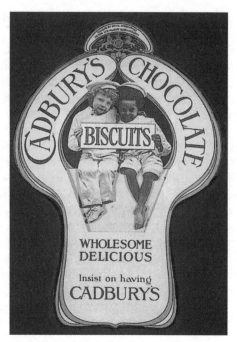

26 Cadbury's Chocolate Biscuits
advertisement, 1910

the Colonial Office was also looking at land policy in the Gold Coast
with the establishment of the West African Lands Committee a couple
of years later.

It is important to note, however, that it was not simply the Quaker
firms whose advertisements seemed to ooze a sense of paternalism.
An advertisement for Epp's Cocoa (n.d.) represents a white girl and a
black boy together (Figure 27). There is no doubt as to who is offering
the instruction in this image. The white girl points her finger in
tuition. She looks at the black boy to see if he is paying attention. He
stares and smiles intently at her instruction. Yet this image conflicts
with the Third Party's perspective on imperial rule by representing
the Westernised top-hatted African, which Kingsley derided. On a
textual level this image seems to relate to Cadbury's image of the
black boy and white girl sitting together on a mat, yet they do not
appear to have adopted the ideology promoted by Cadbury's and Fry's,
but instead conflate Cadbury's perspective with that of traditional
philanthropy, which encouraged the mimicking of European dress
and behaviour amongst Africans. This is hardly surprising since one
Fry's advertisement (n.d.) also represents a top-hatted black boy

27 Epp's Cocoa advertisement, n.d.

(Figure 28). But while the boy in the Fry's image is derided as not having achieved the status of Westernised black man, since he is completely naked apart from spectacles, hat and beads around his neck, the figure in the Epp's Cocoa advertisement is presented in a more respectable way. For Morel: 'The whole notion and policy of Europeanising the inhabitant of the tropical belt of Africa is a profound error of psychology, totally unscientific'.[56] The Fry's boy is clearly still a 'junglee' and seems to affirm the ideas of Morel and the Third Party on the lack of success of Europeanisation.

28 Fry's Cocoa advertisement, n.d.

The conflict of interest represented in soap and cocoa advertising post-1900

Finally, how can we assess the extent of difference between advertisements by the cocoa firms and those of other companies who would have preferred the development of 'direct rule' and a plantation economy. The previous chapter noted how the early years of the 1900s saw the domination of the image of the black baby rather than boy in soap advertising. Although the cocoa images diminish the status of the black man to boy, it is not quite as total as that observable in soap marketing.

It is worth comparing a couple of soap images found in *The Graphic* c.1906–7 with a couple of cocoa images of the same period. This period is important, because of the increasing outcry against Portuguese slavery, the interest by cocoa firms in West Africa at this time, and Lever's campaign in favour of plantations in West Africa, which lasted from 1906 until his death in 1925.[57] This period also saw increasing conglomeration in the soap business, with Lever Brothers purchasing further British soap companies.

On 3 March 1906 an advertisement for Sunlight Soap appeared in *The Graphic*. It depicted two scruffy-looking black boys behind a fence on which was scrawled 'We wash all our clothes with Sunligt Soap' (misspelt) (Figure 29). One of these boys points with his thumb to a washing line behind him on which hang some strings of beads. The implication is clearly that this is all that these uncivilised 'junglees' wear. The stupidity of the expressions on their faces, with round bulging eyes and ridiculous grins, contrasts sharply with Fry's 'peasant producer', who is stereotypical but is at least represented to some degree as productive. These boys, while having been taught what may have been regarded as Western ways, have mastered them imperfectly. Lever certainly believed, as he was to tell Morel in correspondence, that Africans were like children. Lever derided the philanthropic lobby for trying to produce Westernised Africans, as this image suggests.[58] In the light of the outcry against slavery that has been referred to above, it is also worth noting that the Pears image in classical surroundings, first printed in 1887, reprinted with the caption 'Look how the black slave smiles' on 20 January 1907, was during a period in which the opposition to Portuguese slave labour had become almost hysterical following Nevinson's articles (Figure 14).

While it is clear that the ideologies behind the majority of soap and cocoa advertisements are strikingly different, the pervasive racism of the period and the belief in colonisation and Empire, which maintained Britain as educator and civiliser, ensured a certain similarity too. Both Lever and the philanthropist Morel, as has been mentioned, saw Africans as children in need of education and guidance. Their interpretation of how this should affect Europe's relationship with Africa, and their belief in the possibilities of African development, were different. This is indicative of the way in which racism as an ideology is constantly changing and shifting according to contemporary needs and the demands of particular political or economic interests.

29 'We wash all our clothes with Sunligt Soap' (sic),
The Graphic, 3 March 1906

It is clear in observing the totality of images for soap and cocoa advertising that they represent the conflict of actual interests, as well as more general ideologies of the particular period, since the concentrated use of the image of Africans arises at different moments for each product. It is also clear that the use of images of black people on a particular product was never static, either in type of representation or in their overall use. When the climate was right during 1905–10 in particular, cocoa companies had a particular incentive to employ the image of the black boy on their product. It is interesting that after this period, although the cocoa firms were in fact buying their cocoa from West Africa where a peasant system of production was promoted, the number of images of the black boy and 'peasant producer' recedes. Most of the images which predominate later are those of sugary-sweet white boys and girls. You could say that the girl in the first Cadbury's image which was discussed began to fill the whole rug.

Notes

1 K. D. Nworah, 'Humanitarian Pressure Groups and British Attitudes in West Africa 1895–1915', unpublished Ph.D. thesis, University of London, 1966.
2 A. Hopkins, *An Economic History of West Africa* (London, 1975), p. 214.
3 A. W. Knapp, *Cocoa and Chocolate: Their History from the Plantation to Consumer* (London, 1920), p. 7.
4 Jordan Goodman discussed this image in 'Fashionable and Necessary Consumption: The Culture of Tea, Coffee, Chocolate and Tobacco in Eighteenth-Century Europe', V and A Research Seminar, 1993.
5 D. Dabydeen, *Hogarth's Blacks: The Image of the Black in Eighteenth Century English Art* (Kingston upon Thames, 1985), p. 87.
6 J. N. Pieterse, *White on Black: Images of Africa and Blacks in Western Popular Culture* (New Haven, 1992), p. 193.
7 A postcard from a collection at Huddersfield Public Library, for example, shows a picture of black children ready to bathe on the seaside with the title 'Here are some assorted chocolates' (n.d.).
8 Quoted in Pieterse, *White on Black*, pp. 152–3.
9 J. Boskin, *Sambo: The Rise and Demise of an American Jester* (Oxford, 1986), p. 8.
10 *Ibid.*, p. 15.
11 See Hopkins, *Economic History of West Africa*, Chapter 6, and A. Phillips, *The Enigma of Colonialism: British Policy in West Africa* (London, 1989), Chapters 3 and 4.
12 Quoted in Phillips, *Enigma of Colonialism*, p. 71.
13 G. Austin, 'Mode of Production or Mode of Cultivation: Explaining the Failure of European Cocoa Planters in Competition with African Farmers in Colonial Ghana', in W. G. Clarence-Smith (ed.), *Cocoa Pioneer Fronts since 1800* (Basingstoke, 1996).
14 P. Hill, *The Migrant Cocoa Farmers of Southern Ghana: A Study in Rural Capitalism* (Cambridge, 1970), pp. 17 and 176–7.
15 R. J. Southall, 'Cadbury on the Gold Coast 1907–1938: The Dilemma of the "Model Firm" in a Colonial Economy', unpublished Ph.D. thesis, University of Birmingham, 1975.
16 Cadbury to Morel, 12 April 1912, F8, E. D. Morel Papers, London School of Economics (hereafter EDMP), quoted in Nworah, 'Humanitarian Pressure Groups', p. 80.
17 E. D. Morel, *Nigeria, its peoples and its Problems* (London, 1911), quoted in Nworah, 'Humanitarian Pressure Groups', p. 23.
18 Lord Lugard, *The Dual Mandate in British Tropical Africa* (London, 1965), p. 58.
19 Quoted in Nworah, 'Humanitarian Pressure Groups', p. 530.
20 E. D. Morel, *Affairs in West Africa* (London, 1902), pp. 15–16.
21 *Ibid.*, p. 21.
22 E. D. Morel, *Great Britain and the Congo* (London, 1909), pp. 86–7.
23 Lugard, *Dual Mandate*, p. 70.
24 A. McPhee, *The Economic Revolution in British West Africa* (London, 1926), p. 263.
25 E. D. Morel, *The Black Man's Burden: The White Man in Africa from the Fifteenth Century to World War One* (London, 1920), pp. 158–9.
26 E. D. Morel, 'Free Labour in Tropical Africa', *The Nineteenth Century and After*, 75 (March 1914), pp. 629–43.

27 Lugard, *Dual Mandate*, p. 399.
28 *Ibid.*, pp. 399–400.
29 See Southall, 'Cadbury on the Gold Coast', p. 20.
30 Hill, *Migrant Cocoa Farmers*, pp. 170–9; Hopkins, *Economic History of West Africa*, pp. 216–17.
31 No contradiction is acknowledged in these images between the white child's enjoyment of childhood and the black child's labour.
32 Austin, 'Mode of Production or Mode of Cultivation', p. 170.
33 Cadbury's Archive, Bournville.
34 For discussions on black male sexuality see Pieterse, *White on Black*, Chapters 2, 7 and 12; F. Fanon, *Black Skins White Masks* (London, 1986); K. Mercer, 'Imaging the Black Man's Sex', in P. Holland *et al.* (eds), *Photography/Politics Two* (London, 1988).
35 Morel, *Black Man's Burden*, p. 150; W. A. Cadbury, *Labour in Portuguese West Africa* (London, 1910), p. 2.
36 *The Reporter*, November–December 1900, p. 161, quoted in W. Duffy, *A Question of Slavery* (Oxford, 1967), p. 170.
37 I. Williams, *The Firm of Cadbury 1831–1931* (London, 1931), Chapter 8.
38 William Cadbury, Statement to Committee of Planters in Lisbon, 28 November 1907, cited in G. Nwaka, 'Cadbury's and African Cocoa: Social Conscience and Commerce in the Colonial Context', unpublished M. A. dissertation, University of Birmingham, 1972, p. 23.
39 Duffy, *Question of Slavery*, p. 183.
40 *Ibid.*, p. 186.
41 H. W. Nevinson, 'The New Slave Trade', *Harper's* (October 1905), p. 674.
42 Duffy, *Question of Slavery*, p. 193; PRO, FO 367/18, George Cadbury to FO, 27 October 1906.
43 Cadbury, *Labour in Portuguese West Africa*, Appendix A, p. 131.
44 Phillips, *Enigma of Colonialism*, pp. 92–3.
45 Williams, *The Firm of Cadbury*, p. 85.
46 William Cadbury to West African Lands Committee, EDMP, 10,661, cited in Southall, 'Cadbury's on the Gold Coast', p. 55.
47 William Cadbury to West African Lands Committee, EDMP, 10,660, cited in *ibid.*, p. 54, note 12.
48 Hill, *Migrant Cocoa Farmers*, p. 177.
49 Quoted in Phillips, *Enigma of Colonialism*, p. 71.
50 William Cadbury to West African Lands Committee, EDMP, q 10682 African West 1047, 1916, quoted in Phillips, *ibid.*, p. 72.
51 Williams, *The Firm of Cadbury*, p. 150.
52 Phillips, *Enigma of Colonialism*, p. 87; Southall, 'Cadbury's on the Gold Coast', pp. 62–7.
53 M. Taylor, 'John Bull and the Iconography of Public Opinion in England c.1712–1929', *Past and Present*, 134 (February 1992), pp. 93–128.
54 Hill, *Migrant Cocoa Farmers*, p. 179.
55 Phillips, *Enigma of Colonialism*, p. 72.
56 Morel, *Black Man's Burden*, p. 160.
57 Hopkins, *Economic History of West Africa*, p. 211.
58 Lever derided the philanthropic approach in letters to Morel in 1911, quoting Kingsley's ideas in support. See Nworah, 'Humanitarian Pressure Groups', p. 530.

CHAPTER FOUR

Tea advertising and its ideological
support for vertical control
over production

We are told, for example, that free trade will give rise to an international division of labour that will assign each country a production that
is in harmony with its natural advantages. You may think, gentlemen,
that the production of coffee and sugar is the natural destiny of the
West Indies. Two centuries earlier, nature, which is unaware of commerce, had not placed either coffee trees nor sugar cane there.

(Karl Marx, *Discourse on Free Trade*, 1848)

While cocoa companies sported an image of the peasant producer by
1905, tea companies maintained the image of direct vertical control
over plantation production throughout the late nineteenth and early
twentieth centuries. These advertisements highlight the way in which
a particular mode of production that suited tea planters was continuously represented. In consequence, the image of the plantation
labourer became one of the dominant representations of Indians in
the commercial culture of the period. It is particularly interesting for
its emphasis on labour – a rare feature in advertising, where labour is
usually denied. This emphasis on labour was only possible because of
the contemporary belief in racial hierarchy. Just like soap and cocoa,
tea was branded and packaged for the first time during the 1880s.
Unlike the other two products, however, it retains aspects of its colonial identity even today. The advertising of tea also enables us to
observe how the economic and political exploits of planters in the
late nineteenth century shifted the identity of tea from a Chinese
product to an Indian/Ceylonese one. The shift in consumption from
Chinese to Indian and Ceylonese tea, and the consequent changing
identity of tea, did not take place accidentally but was fought out
aggressively. As with cocoa advertising, the intertextual shift in tea
imagery parallels the changing production conditions. To understand
the shift in representation we first need to consider tea marketing and
advertising from the early eighteenth and nineteenth centuries.

Tea as a Chinese product

Before 1838, the only country to cultivate and export tea was China. Tea had been introduced to Britain in the mid-seventeenth century and had become a popular drink during the eighteenth century amongst all but the very poor. While the product was Europeanised in terms of how it was drunk (with for example the adding of sugar), the exotic associations were preserved. When Sylvestre Dufour published his *Traitez nouveau et curieux du café, du thé et du chocolat* he represented tea with the image of a China man.

In illustrations and advertisements, as well as on new tea implements such as tea pots and sugar bowls, it was not only the image of tea as Chinese that was crystallised, but the European image of China. A series of stock in trade symbols of China were always depicted – the port, trading ships, Chinese pagodas and Chinese men (often represented as boys) with triangular hats, pigtails and 'exotic' costumes. While these images began to appear in the eighteenth century, the crystallisation of the stereotype was complete by the nineteenth (Figure 30).

The stereotype of the Chinese man as tea drinker and producer was so total that the early tea entrepreneurs in India fell victim to it, at the very point when their new cultivations would lead to changing associations with tea forever. As Berry White commented in a lecture to the Royal Society of Arts in 1887:

> Acting presumably on the belief that every Chinese man must be an expert in tea cultivation and manufacture, they transplanted all the Chinese shoemakers and carpenters that they could induce to go from Costilloh and other bazaars in Calcutta to Assam; these men were nearly all from the seaport towns of the Celestial Empire, and many had never seen a tea plant before.[1]

The complete association of China with tea meant that when tea began to be produced elsewhere, in aggressive competition with China, it was clear that a strong and new identity would need to be forged for the product.

The beginning of tea in India

The collapse of the East India Company's monopoly on Chinese trade – a trade that was mainly associated with tea in 1834 – led traders and the British government to look for a source of tea production which they could control, as they had the China trade during the previous century. As early as 1822, the Royal Society of Arts had offered fifty guineas for anyone who could cultivate tea in a British colony. The

30 Chinese man holding a scroll advertising imported tea, n.d.

prize remained unclaimed, but in 1834 Lord Bentinck, the Governor of Bengal, appointed a tea committee to 'submit a plan for the accomplishment of the introduction of tea cultivation into India, and for the superintendence of its execution'.[2]

Plants and seeds from China were sent to Assam, which was selected by the botanist C. A. Bruce as the most preferable area for tea cultivation in India. There were also some suggestions that tea was indigenous to Assam, although this has never been categorically proven. Whatever the details, various experiments in cultivation led to the first shipment of tea from India to England in 1838. By 1840 C. A. Bruce believed that tracts in Assam were ready for commercial development and that this would 'enrich our own dominions and pull down the haughty pride of China'.[3] Thirty years later, planting also began in Ceylon.

If we look at imports of Indian, Chinese and Ceylon tea from the late nineteenth century, we can see how dramatic was the change in trade. While 43,806,000 lb of Indian tea was imported into the UK in 1880 as opposed to 114,485,000 lb of Chinese tea, by 1886, 68,420,000 lb of Indian tea was imported, in contrast to 104,226,000 lb of Chinese tea. In 1888 imports of Indian tea at 86,210,000 lb finally exceeded those of China, whose imports had diminished to 80,653,000 lb. From this point onwards the decline in imports and consumption of Chinese tea was dramatic. During this period, Ceylon had only just begun to export tea to the UK. In 1883 1,000,000 lb was imported, in 1886 the figure had increased to 6,245,000 lb and by 1888 this figure had trebled to 18,553,000 lb.[4]

The battle for markets in the tea industry was always aggressive. Both the Ceylonese and Indian planters established organisations to represent their interests and promote the consumption of Ceylon and Indian tea. The Planters' Association of Ceylon was established as early as 1854 to represent the interests of coffee and later tea planters. The Indian Tea Association was formed in 1881 with branches in London and India. Both countries also imposed voluntary and compulsory tea cesses at different times to aid the promotion of their tea. In the third annual report of the Indian Tea Association reference was made to the advertising of Indian teas in the press, and to rivalry with China:

> Advantage has been taken of such opportunities as have presented themselves for advocating the claims of Indian tea in the press, with the view of drawing the attention of the public to the superior merits of these teas over those of China, Java, and Japan.

An example of the rivalry with China can be seen in an advertisement for 'The Indian Tea Bazaar Company' of Glasgow, which declares

'Indian Teas can be relied upon for their PURITY, Chinese teas cannot', and 'Indian Teas are so strong and rich in Flavour that Grocers and Dealers use them extensively to flavour and fortify the Inferior Teas of China'. The only image used in the advertisement contrasts with the Chinese exoticism of the past. It presents the face of what was meant to be an Indian woman. For Ceylon and for India the importance of acknowledging the country of origin in the marketing of tea was crucial for the establishment of their product. They were concerned that their tea should not be simply mixed in unknown blends. In establishing identities for their product they were involved with constructing and representing the countries of India and Ceylon. At the 1886 Colonial and Indian Exhibition, for example, the only product in the Indian section to have its own subcommittee was tea. The Ceylon planters were also heavily involved in the creation of the Ceylon Court. 'The collection of exhibits was placed in the hands of the Planters' Association of Ceylon' (Figure 31).[5] The image that was

1 Ceylon Court, in Frank Cundall (ed.), *Reminiscences of the Colonial and Indian Exhibition*, 886

constructed was therefore in tune with what the planters wanted to see – a place of rich natural resources, but to a degree wild and therefore productively tamed through European intervention. The image of Sinhalese natural servility was also encouraged through the employment of exotically dressed Sinhalese attendants in the court and tea house. This set of representations was to be repeated and refined over the next decades.

Conflicts in the forging of an identity for Empire tea

In the 1880s and 1890s the conflicting identity of tea as a Chinese or Indian/Ceylon product expresses the conflicts of companies with separate interests. Trading companies buying from India, China and Ceylon exploited a complex set of images. Lyons, for example, with planting interests in India as well as trading interests with China, built an Indo-Chinese Pavilion at the Newcastle exhibition of 1887:

> The Indo-Chinese Pavilion, which also belongs to Mr Lyons was designed by Mr J. S. Fairfax of London, and has been constructed under the superintendence of Mr Charles Brooks. Light and elegant, it will be recognised as one of the handsomest buildings on the ground. Externally it is decorated in the Indian style, and combined appearance of domes and minarets, with a profusion of bright colours, produces a very fine effect. Downstairs there is an Indian court, and upstairs a Chinese court, in both of which light refreshment will be sold.[6]

Lyons continued this dual image at the 1888 exhibition in Glasgow, where they also employed 'native' servants to serve tea. The drawing upon a mixture of Chinese and South Asian identities can be seen in a tea sold in 1891 by Kearley and Tonge. A leaflet for 'Ceylindo Tea' in the John Johnston collection presents an image which is definitely not South Asian. While selling a blend of Ceylon and Indian tea, the typeface in which the text is written lends a Chinese feel to the product.

In the 1890s the United Kingdom Tea Company also tried to assert the image of China tea, but the aggressive advertising of Lipton's was to alter the image and taste of middling brand teas for good. Through a perusal of advertisements in *The Graphic*, we can observe the conflicting identities produced by the United Kingdom Tea Company and Lipton's. By 1892, Lipton's aggressive advertising campaign began with triumphal scenes of his tea gardens and images of 'comely' Ceylonese women. In 1893 the imports of China tea had declined to 25,805,313 lb. In contrast India was importing 108,143,602 lb and Ceylon 64,218,061 lb. In 1894, for the first time, China tea imports did not fall, but remained at the same figure as the previous year. Perhaps for this reason, companies involved in the selling of China tea made a last ditch attempt to retain the image of tea as Chinese for the middle market. The United Kingdom Tea Company produced two images in 1894 which encouraged a Chinese association: one of Samuel Pepys declaring as he had in 1660 'I did send for a cup of Tea (a China Drink)' and the other of a Mandarin complete with ponytail pouring a cup of tea out of a Chinese tea pot (Figure 32). In the same year, Priory (a company which had only been established a year before) advertised its tea with handbills depicting images traditional to Japanese block prints that were dropped from a balloon on 16 June 1894. Japanese and Chinese imagery and identity were not clearly demarcated for the British audience, but were rather seen as generally Far Eastern and exotic.

Yet the image of China for mass-consumed teas did not persist much beyond this period. By the end of 1894, the United Kingdom Tea Company had switched its advertising image to one which eulogised colonisation. Britannia, in Roman regalia, sits on tea chests of the United Kingdom Tea Company while men representing China, India, Ceylon and Assam offer her crates of tea (Figure 33). Her control and authority seem total as she sits almost reclining, pouring a cup of tea. She does not look up at the men walking towards her, but they look in anticipation at her, with heads partially bowed and all except China have bare feet.

In developing an identity for Empire tea, the Indian Tea Association and the Ceylon Planters' Association tried to establish ways in which they could present their product as a quality one. In terms of propaganda the Ceylon Planters' Association was on the whole much more forward-looking and more successful than the Indian Tea Association. It used a variety of marketing methods including imperial exhibitions, publicity stunts and advertising for the purpose. At the 1888 Glasgow Exhibition, for example, the Ceylon planters not only organised their own tea house (which India failed to secure), but also scored a trump card in Queen Victoria's public acceptance of a cup of Ceylon tea. The imperial image was consolidated five years later, in 1893, when the Ceylon Association negotiated an agreement with J. Lyons, caterers to the newly opened Imperial Institute, to serve only Ceylon tea 'and none other' for a cash subsidy of £300 for the first year.[7] The Ceylon administration and its Planters' Association also provided the Imperial Institute with 'a large sum for the building of a Ceylon Tea Garden and Rest House with the object of rehabilitating Ceylon teas with the well-to-do classes of the capital'.[8] Whether it was the publicity that Queen Victoria's cup generated, or just the

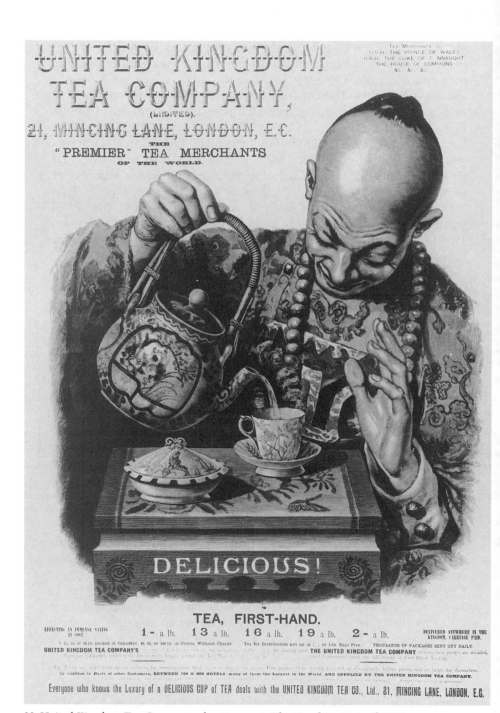

32 United Kingdom Tea Company advertisement, *The Graphic*, 28 April 1894

33 United Kingdom Tea Company advertisement, *The Graphic*, 15 December 1894

BLACKMOOR VALE ESTATE.
PURE CEYLON TEA.

ALTHOUGH the cultivation of the Tea Plant in Ceylon is only of comparatively recent date, the result has abundantly proved that the exquisite climate and fertile soil of this island produces a Tea which, for its delicate flavour and richness of liquor, excels all other growths. Figures, which are indisputable facts, indicate that Ceylon Tea is the Tea of the future. Its rapid advancement into popular favour, and the daily increasing consumption, unmistakably indicate that Ceylon Tea possesses those drinkable characteristics so peculiarly pleasing to the palate of the tea-loving community. The chief one is, perhaps, that when brewed, the liquor possesses the quality of fine China Tea, combined with the strength of the choicest Indian growths—thus, in lieu of the blending that is imperative with all other importations, a Tea is presented to the public absolutely in its original state of production.

Larger areas are yearly coming into cultivation, and the following statistics of the importation for the past three years still further demonstrate the extraordinary popularity of these Teas :

	1884.	1885.	1886.
Imported ...	180,490 lbs.	259,750 lbs.	499,750 lbs.

By special arrangements made with the Proprietors of the Blackmoor Vale Estate, Kearley & Tonge supply the growths of these famed gardens direct to the public in Quarter, Half, and One-Pound Air-Tight Leaden Packages, which are sold throughout the United Kingdom by upwards of 3,000 appointed Agents at the following prices :

1. **THE BLACKMOOR VALE 1/8** (Broken Leaf), Green Label.
2. Do. do. **2/-** (Whole Leaf), Blue do.
3. Do. do. **2/6** do. Brown do.
4. Do. do. **3/-** do. Red do.

As a protection against the many worthless imitations which are being forced on the public as Pure Ceylon Tea, the Proprietors have registered a distinguishing Label, bearing the Fac-simile Signature of the Firm, as follows : without which none is genuine.

Kearley & Tonge

FAC-SIMILE OF LABEL.

F. R. Piggott, South Parade Summertown

34 Blackmoor Vale Estate advertisement, 1890

result of the general marketing of Ceylon tea, by 1890 the name of Ceylon had become a mark of quality.

The image for this imperial tea, however, was still being shaped. In 1890 Kearly and Tonge advertised a tea under the name of Blackamoor Vale Estate (Figure 34). The image appears simply exotic, with a landscape of fairly dense jungle in which a large balconied house establishes the European presence and a boat carries some 'natives' down stream. There are no tea plants and the scene also does not appear to be in a hilly region, where most of the tea in Ceylon was grown. The name of the estate is probably the greatest help in establishing the reason for this rather strange landscape. Blackmoor as a name has far more association with the image of Africans and slavery than with South Asia. The image on this packet and the name of the estate seem to have been directly derived from images of eighteenth- and nineteenth-century tobacco advertising. It is quite possible that this image was part of a printer's stock of images and was simply adopted for this tea label. In fact the plant in the right-hand corner in both the large and the small image that make up the label looks exceedingly like a tobacco plant and no tea plant is depicted at all. It seems clear that at the beginning of the 1890s the identity of Ceylon and Indian tea was still being forged and therefore what would have been translated by the average consumer as a general depiction of exoticism and colonial territory could still be used to advertise tea. This particular advertisement is also interesting because it resulted in the Planters' Association of Ceylon taking Kearley and Tonge to court for selling what was in fact a blend of China and Indian tea as Ceylon tea. The Blackamoor Vale Estate did not even exist.[9] Ceylon in particular made a number of attempts to protect the way in which its tea was marketed as the identity of its tea was developed and consolidated. It is clear that the colonial/Empire identity of Indian and Ceylon tea was a key distinguishing feature from China tea. In developing this identity, tea planters in India and Ceylon drew on contemporary Orientalist and imperialist attitudes towards South Asia that suited their economic interests.

Orientalism and planters' attitudes towards India and Ceylon

Orientalism refers to the study of 'the East' by 'the West'. As Said and colonial discourse theorists have discussed, Orientalist knowledge was not neutral but engaged in a variety of ways with moral, political, military and other forms of power. As terms, 'the East' or 'the Orient' are themselves constructs which were not static, but sometimes referred to the Arab world, sometimes to China and Japan, and at other times to South Asia. 'The East', as Steadman has discussed, does not define a singular community, yet many Europeans have continued to maintain the idea of an Eastern psyche or Eastern way of life pervading all cultures in Asia.[10]

While Said discussed constructs of the Arab world in European thought, Ronald Inden has highlighted the ways in which India was constructed in the European imagination. Like Said, Inden emphasises the way in which Orientalist knowledge of India has been privileged in both the past and the present over knowledge by Indians. Inden notes how the collection of information by Europeans 'enabled the Orientalist and his countrymen to gain trade concessions, conquer, colonise, rule and punish the East'. Drawing on Said's Foucaldian analysis, he comments on how the Indologist, backed by governments, institutions and finance, presents accounts of Indian society which assume the Westerner to be rational and scientific and this encourages his perception of Indians as alien, distorted and irrational.[11] While there has been some justified criticism of Inden's critique of Orientalist, structuralist and Marxist analytic frameworks as equally essentialist and his lack of distinction between European Indologists' constructs of Orientalism and Indian nationalist constructs, the general thrust of his argument provides a valuable insight into the construct of India by Indologists which is useful for analysing tea marketing.[12]

Ronald Inden describes how Indologists repeatedly cited environmental 'racial' and climactic reasons as to why Indians were passive, cowardly, irrational and superstitious. This was seen as the reason for the repeated conquering of India by other states and why 'it was only "natural" for European scholars, traders, and administrators to appropriate the power of Indians . . . to act for themselves'. Inden also cites the obsession of Indologists with religion (particularly Hinduism) and caste in expressing the idea of India as a land 'governed by disorderly imagination instead of a world-ordering rationality'.[13]

Complementing the above representation of India and Indians was the romantic vision of India. In this vision, India is seen as a land of desire and opulence, and while Indian learning is not completely derided, India is viewed as a land of spiritual fulfilment, which could provide relief from the harsh realities of an industrialising West. The hierarchical visions of development and the notion of India as backward are maintained in both Indological approaches, and both were exploited and reaffirmed as the tea companies developed their advertising and marketing for Indian tea.

In defining Orientalism it should be remembered that racist attitudes of the period varied and conflicted. Monogenists believed that all human beings were basically from the same origin, but at different stages of evolution. In contrast, polygenists argued that Africans, Asians and Europeans had separate origins and were therefore intrinsically different. This conflict of opinion amongst racists can be seen in a comparison of two articles from *The Nineteenth Century* published in 1911. The first, entitled 'The East, the West and Human Progress',[14] complains about the idea of 'the East' and 'the West' as concepts and argues that Eastern people are simply at a different stage in the evolutionary process. The second article, 'East and West: A Study of Differences',[15] argues in favour of the idea of intrinsic differences and lists many of the clichéd perceptions about religion, caste and mysticism, as well as other differences between the two areas that Inden also points out. This second article was written by Bampfylde Fuller, the first Lieutenant Governor of Eastern Bengal. Did the idea of the East and West as intrinsically different hold more sway in the tea-growing areas?

It is clear that the tea planters, desiring total control over all production for maximum economic return, affirmed the idea of Indians as intrinsically different, inherently backward and unable to rule and organise themselves. George Barker, for example, in *A Tea Planter's Life in Assam* described coolies as 'lazy and requir[ing] a lot of looking after'. 'Hot days', he continued, using climatic conditions to attribute character, 'are conducive to this spirit of idleness, and many small parties of coolies have to be routed out from under the grateful shade of the nearest tree, where they are to be found stowed away, enjoying the rest from toil'.[16]

The planters were one of the most intractable groups of colonial servants who held on to notions which maintained a rigid racial hierarchy. As George Barker wrote:

> This is the last remaining district where any sort of respect is shown for the Europeans; in all other parts of India the black man is as good as the white, a fact that is speedily brought home to the new comer. It is here, in Assam, that nearly all the old rights of servility that were exacted by Europeans in the days of the East India Company, are still in existence, and flourish to the general better feeling amongst the whole community. Here no heavy babu swaggers past with his umbrella up, jostling you on the way; but with courtly mien, on seeing your pony coming along, furls up the umbrella, steps on one side, and salutes with a profound salaam.[17]

In fact planters were not even particularly bothered about justifying their attitudes at all, as Chamberlain notes:

> the planters' element was not a happy one in Indian society. It was they, for example, who led the outcry against the Ilbert Bill in 1883. Sir George Trevelyan considered that there was not 'a single non-official person in India . . . who would not consider the sentiment that we hold India for the benefit of the inhabitants of India a loathsome un-English piece of cant'.[18]

The Ilbert Bill would have given Bengali officers criminal jurisdiction over European British subjects living in small towns. The planters argued that the Bengali magistrates, whom they stereotyped as 'effeminate babus' who 'do not hunt, shoot, [and] play games', would not understand the 'sporting, public-schooled trained Anglo-Indians who may be brought before them'. A great many cases brought against Anglo-Indians 'involved accusations against Anglo-Indian hunters and sportsmen who were frequently responsible for "accidental" shooting deaths of unwary native peasants; or against Anglo-Indian planters who were accused of using excessive physical force in "disciplining" their native employees'.[19] It was felt that the Bengali magistrate would not understand the 'thoughtless schoolboy spirit in which the injury complained of has been done'. It is clear that the planters exploited and created racist/'Orientalist' constructs that were useful to them. The unbending racial and colonial hierarchies which the planters upheld are perceivable in the rigid systems of order that were represented in the advertising of Lipton's and other tea companies, which formed part of the developing tea industries in India and Ceylon.

The representation of Empire tea – Lipton's advertising

While the United Kingdom Tea Company images discussed above express the shifting representations of older tea traders, the images from Lipton's enable us to explore the representations of Ceylon and India from a company whose interests were always embedded in the imperial products. The most prolific tea advertiser in 1890 was Lipton's. Its aggressive advertising provides an abundance of imagery that was directed specifically at the consumer rather than retailer, since most of its tea was sold in small packets in Lipton's grocery stores. The representations which I will discuss were used by many tea manufacturers and retailers. Lipton's, however, provides an abundance of examples which were directed at the growing group of lower-middle-class consumers. While I will concentrate on Lipton's advertising in this section, I will also refer, where appropriate, to representations by other companies and cartels such as the Indian Tea Association.

The plantation and the representation of vertical
control over production

The first Lipton's tea advertisement in *The Graphic* came out on 30 January 1892, two years after Lipton's first purchase of tea estates in Ceylon (Figure 35). Although it is graphically an uninteresting image, it presents a series of ingredients which were to dominate Lipton's advertising. The image depicts a scene on one of Lipton's plantations. There is a sense of order and serenity. In the gardens, labourers are shown plucking the tea, while on a road through the plantation, a row of women wait to have the tea they have plucked weighed by the European foreman. Buildings are scattered over the

Lipton's Tea advertisement, *The Graphic*, 30 January 1892

picture – all bearing the name of Lipton's on their roofs. On the left, a temple is visible, as well as a section of a port harbour, with boats and ships waiting to transport the tea. The scene is obviously inaccurate, since no tea gardens were on the coast, but it enabled Lipton to reinforce his slogan 'Direct from the tea garden to the tea pot'.

Both slogan and image not only suggest the direct arrival of tea from plantation to European consumer, but also the total control of Lipton's all along the way. While in the majority of advertisements the social relations of production and depictions of labour are deliberately hidden, in Lipton's advertising and other tea advertising of the period it appears to have become exalted. I would like to argue that Lipton's unabashed use was possible because it represented black workers, who within a racialised framework were believed to have been born to labour. Along with this representation of work, it affirmed its support for vertical control over production, which became one of the most dominant representations of this product and its industry. The image affirmed the economic and political interests of planters – plantation production under European control. It was a system that was supported by the Indian government of the time and subsequently the government of Ceylon. The interests of planters were lobbied for continuously and they seem to have won out repeatedly despite conditions for labourers that were often akin to slavery.

From the establishment of tea planting on a large scale in Assam, the government had passed Acts that supported the British planters' endeavours at the expense of local people. Land was given to planters – part free and part at nominal rents – for a period of ninety-nine years from 1838, with even better conditions being established in 1854. While rents to planters were nominal, the rents for ordinary land-owners were not only non-preferential, but were increased in 1867 when there was a labour shortage on the tea plantations, so as to cause deliberate destitution and thereby 'uproot a large section of the cultivators from the soil and force them to work on the tea gardens'.[20] The planters were also not required to cultivate all the land that they obtained on preferential rates, so with the extra land at their disposal they rented plots out to coolies who had completed their period of indenture. These plots, however, were not rented at preferential rates, but at market rates of Rs 1-14-0 per acre.

The coolies were also paid extremely low wages of Rs 5 and Rs 4 per month for men and women respectively. These wages were fixed by the government and contrasted with the Rs 15 per month for indentured labourers in other colonies. Even this meagre wage was often not paid, as the Tea Commissioner Report for 1865 makes clear: 'In one garden, which we visited, the pay of twelve men during the month of September had averaged less than Rs 3 each and out of this rice had to be bought at Rs 2 a maund... Instances of this nature might be multiplied indefinitely.'[21] The labourers were supposed to work nine hours a day but in practice had to work much longer hours because the monthly pay was based on piece work, which could not in fact be completed in nine hours a day.

In 1882 the government supported the planters again by passing what Indian opposition described as a 'Slave Bill in disguise'. The Bill enabled independent recruitment of labourers throughout India through 'sardars'. This independent system left nobody responsible for labourers' welfare between recruitment and their arrival at the gardens and led to large numbers of labourers perishing even before arrival in the tea districts. The Act was eventually amended in 1889 and 1893 in order to ensure some degree of well-being for the labourers since this was also in planters' interests.

The plantation of the Lipton's advertisements white-washed the extremes of exploitation and hardship while at the same time affirming vertical control over production. It presented the plantation as an idealised, ordered world in which there was no conflict. While I have discussed conditions only on Indian plantations due to the limitation of source material on Ceylon, Lipton's had estates in both countries and the conditions for labourers in Ceylon were likely to be no better than those in India. The colonial authorities estimated that between 1841 and 1849 a quarter of Tamil immigrants to Ceylon, indentured to work in tea plantations, died.[22]

Lipton's use of such an image in advertising in the 1890s was even more surprising, since through the 1880s and 1890s criticism of the conditions of coolies were raised in England through the Aboriginal Protection Society, as well as in India by the British Indian Association. In 1890 the conditions of labour on the tea estates in India had also received significant publicity when an article in the *Madras Mail* of 11 September highlighted the high mortality, low rates of pay and extreme punishments given to coolies working in Assam. It noted how in 1886 the Chief Commissioner of Assam, Mr Ward, had remarked how 'the cooly is practically a slave for the whole period of his contract'. The writer also quoted statistics which showed mortality figures for coolies ranging from 200 in every 1,000 to 594 in every 1,000, because coolies were never able to be ill, or they would end up unable to feed themselves. The article also mentioned how a prison for run-away coolies and other punishments were also a regular feature on the estates.

I would like to suggest two reasons which enabled this representation of labour to be possible. Firstly and most importantly, the attitudes to India and 'the Orient' during this period allowed Lipton's to present the plantation as one of idealised labour relations. The idea espoused by Mill and others of the 'natural' ability of European's to rule and Indians to be ruled enabled scenes like this to be read as though they were organic. Development in Ceylon appears entirely down to Lipton; almost every structure is marked with his name. The European obsession with caste as the fundamental institution in India and South Asia also naturalises this scene. 'Better one's duty ill performed', Joseph Campbell quotes from a Hindu text in his *Oriental Mythology*, 'than that of another to perfection'. For the planters this could be interpreted as the coolies' rightful place as labourers, even more so because, as Campbell continued, the 'idea of the great individual simply does not exist within the pale of the system'.[23]

The space for individual greatness is therefore easily preserved for Mr Lipton, who is represented as having brought order and progress to a world of chaos and superstition as represented in the temple. This notion is even further eulogised as late as 1967, by Denys Forrest:

> The mountains may be steep and jagged, the plains luxuriant and steamy, but wherever tea is grown, at whatever elevation, there is one prevailing note – order. What the plantation pioneers evolved in the first place, and what their successors have maintained in the face of all tropical inducements to ease off, *is a self disciplined routine aimed at the production of as much and as good tea as possible from a given acreage of land.*[24] (my emphasis)

The notion of imposed order is indicated in this and other Lipton's advertisements through the regular spacing of the workers lined up in queues, the ordered lines of bushes, and even the three elephants on the left-hand side are spaced evenly apart. Straight lines dominate the drawing; the only contrast to this is the temple and the palm trees, both symbols of the 'other'.

This representation of order and control can also be viewed in the development of a Lipton's advertisement in 1896. In its first appearance on 7 March, the key ingredients of tea garden, tea pickers, coolies, European planter, industrial symbolism (represented by the steam train), and trading ships are all present, but the scene of the gardens in the central circle lacks the sense of order which can be viewed in the image discussed above (Figure 36). On the second and subsequent appearance of this advertisement (4 April 1896 and later), this scene changed (Figure 37). The regulated rows of tea plants and ordered rows of coolies appear in this reworked image, which is also much brighter than the last one, symbolically affirming the notion of progress. Order was also clearly associated with European dominance and total control. The forefront of the previous picture had shown a man and a woman labourer picking tea from the same bush and facing each other. The size of the woman is almost that of the European man standing just outside the scene. There also appeared to be a feeling of togetherness between the two labourers and this relationship was repeated further back with the image of two women working closely together. This scene obviously did not assert a sense of the European planter's control over his labourers, since they appear to have a social interaction which excludes him. In the revised image these labourers are removed and the lines of regimented coolies appear again. Each worker appears isolated in his or her task and their submission to the planter is further affirmed by a coolie who is illustrated as much smaller than the planter and stands to attention on the opposite side of the circular frame looking up at the planter as though waiting for his orders. The insertion of this coolie also stabilises the image. These

36, 37 Lipton's Tea advertisements, *The Graphic*, 7 March 1896 and 4 April 1896

[111]

scenes appear so static and timeless, eradicating notions of conflict or need for change. The representation of Indian tea pickers as obedient workers within an imperial order is an image which many would have seen as entirely natural in late nineteenth-century Britain. At the Colonial and Indian Exhibition of 1886, for example, the exhibition guide, when discussing workers in Ceylon, commented: 'Labour is supplied by the Tamil population who have immigrated from the neighbouring coast of India, whence they are continually obtained; they are a docile and tractable people, well suited for work on the estates'.[25]

Apart from the naturalisation of labour relations through imperial ideology, I would posit that a second reason which permitted this depiction of labour was the romanticised notion of the factory in the garden. In 1879 Cadbury's opened its new factory at Bournville, which was marketed heavily as 'the factory in the garden'. The industrialism of nineteenth-century Britain had seen the working conditions of ordinary people dramatically altered through the move from the countryside to the city, where cramped living conditions, an increasingly poor atmosphere, a lack of greenery and a life regimented by the factory clock made people look back nostalgically at what seemed like an idyllic rural past. With this new factory and its location in the countryside, Cadbury's aimed to keep what was defined as the 'efficiency' of the factory in a rural-like setting. Coming from a Quaker tradition of philanthropy, Cadbury's wanted to provide its British workers with better living conditions and amenities than usually existed for them in the belief that a happy worker was a better and more productive worker.

Lipton's must have been conscious that its advertisements of tea plantations and factories surrounded by countryside echoed this image of British philanthropy. For the British consumer already fed with a diet of Empire, it must have appeared as though the Ceylonese labourers were not only in their rightful place as servants of the Empire, but also that they were being treated relatively well. Lipton's interestingly didn't use the word 'estate' to describe these scenes in its advertisements, despite the currency of this term in Ceylon, but preferred to use the Indian term 'garden' which gave a more favourable and idyllic sounding vision.

The image of plantation life with its imposed and naturalised order, along with a vision of ruralism, dominated Lipton's advertising. Lipton's helped to construct an image of Ceylon which was not limited to its product. Scenes of all-pervading order can be seen in tea images produced by a variety of companies. Tarrant Henderson and Co.'s *Ceylon Tea Report* of 1898, for example, depicts a series of photographs which represents all stages of production. These photographs naturalise an image of plantation life which is tranquil and conditioned by an overarching feeling of regularity, order and stasis (Figure 38). In the late nineteenth century, photographs would have been interpreted by nearly everybody as recording the truth, yet the photographs in this report are consciously orchestrated and framed. An image of regulated coolies and bullock carts can be seen in one of these photographs. Firm triangles and rectangles dominate the structure of the images, along with numerous horizontal axes. The postures of many of the workers along with the images as a whole appear almost classical, adding a sense of timelessness. This timelessness acts to deny the physicality and drudgery of actual labour. In spite of the all-pervading sense of order, the photographs also appear to deny the militarised and mass nature of factory production. An idealised image of three or four workers performing each task is presented. Yet these photographs do not present images of individualised workers. Instead, workers are merely cogs in the machinery necessary for commodity production. The commodification of labour is particularly apparent in a scene called 'Native staff' in which the workers are boxed into a space between crates of tea (Figure 39).

While Lipton was also interested in representing every aspect of production, unlike Tarrant Henderson, he never denied the mass nature of his enterprise. Perhaps Tarrant Henderson aimed to attract a market in fine teas, in contrast to Lipton's drive for a mass market. In a postcard series from 1908, Lipton depicted each stage of production in images which represented a sense of dynamism and order. Above all the sense of vertical integration was paramount, with the Lipton name on every basket crate, bullock cart and building and the white planter frequently depicted surveying the scene. Lipton's appeared to eulogise the mass nature of factory production. Scenes that depict rows of bullock carts or coolies carrying Lipton's teas stretching back as far as the eye can see, as well as scenes that depict crowds of tea pickers (kept in order by the foreman), express the vastness of Lipton's factory and enterprise (Figure 40). The image of European science and order is again contrasted here with postcards that represent Tamil and Sinhalese in states of disorder. A postcard called 'Natives at play' depicts a scene which appears chaotic and full of superstition (Figure 41). Lipton's all-consuming control is particularly expressed in a postcard which depicts an aerial view of coolies arranged in the shape of the word Lipton. Lipton's postcards and advertisements appear to have been one of the only representations of Ceylon in popular culture. For the average British consumer, Ceylon must have simply been one large tea estate, a tea estate that had once been a jungle. This country seemed to have only developed as a result of imperial enterprise and control.

It is worth noting that this series of postcards was not a haphazard marketing exercise. It joined the work of the Planters' Association of Ceylon and the Indian Tea Association in promoting Indian and Ceylon

38, 39 'Hand sifting by women' and 'Native staff', Tarrant Henderson and Co., *Ceylon Tea Report*, 1898

tea in reaction to the establishment of a China Tea Association in 1907, which attempted to promote China tea as healthier than Indian/Ceylon tea, because it was less astringent. The Ceylon Planters had voted £2,000 for 'repelling this Chinese menace',[26] and the Indian

40, 41 'Weighing the plucked tea, Ceylon' and 'Natives at play, Ceylon tea estate', postcards, Lipton series, 1908

Tea Association, although not voting funds to promote tea, decided that 'much useful work might be done in the way of pushing British-grown teas in the United Kingdom by judicious advertisements in the shape of leaflets, pictorial postcards or pamphlets'.[27] Copies of the paintings for Indian Tea Association postcards exist in the Public Record Office National Art Register files. It is interesting that these paintings do not represent the sense of order that Lipton's creates in its images, although many of the images reflect an exoticism and romanticism of labour. It is clear that Lipton's postcard series must have been part of this thrust to promote the Empire more aggressively. It clearly aimed to promote both the market for imperial goods, and the ideology of vertical control which was essential for the maintenance of planters' interests.

Imperial exhibitions also promoted plantation culture. Along with the tea houses at the Franco-British exhibition of 1908, the Indian Tea Association commissioned a well-known scenic artist to paint a large tableau depicting a scene for a tea garden (Figure 42). While

42 Indian Tea Association Panoramic Tableau, *Franco-British Exhibition: Report on the India Section*, 1909

representing a degree of order through the lines of bushes at which the pluckers work, the image of an idyllic rural vision dominates. Just like in the Tarrant Henderson photographs, there is a quietness and classicism about the tableau which gives Indian tea production a historicity as well as denying the harshness of plantation production. The image of India as jungle is dominant through the side panels of vegetation, which encroach on the garden. It is as though classical European order has been bestowed on the untamed jungle. Although the image was painted from a photograph, its symbolic referencing of India and plantation production pulls the scene away from a documentary style. Yet in the *Report of the India Section*, the Princess of Wales is reported to have 'admired the Tea Garden scene, remarking that it vividly reminded her of her visit to the Indian tea districts'. This kind of projection obviously asserted these images as 'true' representations of plantation life and increased their ideological effectiveness. The tableau from the exhibition also draws out another reason why the representation of plantation production may have been so strong. As I have mentioned, the side panels represented the typical notion of tropical abundance in the untamed jungle that was often used to undermine the work and knowledge of 'native' farmers all over the Empire. The European planters in India and Ceylon must have wanted to qualify this idea of natural abundance so as not to undermine the importance of their own contribution. The image of the plantation, run with scientific rationality and vertical control over production, was the most efficient way of expressing the value and necessity of their involvement in the development of what became a massive industry. The centrality of this image for the identity of Lipton's can be seen through its repeated use on promotional tins produced by Lipton's. These images were recently reproduced on an advertisement for Lipton's centenary year in 1990, reaffirming their importance.

Imperial pageantry and a romantic image of India
While the depiction of plantation life, with its order and vertical control over production, was the strongest of all tea marketing images, Lipton's often combined this with images drawn from broader representations of India and 'the Orient'. Plantation scenes were eulogised further through scenes of pageantry, for example, which depicted trumpeting elephants. Imperial pageantry had increased in the mid 1880s with the development of a more aggressive imperialism. The 1887 Jubilee celebrations, as well as exhibitions such as the Colonial and Indian Exhibition discussed above, 'were enacted with considerable pageantry, replete with imperial trappings'. In this kind of

advertisement Lipton's joined in the contemporary imperial jingoism, declaring in the banner above the elephants that Lipton's was 'Victorious over all others'. Lipton's was obviously referring to the sale of its tea, but the colonial exploits of Europeans during this period give the phrase military overtones. Lipton's seems to have cultivated an image of imperial pomp, often mentioning medals won by Lipton's at imperial exhibitions in its advertising. This advertisement, for example, was adapted to celebrate the gold medal that Lipton's won at the Chicago exhibition of 1893.

The sense of pomp and ceremony in these advertisements also drew on the romanticised image of India. This image, while rejecting the complete attack on Indian civilisation made by the anglicists and the utilitarians, still viewed India as Europe's other and saw it as a land which outsiders desired to possess. As Hegel wrote:

> From the most ancient times downwards, all nations have directed their wishes and longings to gaining access to the treasures of this land of marvels, the most costly which the Earth presents; treasures of Nature – pearls, diamonds, perfumes, rose-essences, elephants, lions, etc. – as also treasures of wisdom . . . Those wishes have been realised; this Land of Desire has been attained; there is scarcely any great nation of the East, nor of the Modern European west, that has not gained for itself a smaller or larger portion of it.[28]

Hegel concludes: 'The English, or rather the East India Company, are lords of the land; for it is the necessary fate of Asiatic Empires to be subjected to Europeans; and China will, some day or other, be obliged to submit to this fate'. The tamed and controlled elephants, parading to extol Lipton's achievements at the Chicago exhibition, appear to represent symbolically Britain's control over this 'land of desire'. The image of pomp and pageantry on Lipton's advertising and marketing was heightened at imperial exhibitions. The Planters' Association of Ceylon and the Indian Tea Association exploited similar representations in their marketing of tea at imperial exhibitions.[29] A programme for the Franco-British Exhibition's Indian Arena depicts a scene of pageantry, as well as a hunt. The symbols of India as wild and full of jungle, as well as an opulent East, are present. On the inside of the programme, flanking the details of a 'spectacular pantomime' on 'Our Indian Empire', Lipton's advertised both an Indian and a Ceylon tea room.[30] The glamour and drama of the pantomime, along with its imperial identity, were transferred through juxtaposition to Lipton's.

Lipton's never missed an opportunity to associate its product with exoticism and glamour. In the 1890s Lipton's also used the image of a trumpeting elephant carrying crates of Lipton's tea on its packaging.

In fact Lipton's repeatedly used the image of trumpeting elephants. As Alex Waugh notes, when one of the managers of a Lipton's store was perplexed as to how he could get a 3-ton cheese from the docks to the store, Lipton, who had noticed that a circus was in town, promptly suggested that he should hire an elephant: 'His manager acquired the services of the elephant for seven dollars and a half, and a procession of jubilant small boys attended the triumphal progress of the monster cheese'.[31]

The Orient as female and the representation of the Tamil woman tea picker

While exploiting the image of imperial triumphalism, a more dominant and enduring image for Ceylon tea, along with the image of plantation production, was the use of the image of the Tamil woman. 'The Orient', whether Arab or Indian, was often identified as female in European thought. The qualities of reason, intellect, action, dynamism and natural leadership that were associated with the West were also perceived as masculine in Victorian England. In contrast, the East, which Victorian Britain believed to be organically feminine, was irrational, spiritual, decorative, passive and servile.

Inden has highlighted the language which writers such as Percival Spear and Charles Eliot used to describe India and Hinduism. Spear, for example, defines Hinduism as a vast sponge that 'has no clear outline on its borders and no apparent core at its centre', in contrast to the 'Western love of definition'. As Inden comments, 'implicit here, is also the idea that Hinduism is a *female* presence who is able, through her very amorphousness and absorptive powers, to baffle and perhaps even threaten Western rationality, clearly a male in this encounter'.[32]

With this background of representations, the otherness of South Asia could best be represented for Lipton's through the image of a Tamil woman tea picker. The advertisement from *The Graphic* on 10 September 1892 is described in the Lipton's archive as Lipton's first advertisement (Figure 43). Although it was not, the fact that it has been described as such indicates the enduring nature of the image as well as its impact. The woman appears decorative, exotic and submissive. Interestingly she does not appear to be a worker on the plantations but instead is decked out with jewellery and holds a cup of Lipton's tea. Alex Waugh notes how Lipton, in his early advertising, 'visualised an attractive label of a Tamil girl with a basket on her head. He had his slogan ready: "Direct from the tea garden to the tea pot".'[33] The emphasis on the image of an exotic woman in both contexts expresses the endurance of this image.

43 Lipton's Tea advertisement, *The Graphic*, 10 September 1892

For the European, while the 'Orient' was feminine, the 'Oriental' woman was viewed as an ideal object for fantasy, particularly erotic fantasy. As Rana Kabbani notes, in Victorian prejudice,

> all women were inferior to men; Eastern women were doubly inferior, being women *and* Easterners. They were an even more conspicuous commodity than their Western sisters. They were part of the goods of Empire, the living rewards that white men could, if they wished to, reap. They were there to be used sexually, and if it could be suggested that they were inherently licentious, then they could be exploited with no qualms whatsoever.[34]

While the woman in this advertisement does not appear highly eroticised, her exoticism is certainly sexualised through her jewellery, loose hair, and open lips. Along with this sexuality, she also appears slightly innocent with her wide eyes and demurely cocked head. As a domestic and family product it would not have been appropriate for Lipton's to have adopted a highly eroticised image for its tea. In selecting this representation, Lipton's appears to have adopted an image which recalls that of Scheherazade, whom Kabbani describes as the only 'saving stereotype' of the 'Oriental' woman in European culture.[35] As Kabbani describes, she is both good and physically desirable, intelligent, pious, learned and dutiful. Yet her innocent nature is in sharp contrast to the bawdiness of her stories . . . She is exemplary in all the domestic roles; dutiful daughter, considerate sister, loving wife and caring mother. Although she is highly learned, her learning serves only to please and placate a man – it has no other function at all.[36]

The Arabian nights were probably the best known stories of Arab literature in the West, and if it appears strange to suggest that Lipton's could have exploited an Arabian image for a Ceylonese product, we should remember that representations of 'the Orient' were both generalised and particularised and Lipton's was drawing on an Arabian stereotype here, since the woman represented is decorated in jewellery that does not appear Tamil or Sinhalese, but is much more representative of North Africa.

The image of a generalised feminine exoticism which is represented in this image captured a Europeanised image of the East that was acceptable for family life. While this was an attractive image for tea, it appears from other advertisements that Lipton's also wished to continue to assert its belief in the plantation system and vertical control over production. In two advertisements published around 1901, one a poster and the other for print media, Sinhalese women are represented in order to give the product exotic appeal. In both images, the plantation can be glimpsed in the background. The advertisements are also interesting since they appear to represent two very different exotic women. In the print advertisement the woman is reasonably well dressed but in a plain outfit. She carries a palm leaf behind her, which frames her face, a bit like a fan. She sits smiling at the viewer with her body turned towards us in a typical portrait-like stance. Although there is a basket at her feet, she does not appear to be a worker by the way she sits with her feet delicately crossed.

In contrast to the newspaper image, there is no ambiguity about the woman's position in the poster, which represents an exotically dressed woman with flowers in her hair, who carries a Japanese-style parasol behind her head. Her posture and dress, as well as the feel of the poster as a whole, clearly suggest that her class position is not that of a worker at all. Is she the exotic wife of a planter? She is simply identified at the bottom as 'the Belle of Lipton's Dambatene Ceylon Tea Gardens'. Both women clearly offered the brand exotic appeal, but the woman in the poster also seems to present an image which suggests quality and also appears Far Eastern, with her parasol and the delicately potted plant behind her. This conflict of identity and imagery may be a result of the audiences for which they were intended. The print media image was aimed at a mass market. It was headed 'Millions drink it daily'. Fewer people would have viewed the poster. The refinement of the woman in the poster, along with the slightly Far Eastern style imagery, seems to reflect Lipton's desire to capture the elite market for tea, which was still dominated by China tea. Apart from Lipton's brand advertising to this market, generic advertising for Ceylon tea by the Ceylon administration and its Planters' Association also aimed at capturing this market. At the turn of the century, for example, Ceylon had provided the Imperial Institute with money to build a tea garden in order to encourage the drinking of Ceylon tea amongst the 'well-to-do' classes of the capital.

While the representation of these women situated on the plantation provided both an image of exoticism and the exaltation of plantation production, the two symbols were still essentially separated within the image. Sinhalese women were not employed as labourers on the plantations. With the representation of the Tamil woman tea picker, Lipton found an exotic identity with a degree of sensuality and an assertion of the plantation labour system, in one image. The exoticism of the woman tea picker not only found space in pictures but also in texts on plantation life in both India and Ceylon. As George Barker wrote on Assam in 1884:

> The women, of whom there is always a fair sprinkling in every batch, take more pride in their appearance than the men. This they manifest by the care with which they will arrange their hair, the gaudy-coloured raiment, the gaudier the better, that they affect, and the enormous silver or brass bangles studding their arms and ankles. Love of finery usually takes the form of bangles or earrings. Both of these articles of adornment assume gigantic dimension.[37]

In *Golden Tips*, Henry Cave, writing about Ceylon, also referred to the exoticism of the women and their suitability for plucking:

> Women are preferred to men for this work . . . They look very picturesque, with their fine glossy hair and dreamy black eyes, their ears, necks and arms, and ankles adorned with silver ornaments, and their gay cloths of many colours falling in graceful folds while standing intent upon their work among the bushes.[38]

As late as 1967, Forrest defended the exoticised image of the woman tea pickers:

> Travellers, by the way, who have only seen [the tea pickers] in their foul weather garb or among the chillier heights of the Up-country, are inclined to dismiss as 'phoney' any coloured photograph or film which shows them in bright saris, set off by golden neck, arm, ear and nose ornaments. But the gayer and the more sombre picture are equally authentic – it is just a matter of weather!

> Women pluckers ... bright saris ... dark cumblies ... such are the familiar ingredients of the plucking scene.[39]

From 1910 onwards, a variety of versions of the Tamil woman tea picker's image appeared in Lipton's advertising. In all of these images, the Tamil woman was shown smiling gently in a lush plantation. She is the acceptable face of production through the genderising of labour relations and imperial hierarchy, and as such could survive the crisis of British imperialism of the 1920s, the increasing questioning of Empire and the period of decolonisation. The Tamil woman plucker as the acceptable face of production appears to be the point of contact between consumption and production. In one image from the 1920s, the Tamil woman even stretches her basket out of the plantation scene for the European woman consumer to select her tea, fresh from the garden, for her pot (Figure 44). She is framed and contained in contrast to the European consumer. She is the worker in contrast to the leisured European woman. This image also represents the growing belief and promotion of Empire as a complementary and supportive unit in which the colonies provided the metropolis with raw materials in return for manufactured goods. This idea, propagated by the Empire Marketing Board (EMB) in the 1920s and 1930s, will be further discussed in the next chapter, although it is worth noting here that an EMB series of tea posters reflected the notion of producer and consumer that can be seen in the Lipton's image.

The Tamil woman tea picker as point of contact between producer and consumer also offers an explanation for another 1920s advertisement which represents an Indian woman tea picker dressed in the traditional saris and bangles (Figure 45). In facial features and hairstyle, however, she is the fashionable young British woman of the 1920s. Here, the two separate women (producer and consumer) are collapsed into one, romanticising and neutralising labour relations even further. This collapsing was doubly easier because of the frequent insertion of European models into 'Orientalist' scenes by European painters. It also enabled Lipton's to focus on the consumer as increasingly happened in 1920s advertising, without ditching the historical development of Lipton's and Empire tea imagery.

Another reason for the collapse of producer and consumer into one figure could also be the visual referencing of a general association between women and gardens (particularly flowers) that was commonplace in Victorian and Edwardian culture.[40] These images formed part of a general association between women and nature, yet for white women these were invariably associations of leisure and pleasure, in contrast to the Tamil woman's relationship of labour. In the Lipton's

44 Lipton's Tea advertisement, *Pearson's Weekly*, 12 December 1925

45 Lipton's Tea advertisement, 1922

tea image of collapsed producer/consumer, the woman appears to enjoy picking leaves selectively, as though at leisure. The regimented order of the late nineteenth-century advertisements is not apparent here, although the naming of Lipton's on all constructions within the natural environment and the representation of a woman maintains the male and imperial hegemony of Lipton's.

Lipton's, of course, was not the only company or organisation to use the image of the Tamil woman tea picker. The Planters' Association of Ceylon, 'Salada' Tea, and Tarrant Henderson and Co., for example, all used this image, sometimes in a seemingly matter-of-fact style and at other times in dreamy, exoticised ways (Figure 46). The image of the Tamil woman tea picker has remained the most enduring image for sub-continental tea, as well as one of the most pervasive images of India and Ceylon in British consumer culture.

By the 1920s, the image of the Indian woman tea picker may have provided more than an exotic and alluring image. Her representation may have been viewed as symbolically asserting the need for Empire. With the growing demand for self-rule, the subordination of the Indian

46 'Coolie plucking leaf', Tarrant Henderson and Co.,
Ceylon Tea Report, 1898

woman was used to legitimate colonial rule. The idea of the English
woman's 'imperial burden' had been voiced throughout the nineteenth
century. A variety of women's journals concerned themselves with
what they saw as the plight of the Indian woman, publishing articles
about India and women in India, as well as encouraging white women
to 'help' them. The *Women's Suffrage Journal*, for example, had articles entitled 'How to help Indian women'.[41] Katherine Mayo's book
Mother India, published in 1927, reaffirmed the idea that the abuse of
women by Indian men was to blame for India's plight, at the moment
when the Indian independence movement was growing in strength:
'The whole pyramid of the Indian's woes, material and spiritual . . . rests
upon a rock-bottom physical base. The base is, simply, his manner
of getting into the world and his sex life thenceforward.'[42] Mayo and
others ignored the abuse and subordination that Western women
faced and suggested imperialism as a way to save Indian women from

[125]

their men. British Rule was represented as encouraging liberalisation, although as Liddle and Joshi point out, the British position was contradictory and was above all concerned 'with the way the divisions of gender mediated the structure of imperialism'. In using an image of a Tamil woman worker, Lipton's was inevitably not only representing the image of the Tamil woman as alluring and sensual, but through her apparent contentment and productivity in an ordered environment symbolically affirmed the need for Empire.

The collapsing of the representation of Ceylon and tea

The power of tea advertising and marketing not only affected the public's perception of tea, but also impacted on the popular image of Ceylon, in particular. To the ordinary British consumer, Ceylon, as Denys Forrest has indicated, must have appeared to be one large tea estate. Forrest attributes this image especially to Lipton's and suggests that Ceylon almost appeared 'a Lipton rather than a British colony'.[43] The collapse of representations between Ceylon and tea seems to have appeared frequently. Here I will discuss two examples. The first is Henry Cave's *Golden Tips: A Description of Ceylon and its Great Tea Industry*, first published in 1900. The book is presented as a travelogue and describes the landscape, flora and fauna of the country, as well as its people. Interspersed is a discussion about the tea industry and its production. The shifts between travel writing and a discussion of the industry appear so natural that the two cannot be separated, and in this process the conditions of the tea workers are also aestheticised as enviable and beautiful:

> The height of Allagalla is 3,394 feet. Tea grows upon its steep acclivities, and those who are occupied in its cultivation on these giddy heights are enviable witnesses of the most varied and beautiful atmospheric scenes that are to be found in Ceylon.[44]

> Although in visiting Labookellie we have approached to within seven miles of Nuwara Eliya, the famous mountain sanitarium to which considerable reference will be made later, we must now return to Gampola and thence proceed through the central and largest of all the tea districts.[45]

In *Golden Tips*, through descriptions such as the above, Ceylon is reduced to being one large tea estate with recreational countryside. Britain's involvement in developing the tea industry is also used in the travelogue to justify imperial control:

> Fruit and flowers of forms quite strange to the visitor grow in profusion everywhere, impressing one with the idea of luxury and plenty. We feel,

as we roam along the paths, how happy and contented the people must be who live amidst such surroundings; and we reflect upon the contrast which it all bears to the barbarian and poverty-stricken Kandy under the tyrant kings, when the food of the people chiefly consisted of bark and roots, and their homes were squalid beyond conception. Such transformation as this influx of wealth and comfort under British rule must be a convincing proof to the intelligent natives that their citadel at length fell to worthy conquerors, and a matter of proud satisfaction to every Briton who reflects on the result of the enterprise.[46]

The endurance of this identity for Ceylon can be seen in the film *The Song of Ceylon* (1933) directed by Basil Wright and funded by the Empire Marketing Board. Produced by Grierson's Film Unit, this haunting film reproduces all the images of Ceylon which have been discussed above. Ceylon is represented as untamed jungle, with inhabitants who lead a simple life dominated by religion and superstition. The first part is in fact called 'The Buddha' and traces a group of Sinhalese on a pilgrimage. It is then followed by a section entitled 'The Virgin Island' which enhances the typical colonial image of an idyllic, untouched and almost unpopulated island upon which the tea industry, commerce and Europe intrude in the third section – 'The Voices of Commerce'. Although the film certainly romanticises the pre-commercial world of Ceylon through imagery and music, and presents the British trader and his world as dry and cold (a world dominated by statistics, telexes and telephones), no proper evaluation is made of the impact of commerce on the lives of the local people. West and East are also crystallised as rational and irrational; developed and underdeveloped; ordered and disordered; industrialised and rural respectively. Importantly, the planter is not represented in 'Voices of Commerce', but rather the trader. This dissipates and denies the appropriation of land by planters and the reduction of Sinhalese and Tamil men and women simply to hired labourers, since, as the film mentions, most men would consider this demeaning, in comparison to working for themselves.

Finally, in the fourth section 'The Apparel of God', the film fails to express any effect that the tea and other industries have had on the local population. Tea simply seems to be absorbed into the landscape and its production becomes a new form of pilgrimage, with images of the lines of tea pickers returning from the estates being compared to earlier images of pilgrims climbing up a hill through the use of the same music. Asserting Orientalist doctrine, the Ceylonese appear to continue in a static world that remains superstitious and religious. It is as though the worlds of commerce and idyllic ruralism live side by side without impinging on each other. A sense of complete stasis is also achieved by the film ending as it began with an image of jungle and palm leaves. It is as though the film just pushed back the dense jungle for a moment to capture a glimpse of 'Ceylon and her tea industry' – the representations of which elide at moments and conflict at others. The return to the jungle suggests Ceylon and its people are part of an untameable world, which will always run wild unless constantly held in check – by Europeans.

Film and travel literature emphasise even more than standard advertising the completely transformed representation of tea from a Chinese product to an imperial and Ceylonese one. While the vastness of India could not allow such a total collapse of identities, we should remember that the relationship between representations of Indian and Ceylon tea were strong, as was the relationship between representations of the two countries.

The collapsing of identities for both countries into this commodity was clearly apparent at the Glasgow Empire Exhibition of 1938. The only representation of both India and Ceylon at the exhibition was in the Empire Tea Pavilion, which depicted 'a three dimensional diorama incorporating typical mountain scenery in India and Ceylon where the finest Empire tea is grown', as well as photographs of production, maps and statistics. Although in a modernist setting, unlike previous Empire exhibitions, the exoticism of the product was retained. As the official guide noted: 'Displays lent by the Govt. of India and Ceylon of arts and crafts typical of these famous tea-producing countries give colour to the exhibits'. Along with this exoticism, films 'about life in India and Ceylon and the production of tea' were shown in a small cinema.[47] It is unclear whether there were different films about life in the countries and about tea production, or whether films like *Song of Ceylon*, which discussed both, were on view. It is quite likely that *The Song of Ceylon* would have been one of these films since it had only been made five years earlier. Whatever the films shown, the context within the pavilion encouraged a collapsing of identities between tea and the countries of production. The joint nature of this pavilion also ensured a singular identity for Empire tea, which, although grown in parts of Africa too,[48] was depicted as an entirely sub-continental product produced by the European.

In a period of less than thirty years, Empire tea producers radically altered the identity of tea from a Chinese to an Indian and Ceylonese product. Apart from actual advertising, the image of Indian and Ceylon tea was created through imperial exhibitions, postcards, travel writing and film. For Ceylon, in particular, these cultural products all encouraged the collapsing of the identities between Ceylon and tea. Tea advertising and marketing not only created a sub-continental image, but also affirmed the plantation economy and vertical control over production as an almost natural response to racial difference. This attitude never really altered throughout the period of Empire, although by the 1920s scenes of rigid order were replaced by the image of the Tamil woman tea picker. She symbolically maintained an affirmation in plantation production and imperial control through a gendered hierarchy and was a dominant representation of Indians in British commercial culture of the time.

Notes

1   P. Griffiths, *The History of the Indian Tea Industry* (London, 1967), p. 50
2   E. Brammah, *Tea and Coffee: A Modern View of Three Hundred Years of Tradition* (London, 1972), pp. 81–2.
3   Griffiths, *Indian Tea Industry*, p. 58.
4   Figures from the 'Detailed Report of the General Committee of the Indian Tea Association' , year ending 1893, PRO.
5   Frank Cundall (ed.), *Reminiscences of the Colonial and Indian Exhibition* (London, 1886), p. 36.
6   *The Jubilee Chronicle of the Newcastle Exhibition*, 1887.
7   D. Forrest, *Tea for the British* (London, 1973), p. 179.
8   J. MacKenzie, *Propaganda and Empire: The Manipulation of British Public Opinion 1880–1960* (Manchester, 1984), p. 127.
9   D. Forrest, *A Hundred Years of Ceylon Tea 1867–1967* (London, 1967), pp. 170–1.
10 J. Steadman, *The Myth of Asia* (New York, 1969), pp. 25–6.
11 R. Inden, *Imagining India* (Oxford, 1990), pp. 36–8.
12 L. Mani, Review of *Imagining India*, in *Journal of Asian Studies*, 50 (1991), pp. 435–6.
13 Inden, *Imagining India*, p. 49.
14 E. Bevan, 'The East, the West and Human Progress', *The Nineteenth Century* (August 1911), pp. 350–66.
15 B. Fuller, 'East and West: A Study of Differences', *The Nineteenth Century* (November 1911), pp. 860–70.
16 G. Barker, *A Tea Planter's Life in Assam* (Calcutta, 1884), p. 138.
17 *Ibid.*, p. 87.
18 M. E. Chamberlain, *Britain and India: The Interaction of Two Peoples* (Newton Abbot, 1974), p. 127.
19 M. Sinha, *Colonial Masculinity: The 'Manly Englishman' and the 'Effeminate Bengali' in the Late Nineteenth Century* (Manchester, 1995), p. 42.
20 *Tea Commissioners Report*, 1868, cited in S. K. Bose, *Capital and Labour in the Indian Tea Industry* (Bombay, 1954), p. 14.
21 Cited in Bose, *Capital and Labour*, p. 75.
22 World Development Organisation, *The Tea Trade* (London, 1979), p. 10.
23 J. Campbell, *Oriental Mythology* (New York, 1962), pp. 339–40.
24 Forrest, *Ceylon Tea*, p. 19.
25 T. H. Wood (ed.), *Colonial and Indian Exhibition – Reports on the Colonial Sections* (London, 1887), p. 156.
26 Forrest, *Ceylon Tea*, p. 212.
27 Griffiths, *Indian Tea Industry*, p. 602.
28 G. W. Hegel, *The Philosophy of History* (London, 1956), p. 142, quoted in Inden, *Imagining India*, p. 70.

29 See A. Ramamurthy, 'Representation of Colonial and Imperialist Ideologies through the Images of African and Asian People in British Advertising 1880–1960', unpublished Ph.D. thesis, Lancaster University (1999), pp. 155–65.
30 See Tea and Coffee, Bodleian Library, John Johnson Collection.
31 A. Waugh, *The Lipton Story* (New York, 1950), p. 63.
32 Inden, *Imagining India*, pp. 85–6.
33 Waugh, *Lipton Story*, p. 58.
34 R. Kabbani, *Europe's Myth of Orient* (London, 1986), p. 51.
35 L. Jardine, *Still Harping on Daughters* (London, 1983), p. 169, quoted by Kabbani, *Europe's Myth*, p. 50 .
36 Kabbani, *Europe's Myth*, pp. 50–1.
37 Barker, *A Tea Planter's Life*, p. 165.
38 H. Cave, *Golden Tips: A Description of Ceylon and its Great Tea Industry* (London, 1900), p. 152.
39 Forrest, *Ceylon Tea*, pp. 23–4.
40 P. G. Nunn, *Problem Pictures: Women and Men in Victorian Painting* (Aldershot, 1995), pp. 28–48.
41 A. Burton, 'The White Woman's Burden: British Feminists and the Indian Woman 1865–1915', *Women's Studies in International Forum*, 13:4 (1990), pp. 295–307.
42 K. Mayo, *Mother India* (New York, 1927), p. 32, quoted in J. Liddle and R. Joshi, 'Gender and Imperialism in British India', *South Asia Research*, 5:2 (1985), p. 147.
43 Forrest, *Ceylon Tea*, pp. 152–3.
44 Cave, *Golden Tips*, p. 53.
45 *Ibid.*, p. 113.
46 *Ibid.*, p. 60.
47 *Empire Exhibition Official Guide* (Glasgow, 1938), p. 150.
48 For details of the development of the African industry see C. Harler, *The Culture and Marketing of Tea* (Oxford, 1964).

CHAPTER FIVE

The Empire Marketing Board, tobacco advertising and the imaging of the white male imperial archetype

In the period prior to 1914, images of black people and Empire in commodity advertising represent the conflicting ideological interests of companies. They highlight the different attitudes and approaches of companies to colonial policy and imperialised labour relations. During this period, it appears to have been private enterprise, rather than the government, that was powerful in shaping images of Empire and black people. In the inter-war period, however, the government's propaganda experiment, in the shape of the Empire Marketing Board (EMB), radically altered this state of affairs. The British government, through the EMB, became the defining force in representing the image of black people and Empire, to which private enterprise responded. This chapter will trace the reasons for the government's direct involvement in marketing an imperial ideology and assess the ways in which the EMB sold the idea of 'imperial partnership' to the nation. Through a perusal of tobacco advertising by both private enterprise and the EMB, it will consider the response and attitudes of private enterprise to the EMB ideals. Tobacco has been chosen because it is a product which depicted Africans in its marketing as early as the eighteenth century, yet during the inter-war period these images were almost completely dropped from tobacco advertising and replaced with the image of the white male imperial archetype. Tobacco is also an important product because it was the first commodity to be singled out and actively pushed by the EMB. It marked a shift in EMB policy towards the promotion of specific commodities. First we need to consider why the EMB was established.

Empire as a solution to the economic crisis in the inter-war period

By the early 1920s, the high unemployment of the immediate post-war period was recognised as not just a temporary situation caused by the return to peacetime conditions, but a more fundamental problem. The development of an 'imperial partnership' was seen by many as the long-term solution to Britain's economic problems. Colonial development, it was hoped, could be used to stimulate demand for British goods, halt Britain's industrial decline and as a consequence end the critical problem of unemployment that was causing hardship and destitution in Britain. The Colonial Development Act of 1929, for example, aimed to provide loan funds for the development of transport and other facilities, which would develop the colonies for the benefit of Britain. As the Parliamentary Under-secretary of State stressed, with regards to the Bill:

> I hope that the House will agree to this Bill and that we shall not be delayed too long, as we are anxious to see the schemes of development begun and useful work provided for many of our people as we believe it will be – useful work for those who are unemployed or partially employed today.[1]

The promotion of Empire was not only believed to be important as a solution to unemployment but was also crucial in the conflict and attack on socialism after the Russian Revolution of 1917 and the militancy of trade unions in 1920s Britain which led to the General Strike of 1926. As Constantine notes, for Amery, Secretary of State for the Colonies and the Dominions from 1925 to 1929, 'Imperialism offered a solution to more than one economic problem. . . . Imperialism and patriotism had been consciously used before and during the First World War to try to distract a working-class electorate from notions of class conflict and anti-capitalism.'[2]

By the 1920s, it was clear that the era of free trade had past. As early as the Imperial War Conference in 1917, resolutions in support of imperial preference and the development of Empire resources were passed. Yet in the post-war political climate, all that the government was able to promise its colonies was that 'a preference will be given to our colonies on existing duties and upon any duties which for our purposes may be subsequently imposed'.[3] While wishing to impose imperial preferences, it was difficult for the government to impose tax preferences, which would inevitably lead to the rise in cost of a wide variety of goods. Advocating such a policy lost the Conservatives the election in December 1923, bringing in a Labour government for the first time. Baldwin was only able to return the Conservative Party to power in September 1924 by renouncing protection. Instead, the government established an Imperial Economic Committee (IEC) in December 1924 'to consider the possibility of improving the methods of preparing for market and marketing within the United Kingdom the food products of the overseas parts of the Empire with a view to increasing the consumption of such products in the United Kingdom in preference to imports from foreign countries and to promote the interests both of producers and consumers'.[4] The following year, the IEC recommended the establishment of an executive commission to develop a 'national movement' to encourage Empire buying. Established in 1926, the Empire Marketing Board tried to achieve through propaganda what could not be achieved through economic reforms. Both the Labour and Conservative governments maintained the organisation until 1933.

The Empire Marketing Board

For the first time during an era of peace, a government department was established to sell the people of Britain an idea and this was repeatedly stressed in its publications:

> The Board's task is to advertise an idea rather than a commodity ...
>
> The purpose of the Empire Marketing Board is clear and definite. It is to improve the quality and increase the quantity of Empire products marketed in the United Kingdom and to make Empire buying a national habit.[5]

To achieve this, the EMB set up three sub-committees: (a) a Research Sub-committee which was involved with sponsoring research into breeding and cultivation problems affecting Empire food production; (b) a Marketing Sub-committee which investigated issues affecting the supply and demand of Empire foodstuffs and published information bulletins for trade organisations; and (c) a Publicity Sub-committee which aimed to sell the idea of Empire through a variety of means.

It was the work of the Publicity Sub-committee, which was the best-known part of the EMB's work. As Amery commented, 'the conspicuous success of our publicity schemes tended to impress the general public with the idea that they were the main part of our work'.[6] The public was certainly not far off the mark in reaching this conclusion, since the publicity work absorbed £1,224,562, that is approximately 40 per cent, of the total money spent by the EMB during its brief existence between 1926 and 1933. Its propaganda role was paramount, and this was impressed upon the Cabinet: 'Forty millions of people had to be induced to change their habits'.[7]

It was impossible, however, to judge the extent of economic changes which the work of the EMB may have affected, as the often apologetic sounding statements in the annual reports show:

The question is often asked whether the work of the Board has increased the consumption of Empire products in the United Kingdom in
a degree commensurate with its expenditure. The programme of the
Board, as will be seen from this report, is planned to take effect over a
considerable period, and much of its work could not have shown direct
results within two years. In any case the question is one which cannot
well be answered in any simple statistical form.[8]

If the economic benefits could not be measured, one thing which was
certainly intense was the ideological impact. Perhaps it was this
impact to which the above reference about not being able to quan-
tify the EMB's work in statistical form refers. The EMB used almost
every conceivable form of publicity – posters, print advertisements,
Christmas cards, postcards, leaflets, lectures, radio broadcasts, film
screenings, Empire shopping weeks and exhibitions. The success of
the publicity work, especially that of the Poster Sub-committee, can
be seen by requests from both overseas educational establishments
and schools in Britain for materials produced by the EMB. There were
9,000 requests from schools for copies of EMB posters in the first year
of operation, and by 1928 17,000 schools in Britain were on the EMB
mailing list. In May 1933, just before the EMB was wound up, there
were 27,000 schools on its mailing list – that was about three-
quarters of all the schools in Britain. It was not only institutions that
responded to the EMB, but the general public too. By 1928, 80,000
copies of a leaflet depicting an Empire Calendar of Fruits and Vegetables
had been distributed, and following a radio broadcast in 1929 on recipes
using Empire produce, the EMB received 20,700 letters for copies of
the recipes with Empire sources of supply for the ingredients. During
its height, the EMB distributed an average of two million leaflets a
year. It seems to have targeted all sections of the population including
children. There is evidence that it commissioned a children's alphabet
and illustrated poems on Children of the Empire, and on 16 June 1927
an Empire nursery set of posters was approved.[9]

While the EMB used a variety of forms of publicity, it is clear that
two of the most important were the posters and press advertisements,
on which over two-thirds of the annual publicity budget was spent.
The posters, in particular, must have had a profound impact on the
general public, since for the first time special hoardings were erected
in almost every town of the United Kingdom. The hoardings incor-
porated an elaborate set of five frames, made to unique specifications,
and allowed the posters to depict a narrative or express complex ideas
through juxtaposition. They were made up of three large landscape-
format poster frames, which were broken up by two smaller portrait-
format frames. By 1928, 1,500 special poster frames had been erected

in 270 towns. By 1932 this had increased to 1,700 in 475 towns. The impact of these posters was not only from their unique public situation, but also because of the stunning designs of many of the posters, which were commissioned from some of the most prominent graphic artists of the day. Amery and other government officials who sat on the EMB realised that in order to get the best results, it was essential to look for expertise in the commercial world. The Poster Sub-committee included businessmen such as William Crawford, head of one of the major advertising agencies in the 1920s, and Frank Pick, who had been responsible for the memorable advertising and marketing of the London Underground.

The key concept for the Publicity Sub-committee was to 'bring the Empire alive' for the British public. W. S. Crawford wrote repeatedly of the way in which he wanted 'the Empire in its economic aspects [to] "come alive" before the eyes of the public'. He saw the posters in particular as mobilising an imperial sentiment, to create an 'Empire-conscious people' who would then respond to more specific campaigns.[10] In bringing the Empire alive, the EMB advocated Joseph Chamberlain's concept of the complementary economics of Empire. This notion of 'complementary economics' saw the colonies and Britain in separate roles as producers of raw materials and manufacturer respectively, and both, it was believed, would develop best through fostering this relationship. In 1895 Chamberlain had declared:

> I regard many of our Colonies as being in the condition of undeveloped estates and estates which can never be developed without Imperial assistance . . . [T]hose estates which belong to the British Crown may be developed for the benefit of their population and for the benefit of the greater population which is outside.[11]

It was believed that the colonies could produce everything that Britain needed in the way of foodstuffs and raw materials, and in turn could provide markets for Britain's manufactured goods. Therefore, if Britons bought Empire goods, it would enable the colonies to buy from Britain, or so the logic ran. As Havinden and Meredith point out, by the 1920s the colonies fulfilled the role of 'complementary economics' to a greater extent. The task for the EMB was, therefore, to illustrate this economic relationship and encourage the British consumer to foster this development by buying Empire goods. The promotion of this concept can be seen in the titles for many of the poster series: 'Empire buying brings prosperity'; 'Empire buying makes busy factories'; 'Today trade builds the Empire'; 'Colonial progress brings home prosperity'.

In presenting this 'complementary' relationship, 'the racial division of labour, inherent in Chamberlain's programme, was still very much alive'.[12] The posters repeatedly depicted black people as labourers serving white consumers, as one of the first sets of posters entitled 'Empire buyers are Empire builders' represented. It depicted tea and rice fields from the colonies on the side posters, with a scene of a British shop in the centre. Apart from representing black people as producers of raw materials for white consumption, black people were always represented as manual workers in contrast to whites in supervisory roles. On the rare occasions when white labourers were presented, they were surrounded by machinery to distance them from black workers who were often shown involved in heavy manual tasks. This contrast is particularly noticeable when we compare two scenes of ships being loaded, one depicting Ceylonese workers in Colombo using all their manual strength to move cargo and the other depicting white workers in Britain loading a ship with the help of machinery.[13]

Finally, one crucial effect of the EMB was that it made everything consciously imperial, including ordinary products like milk and butter and everyday activities like shopping and cooking. Images of mothers cooking with Empire products, local grocery stores selling Empire goods and scenes of the English countryside were as much a part of the imperial vision as orchards of South African oranges. The application of all people, whether through consumption or production, appeared to create a prosperous Empire. Through its variety of images including many domestic ones, the EMB, in John Grierson's words, 'chang[ed] the connotation of the word "Empire". Our command of peoples became solely a co-operative effort in the tilling of soil, the reaping of harvest and organisation of the world economy. For the old flags of exploitation it substitutes the new flag of common labour.'[14]

The Empire Marketing Board and the promotion of Empire tobacco

While adhering in principle to the notion of selling a general imperial idea, on 14 June 1928 the Poster Sub-committee, in direct conflict with this aim, commissioned a poster series on tobacco (Figures 47 and 48). This heralded the beginning of the EMB's involvement, however reluctant, in the promotion of particular commodities. The commissioning of this series must have been the EMB's attempt to help the crisis in trade facing Rhodesian farmers in that year. While tobacco had first been cultivated in Rhodesia by Europeans in the 1890s, it had only been around 1924, after the favourable comments which Rhodesian tobacco had received at Wembley and the sharpening of relations between Rhodesian farmers and the United Tobacco Company which had previously sold the bulk of the crop, that Rhodesia

47, 48 'Smoke Empire tobacco' and 'Tobacco plantation in Nyasaland', EMB posters, June 1929

had looked to Britain to increase its exports. These had previously been confined to South Africa. When Britain increased the imperial preference on tobacco by 50 per cent in July 1925, so that Empire leaf only paid three-quarters of the standard duty, Rhodesians must have felt that this was their chance. At the 1924–25 Empire Exhibition at Wembley, the government had also promoted Rhodesia as an area for continued settlement. In 1926 the tobacco yield was 5,000,000 lb, in 1927 it had shot up to 18,000,000 lb and in 1928 it reached 24,000,000 lb. While Britain had been able to absorb large quantities of tobacco in 1926 and 1927, by 1928 the reserves of Southern Rhodesian tobacco were so large that almost none of the 10,000,000 lb sent to Britain proved saleable. The EMB's concern for the economic disaster which faced the Rhodesian farmers must have been increased by the fact that its chairperson, Leo Amery, as Secretary of State for the Colonies in the previous year, had cavalierly declared at the Salisbury Agricultural Show on 12 August 1927 that:

> The time may perhaps come, and you have got to consider it, when you may be producing more than the British market can take; but at any rate it can take six, or eight or ten times as much as you produce at this moment before our market is anything like filled up.[15]

The crisis in the Southern Rhodesian tobacco trade clearly prompted this poster series, since in the initial discussion for the series, the only country to be depicted was Southern Rhodesia:

> it was agreed that the idea of the designs for this set might be based on the labels of cigar boxes; the left hand 60 × 40 poster depicting a scene of tobacco production in Southern Rhodesia, the centre 60 × 40 a list of the Empire countries where tobacco is grown together with the types of tobacco they produce, illustrations of the kinds of tobacco leaf and figures showing the growth of Empire tobacco trade in the last few years, and the right hand 60 × 40 poster, bales of tobacco in a warehouse, all three being enclosed in a florid design such as is used in cigar boxes. The two double royal posters might consist of a message urging the smoking of Empire tobacco. It was arranged that the secretariat should proceed with the preparation of the necessary photographic and statistical material for this set.[16]

It is worth analysing this series in detail to consider both the representation of EMB ideology within the series as well as its support for a particular trade that was in crisis. The minutes of the meetings at which the posters were discussed are also worth analysing in detail, since they allow us to recognise the control the EMB maintained over the poster designs and highlight what its members saw as important. The description I have quoted above, for example, is not only interesting from the point of view of the details discussed, but also in its references to 'photographic and statistical information'. This was collected for every set of posters, and indicates the way in which the Poster Sub-Committee believed that it was representing a degree of 'reality'. It took great care to ensure the accurate depiction of plants and animals etc. within the posters. Juxtaposed with this seeming scientific reality, however, was the ideological push which is particularly noticeable in the discussion which took place on this set two weeks later, when it was decided that the large posters on either side should be scenes of Rhodesia and Nyasaland, with 'an allegorical group in the centre'.[17]

After having decided on the format and content, the sub-committee looked for an artist to carry out its requirements. For the tobacco posters, Frank Pape was interviewed, and while the sub-committee looked favourably at his designs for the scenes of tobacco production on the two flanking 60 × 40 posters, it was not afraid to criticise aspects of his work where it perceived he had misunderstood its requirements. He was asked to resubmit his work: 'Mr Frank Pape had not grasped the intention of the sub-committee in regard to the cigar-box label designs, which should form the key note of the set, nor the allegorical nature of the centre poster'.[18] The following week, after Pape had made the required alterations, the set was approved. The strict vision of the sub-committee is further shown by its unwillingness to compromise on the design of the posters on discovering that the large quantity of gold in the design, due to the cigar box borders, would cause particular printing problems. At a meeting on 20 December 1928, the sub-committee decided that the gold was important (this was not simply graphically, as we shall see, but also in terms of the posters' message) and therefore decided to find a special printer to take on the job.

Let us take a closer look at the messages constructed in the set of tobacco posters. To begin with, the allegorical set in the middle symbolically represents the EMB ideology perfectly (Figure 47). A white and a black man flank an image of the globe, in which Africa is highlighted. The two men are the same height, have practically the same-coloured khaki shorts and shirt and face each other. The initial impression is one of unity, but it is clearly not a unity of equals. The white man is depicted holding a spade on which he rests his left foot. He stands up straight with his chest pushed forward which gives him an aura of authority. He appears in control, in contrast to the black man who stands with naked feet together opposite him. In contrast to the white man's spade (an allegorical reference to technology), the black man holds a bright yellow-green tobacco leaf (an allegorical

reference to the raw material of Empire). The leaf curves gently down-
wards, echoing the man's lowered gaze, which makes him appear
passive and servile in comparison to the arrogant assertiveness of the
white man, who gazes upwards. Other differences between the two
include the hat, socks and shoes which the white man wears in contrast to the black man's naked head and feet; the pen knife (another
symbol of technology) which hangs from the white man's belt in
contrast to the African man's lack of any implements; and finally the
tailored shirt on the white man in contrast to the simple T-shirt on
the black man. In a simple graphic, the image of the colonies as
producers of raw materials and Britain as the industrial workshop is
presented. At the same time the notion of a seeming unity is imaged,
while still asserting and naturalising white supremacy. Above the
globe, a sun shines brightly, across the various pink splashes graphically representing the notion of the sun never setting on the Empire.
Below is the image of a sailing ship, a centuries-old emblem for trade,
highlighting trade as central to the success of the Empire. Finally, the
elaborate gilded tobacco leaf border gives the image a feeling of high
quality and tastefulness. It was important for Britain to represent this
tobacco as a quality one, and this may explain why the sub-committee
was so keen to have florid cigar box borders in spite of their cost.

The poster is simple yet at the same time highly sophisticated in
its meanings. Its detail and sophistication are further enhanced by the
colour of the tobacco leaf held by the African man. Its colour is so
bright, in the actual poster, that it is almost garish. This was certainly
not because the colouring was badly done, since as we know it was
printed by a specialist printer, but because the leaf was referencing
a specific type of tobacco which was being cultivated in Southern
Rhodesia and Nyasaland as a result of the increase in cigarette production and consumption which needed bright Virginian-type flue-
cured tobacco. This emphasis was particularly important because the
early tobacco from Southern Rhodesia had been regarded as very strong,
and of little appeal to European taste. This bright flue-cured tobacco
was called 'leaf of gold' in Rhodesia, another reason why the committee may have insisted on printing the gold borders. The highlighting
of Africa is also important, since this was certainly not the only area
of the Empire in which tobacco was grown, yet while a fairly substantial quantity of tobacco was grown in India, most of it was consumed
locally, in contrast to Southern Rhodesia and Nyasaland, which were
almost entirely dependent on their trade with Britain.

The concepts represented in the allegorical panel continued into the
other large posters, which depicted plantations in Southern Rhodesia
and Nyasaland (Figure 48). Even in the cigar box style borders, the

idea of African and British 'exchange' is represented by the combination of the image of an African head and a British Unicorn. The symbol of the sun was also used again in the border, shining down on all corners of the Empire. In the images themselves, the notion of advanced British technology is maintained by the presence of a jeep in the Southern Rhodesian scene where a white planter is represented, in contrast to the bullock cart and horse on which the Africans ride out a consignment of tobacco. The idea of Africans as labourers and British as supervisors or scientists is also maintained. While Africans carry cut leaves, and bales of tobacco, the Europeans stand at ease in the shade, or are involved in what look like skilled complicated tasks. The notion of black labourer and white consumer is also maintained in the Nyasaland picture, which depicts the only two people smoking in the whole series – the two white supervisors or buyers. While the poster series presents scenes of labour, the image that it conjures is of a rural idyll. There are no hints at exploitation or hard labour. Instead an image of a young man waving goodbye to his wife and children as he travels away on the cart of tobacco dominates the scene of the Nyasaland plantation. One of the two white men who stand in the shade look across at the scene, as though to suggest that the peace and tranquillity represented is as a result of British imperial involvement. The paternalistic glance is heightened by the size of these two white men in the foreground, who are at least a third taller than any other figure. Their authority is further asserted by the relaxed manner in which they appear to control what is happening – both stand at ease smoking pipes. The only image of physical labour is that of three African men on the left-hand side who carry a bale of tobacco, but their presence is diminished by the way in which they are squashed into the edge of the picture.[19] The availability of bright flue-cured tobacco is also referred to through the same bright lime green colour that covers the Nyasaland harvest image. Finally the cultivation scene in Southern Rhodesia suggests the idea of a quality tobacco. It shows careful, scientific work being carried out – under European guidance, of course – in order to ensure crops of quality leaf.

While this set of posters was being developed, the EMB had already started to advertise Empire tobacco through advertisements in the press. In fact a special advertisement was placed in *Punch*, a magazine with which the EMB seems to have had a special relationship.[20] It declared 'Smoke Empire tobacco' and encouraged consumers to write in to the EMB to receive copies of a list which named brands that were 'made largely from Empire tobacco'. The list included 319 kinds of pipe tobaccos, 54 brands of cigarettes and 112 brands of cigars.[21] At the same time, the EMB also issued a specific advertisement for

Southern Rhodesian tobacco. It is clear that by the end of 1928, the EMB had realised that it would inevitably need to advertise specific commodities at times, but this was a role which it resisted, as the minutes indicate:

> following an application from Southern Rhodesia, it was proposed to issue an advertisement in the normal schedule of media in favour of Southern Rhodesian tobacco. The Sub-Committee approved this proposal but felt that no further incidental advertisements should be issued until the Board's future press advertising policy had been considered by the subcommittee.[22]

The advertisement referred to above appeared in twenty-two national newspapers in the week ending 8 December 1928. The image on the advertisement simply showed a bunch of tobacco leaves, but the text of this press advertisement for Southern Rhodesian tobacco is worth quoting in full, because it expresses so clearly the responsibilities and attitudes which the British government tried to infuse in consumers, especially those with a degree of clout such as the readers of *The Times*:

> Look at this picture of a tobacco plant, with its strong healthy leaves and delicate white flower. Now carry your mind to a tobacco farm in Southern Rhodesia. As far as the eye can see, row upon row of tobacco plants are lifting their broad green leaves to the African sun, till they disappear in the distant blue of the hills. The farmer is gazing at his crop. He knows his Rhodesian Virginia is equal in quality to any tobacco in the World.
> *Will he be able to sell it? Who will buy?*
> English, Welsh, Scotch or Irish, he is British born and bred. His thoughts wander thousands of miles away to his home, his family, his friends, his fellow countrymen.
> Do they know that Britain consumes one hundred and forty million pounds of tobacco in a year, and that of the ninety million consumed as cigarettes, ninety-nine percent is foreign?
> Surely the British Smoker will prefer to buy from his friends and relations in Southern Rhodesia, who obtain nearly half of their imports from the United Kingdom, and more than half the remainder from other Empire countries.
> *Southern Rhodesian tobacco is as good as any in the world*
> *Its purchase means more orders for British Industries and more homes and employment for British settlers*
> BUY RHODESIAN TOBACCO

The text of the advertisement acts as a beautiful interpretation for the harvest scene of Frank Pape's poster series. The public as viewers of the poster, as well as one of the white men standing in the foreground of the image, not only look at the seemingly happy African workers, but also at the endless fields of bright lime green tobacco, which stretch into the distance, up until 'the distant blue hills' mentioned in the text above. The emphasis on land in EMB posters as a whole is significant. The imperial gaze is frequently depicted running across orchards of oranges, fields of cotton or ports in imperial possession. Here, across the fields of tobacco, there is a gaze not only of possession but also of satisfaction – the man is smoking a pipe of presumably Rhodesian tobacco. The interpretation of the poster, however, does not stop there. Below the description of a Southern Rhodesian farm in the press advertisement is a series of questions about how the farmer will sell his crop, thoughts which must also be in the minds of these men in the poster as they watch a cartload of tobacco leave for market. Their hopes in selling are directed at the British market, at 'his family, his friends, his fellow countrymen'. And as though to mirror this suggestion, the second farmer depicted in the poster looks out at us just before he lights his pipe. While there is no doubt that Pape's posters were ready when this press advertisement was produced and released, and they may have encouraged the civil servant writing the advertisement, I would not for a moment want to suggest that the text was a direct description of the poster. What is important is the singular EMB ideology represented and the way in which the poster designs were rigorously controlled to express the EMB ideology.

Empire tobacco as a whole and Southern Rhodesian tobacco in particular was a heavily targeted commodity. The poster display, press advertisement and the tobacco list referred to above were not the only attempts to promote it. In 1929 the Publicity Sub-committee also agreed to a series of advertisements to promote particular commodities which were 'considered to be in particular need of advertisement and which [were] susceptible to being assisted in this way'. The advertisements ran throughout the year and included another one for Southern Rhodesian tobacco. Interestingly, the Southern Rhodesian image did not depict any African labourers but instead featured the white planter/settler standing proudly behind tobacco plants. He looks out at the viewer with one arm akimbo (Figure 49). Below the text begins: 'The British colonists in Southern Rhodesia grow a Virginia tobacco, the leaf of which is equal in quality to that grown in any other part of the world'. Part of the reason of this focus on the colonists may have lain in the fact that the British and Imperial Southern Rhodesian governments were still publicising Southern Rhodesia as an area for settlers. One EMB lecture was even dedicated to this subject, and was entitled 'Rhodesia, the land of promise'. In line with the identities developed in other settler colonial states, the images of

EMPIRE SHOPPING

SOUTHERN RHODESIAN
Tobacco and Cigarettes

The British Colonists in Southern Rhodesia grow a Virginia tobacco, the leaf of which is equal in quality to that grown in any other part of the World.

Southern Rhodesian tobacco is raised from the finest seed, dried, cured, and graded under expert advice, and exported to Britain, where it is manufactured into cigarettes and pipe tobacco.

There are brands and varieties of Southern Rhodesian cigarettes to suit every taste, but one and all are made from pure tobacco, under ideal conditions.

Southern Rhodesian tobacco and cigarettes can be bought at all the best tobacconists.

Give this purely British industry a fair trial by asking for Southern Rhodesian tobacco and cigarettes.

Write for the Southern Rhodesian Tobacco Book, *From Seed-bed to Smoker*, with brands and prices, post free on application to the Empire Marketing Board, Westminster, London, S.W.1.

Empire Quality
Buy
Southern Rhodesian Tobacco and Cigarettes

49 'Empire shopping – Southern Rhodesian tobacco and cigarettes', EMB press advertisement, *Punch*, 24 July 1929

EMPIRE TOBACCO
FROM
NORTHERN RHODESIA & NYASALAN

50 'Empire tobacco from Northern Rhodesia and Nyasaland', EMB poster, 1930

Southern Rhodesia did not concentrate on representing African labour or people, despite the history of representing Africans in tobacco advertising. As in all settler colonies, propaganda and identities were fostered to deny black people's history, presence and development.

The presence of the white settler is also strong in one of the smaller posters from a series by Adrian Allinson. The poster depicts Northern Rhodesia and Nyasaland tobacco (Figure 50). A white man dominates the scene. He takes up nearly half the poster and is depicted sitting fully dressed and relaxed. He smokes a pipe and talks to a young African boy, who stands to attention in front of him with hands clasped behind his back, wearing only a loincloth. Our association is inevitably with the white man who faces us, in contrast to the boy whose face we cannot see. He appears to beckon the young boy in a paternal fashion. Development and European involvement appear to go hand in hand. Again notions of technology as being the domain of Europeans are symbolically addressed by the white man's watch, which is prominently displayed on his arm.

With the continuing need to promote Empire tobacco and the increasing degree to which the EMB got involved with commodity publicity, a letterpress poster series entitled 'What do you smoke?' was also designed by C. Burton in 1931. A 1928 series of posters for factories encouraging workers to buy Empire goods also included one about Rhodesian tobacco. The EMB push for Empire tobacco was heavier than that for any other product. While cocoa farmers in West Africa had experienced a collapse in the price of cocoa that was to leave many of them almost destitute, the EMB did nothing to support them and encourage a fair price.[23] While it is true that the EMB was not concerned about 'fair' prices for products, it is also clear that the EMB's almost fatherly concern for Southern Rhodesian farmers' was because they were white. In the press advertisement for Southern Rhodesian tobacco that came out at the end of 1928, the EMB did not simply discuss the complementary relationship of Empire, but appealed to the public to support their 'friends and relations' and discuss the mutual trade as providing more homes and employment for British settlers.

Yet how did commercial tobacco companies respond to this EMB drive to buy Empire tobacco? In order to analyse this effectively, it is important first to consider representations of black people and Empire that existed in previous tobacco advertising, as well as the general image of black people in inter-war advertising, so that we can understand the inter-textual shifts and breaks that appear.

Early tobacco advertising and the representation of Africans

The earliest representations of Africans in British advertising were to be found on tobacco labels and signs. Crude representations of black men hoeing fields, rolling hogs heads of tobacco or smoking pipes were often used in tobacco advertising throughout the eighteenth and nineteenth centuries. Tobacco, along with sugar and cotton, relied upon slave economies for massive profit and those slaves were in turn represented adorning tobacco packets and advertising.

One interesting factor about many of these eighteenth-century images is that while alluding to the relationship between master and slave, many of the tobacco labels also represented the black man as a prince. A substantial number of labels represent Africans wearing royal cloaks and in one case he is even enthroned. This is not to suggest that these images ever presented black and white men as equal, for the black man's authority was always diminished by his nakedness. What is interesting about these images is their existence in the eighteenth century, but their disappearance by the end of the nineteenth century. The other common feature on eighteenth-century labels is the representation of the black man or boy smoking a pipe. While a small number of these continue into the late nineteenth century, after 1919 this image was non-existent apart from on tobacco logos whose design originated from the 1880s.

Although black people continued to be represented frequently on tobacco products in the late nineteenth century, the struggle against slavery affected the imagery profoundly. The ubiquitous 'sambo' caricature replaced the previous images of naked black boys and men in skirts of tobacco. While nakedness ceased to be a dominant symbol for black servility, these new images represented blacks as carefree and irresponsible 'sambos' (Figure 51). In the 1880s, many tobacco brands also continued to use the image of the black man as a logo on their packaging, usually in a mock eighteenth-century woodcut style. Most of these images represented them in period costume,[24] yet to my knowledge in none of the eighteenth-century images was the African

51 W. D. and H. O. Wills, Old Friend tobacco label, 1890s

Wills's Fine Shagg showcard, turn of the century

man presented in gentleman's dress. This image, while suggesting an eighteenth-century American world, was a nineteenth-century mythification and sanitisation of slave experience.

Alongside this representation were images of nostalgia for an idyllic past. This can be seen in the showcard for Wills's Fine Shagg dating to the turn of the century (Figure 52). A scene of idyllic ruralism is represented. Two black men stand in a field of tobacco that has the impression of a family enterprise rather than a large plantation. One man props himself up with a stick, while the other is bent gently over a leaf. The pace of life appears beautifully slow. All suggestions of exploitation and slavery are banished from the image. On the left-hand side, an insert depicts three packets of the shagg with its logo in woodcut style representing a black man in eighteenth-century dress smoking a pipe. An image of idyllic ruralism was also used on tobacco labels for Rhodesian tobacco in the late nineteenth century. An advertisement for Matabele Mixture[25] represents a scantily clad family relaxing outside a straw hut. Nakedness and the straw hut act as signifiers of underdevelopment. What is important about this

[147]

53 Ricketts and Co.'s Superfine Shagg label, n.d.

image, when we compare it with inter-war images later, is the depiction of Africans on a Rhodesian tobacco product.

There is one other image which emerges in the late nineteenth century that is worth pausing on briefly: the image of a black woman on tobacco labels. She is never represented in dignified costume, but is always depicted as a 'loose woman'. She has all the symbolic accoutrements of a prostitute – earrings, beads, loosely worn clothes, and sometimes a bare shoulder. In an image for Ogden's, the black woman, although better clothed than in Wills's image (Figure 53), smokes a pipe, something which would have been considered unbecoming for a lady at the turn of the century in European society and would also have been associated with a 'loose' woman. It is worth noting that both these women are depicted on packets for shagg tobacco. While I can't find reference to the date of the term's sexual meaning, the *Shorter Oxford Dictionary* notes that by 1784 it was used to mean roughness and brutality of manner. It may be safe to assume that there was an intended sexual innuendo through the use of the image. These women, while represented as prostitutes, also draw attention to the black female labour that was so often used on tobacco plantations. What is interesting, however, is that these images emerge at the point when black women in North Carolina, for instance, were trying to stop working in the fields and particularly stop doing hired work, confining their labour to the household. As one farmer from Granville noted: 'Very few females engaged in farm work. They will not hire for regular work.'[26] It is almost as though at the point when black women in tobacco areas were attempting to better their class position through avenues that they perceived best, these images appeared to ridicule their achievement.

What is striking about all these images is their practical disappearance from tobacco advertising after 1919. While the EMB imaged labour relations and scenes of work in its posters repeatedly, commercial tobacco advertising ceased to represent either scenes relating to aspects of production, or Africans as workers or consumers. There are a number of possible reasons for this change, which I shall explore. Firstly, the shift in advertising, from one that emphasised product qualities to one which increasingly focused on the consumer and symbolic qualities which products could lend to the consumer, undoubtedly influenced these changes. Secondly, perhaps the increasing number of anti-colonial voices which began to be heard by the 1920s raised objections to the excesses of racism and began to campaign for black rights. These tobacco images had emerged during the period of the transatlantic slave trade, which may have made them unpopular, although this could not account for their complete banishment from advertising imagery. Finally, the impact of the Empire Marketing Board cannot be underestimated.

Advertising and the inter-war period

It was not just tobacco advertising which drastically altered in the inter-war period, but advertising as a whole. Leiss, Kline and Jhally have described how 'marketing thought [began] to shift towards the non rational or symbolic grounding of consumption' during this period, 'based on the notion of appeals or motives, putting less emphasis on the product and its uses'. Products were made to '"resonate" with qualities desired by consumers – status, glamour, reduction of anxiety, happy families – as social motivations for consumption'.[27] One key value which permeated the identity of many products but of tobacco especially was that of Empire and imperialism.

It was not just in the context of advertisements that tobacco was associated with the imperial image. As Jeffrey Richards commented with regard to cinema:

The Imperial hero figure conforms to a definite physical and spiritual archetype. He is tall, thin, square-jawed, keen eyed and almost always equipped with pipe and moustache. It is difficult to overestimate the importance of the pipe and the moustache. They are what the horse and gun are to the Western. They are the key icons of the Imperialist, lending him a dignity and dependability, which their removal likewise removes.[28]

The pipe in particular appeared to offer the imperial figure an image of authority even at a moment of rest and relaxation. The notion of imperial authority which the pipe conveyed was also used in an EMB poster that was not directed at selling tobacco. In Adrian Allinson's 'East African transport new style',[29] the white supervisor, complete with pith helmet, holds a pipe as he directs the building of a bridge. The relationship of the pipe to imperial authority is especially apparent if we bear in mind that the image was slightly altered after the EMB's approval, when the East African Commissioner objected to the horsewhip that was originally in the white man's hand. The whip was removed and a pipe inserted instead. The pipe does not look out of place despite its last-minute insertion into a figure that was designed to reflect uncompromising and almost brutal imperial authority. As the imperial archetype, the pipe appears to sit quite naturally in his hand, emphasising his role as supervisor and further distancing him from the African workers around him who are involved in manual work.

Why was this identity so attractive to the average British, particularly male, consumer of the 1920s? In the shadow of the Great Depression, Britain's major industries such as iron and steel, cotton, and shipbuilding were in decline, leading to high unemployment, especially after the return of millions of soldiers from the front. This recession affected attitudes to Empire and imperialism as well as the growing black community in Britain. For unemployed or low-paid British male workers who saw a world that did not appear to be 'fit for heroes', the image of themselves as imperial heroes must have provided a degree of glamour as well as an expression of individualism which would mobilise their support away from the collectivity of socialism.

The emphasis on whiteness also reflected the growing racism exhibited towards the now sizeable black community in Britain. At the end of the First World War, white workers deliberately scapegoated black communities in Britain. It led to riots in 1919 and racist legislation in 1925, making it almost impossible for black Britons to find work. Perhaps the riots in 1919 in towns such as Cardiff and Liverpool left the 'sambo' caricature no longer an image of harmless fun for white Britishers. Whatever the reasons, the disappearance of advertisements representing black people in a British context is striking. The image of black and white children by the seaside, or drinking cocoa, or even washing themselves, disappeared. Even images in an Americanised context, where black residency was not questioned, do not appear in British advertising in the inter-war period. It was as though advertisers took up the call for the repatriation of black people, popular in the early 1920s, by banishing them from advertisements which image Britain. In doing this, advertisers also did what they always do – avoided conflict. By the 1920s black people in Britain had begun to express their attitudes and ideas through organisations such as the West African Students' Union. They expressed their discontent with the violence and riots that had taken place in black communities, as well as with Empire and racist attitudes. In 1924, for example, the Union of Students of Black Descent complained to the Colonial Office about the portrayal Africans at the Empire Exhibition at Wembley.[30] The aggressively racist images of previous years were therefore less acceptable. In this climate of conflicting opinion, advertisers responded by avoiding black representations.[31]

The only dominant representational reference to black people in a British context during this period was that of the golliwog. This image, which originated in children's storybooks by Mrs Upton written between 1895 and 1908 (the heyday of colonial and imperial aggression), sanitised and domesticated Empire. The figure was never copyrighted[32] and was used to advertise everything from Mansion polish and geysers, to soap, toothpaste, marmalade and cream. In these advertisements the golliwog was often the butt of jokes about colour, but at times he was there simply as an image of domesticity and childhood and shows the way in which imperialism and racism became naturalised in mainstream 1920s culture. Between 1920 and 1926, eleven different companies advertised in *The Graphic* using the golliwog. Reduced to a doll, the African was symbolically represented as available for total manipulation by the white child owner. As a doll, he could pose no threat and could be cared for or thrown around at will. It is important to note that most of the advertisements which used golliwogs were directed towards the child or female consumer. On one occasion, the Imperial Tobacco Company also used the golliwog to convey an image of domesticity in a Gold Flake advertisement that was designed to attract women to the brand (Figure 54). While the white female consumer digested the Empire both literally through her domestic products and metaphorically through the advertisements of golliwogs and exotic dreams, the male consumer was bombarded with images of imperial adventure and grandeur in which it appeared he could take part.

54 Gold Flake Cigarettes advertisement, *c.* 1930

Commercial companies and the production of Empire tobacco/cigarette brands

The abrupt decline in use of the image of the African in tobacco advertising is matched to some degree by the rising use of the image of the white male imperial consumer. Was this rise wholly or partly the result of the EMB propaganda? The Imperial Tobacco Company and other leading manufacturers were certainly not driven by economic investments within the British Empire to use Empire leaf, but the preference for Empire leaf that was established in 1919 and increased in 1925 did stimulate some manufacturers to use it, especially in pipe tobacco. Yet with the rise of cigarette consumption, the challenge was also to encourage Empire cigarettes. In 1922 Rothmans did launch Rothmans' Rhodesian Virginia cigarettes, but most cigarette manufacturers were reluctant to do the same because rightly or wrongly manufacturers were also worried by the consumers' reaction to Empire leaf, some of which was regarded as inferior in taste and was believed to harm the throat.[33]

By 1920, however, the major tobacco companies in Britain, both in and outside the Imperial Tobacco Company, also had a large range of established brands which used American grown leaf. They undoubtedly did not want to tamper with their most valuable lines for the sake of patriotism, especially as the 1920s saw fierce competition and a price war amongst cigarette producers which ran until 1933. While the production of Empire-grown leaf was of great interest to British manufacturers since they did not want to see America monopolising this part of the industry and controlling prices, Imperial (which sold 73 per cent of all tobacco products in the UK) also had substantial investments in the American Leaf Organisation which it undoubtedly wished to protect. Imperial was therefore in a contradictory position of 'cautiously encouraging Rhodesian and Canadian growers'[34] during the 1920s while not wishing to buy more Empire leaf. In 1906, Imperial had established an Africa Leaf-Buying Organisation and a processing factory at Limbe in Nyasaland. Rhodesia was probably hopeful that it might do the same there. However, as opposed to the three factories at Limbe, Imperial possessed thirty-one factories in the states of Georgia, North and South Carolina, Virginia, Kentucky and Tennessee.[35] Its support for Empire-grown leaf was clearly tentative. With the size of its market share, however, the support of Imperial in increasing trade with the Empire was obviously crucial to the EMB and the government.

Despite the tentative support of Imperial, the success in establishing Empire brands of pipe tobacco was substantial, especially amongst small manufacturers. These brands, both in and outside Imperial used a mixed bunch of images to advertise Empire blends. To begin with, many of the leading brands had 'sister' products called, for example, St Bruno's Empire Blend or Capstan Empire. These products simply maintained the imagery normally used for their respective brands. Some smaller companies which sold Empire brands, such as Lloyd's Magpie Shag or Adkin's Filbert Shag, used banal images of Magpies or Filberts, with no connection to the image of Empire. Other brands such as EG (Empire Grown) simply used the picture of tobacco leaves in its advertising and packaging. While it is clear that commercial companies did not simply advertise Empire brands with patriotic and imperial imagery, a significant number of Empire tobacco brands

55 Adkin's Rhodesian Mixture advertisement, *Tobacco*, 1 July 1928

exploited patriotic images or images of the 'settler colonial'. Flag evoked the popular notion of trade following the flag and therefore appealed to the patriotic conscience of the consumer. Afrikander, Fireside, Digger, Melsetter, Adkin's Rhodesian Mixture, and Stockrider, to name a few, all evoked the image of the pioneering 'settler colonial' (Figures 55 and 56). Some brands depicted him with pith helmet, moustache and pipe; others depicted him standing triumphantly in a rancher's hat; at other times he was portrayed sitting by the fire in a log cabin. Significantly none of these brands represented Africans. Of course Empire tobacco was not simply grown in Africa, but in Canada too, yet none of the brands that define themselves as Rhodesian, for example,

56 Melsetter Rhodesian Tobacco advertisement, *Tobacco*,
1 April 1930

represent any African people. In back issues of the trade journal
Tobacco, during the period of the EMB, the only advertisement that
featured a black man was a Virginia cigarette called Prize Crop. Perhaps it was the image of black people on past cigarette marketing,
and the desire to create an identity which would differentiate Empire
tobacco from American-grown leaf, that also displaced the image
of the black man from many tobacco products in the 1920s and 1930s.
It was also, however, the promotion of the 'settler colonial', and the
cultivation of the consumer's identity with him, that undoubtedly
took place.

[155]

In order to look at the images of Empire adopted by Empire brands, I will discuss two particular brands that were promoted as using Empire tobacco after the introduction of imperial preference. The first is Digger, launched by Players in 1917 when imperial preference was first introduced, and the second is Rhodian, launched by Lambert and Butler in 1928. Early advertising for Digger, launched during the First World War, was inevitably jingoistic, but this was an image which was also retained into the 1920s and 1930s. A showcard for Digger from 1932 depicts the typical image of an early settler with hat, rugged complexion, red cheeks and a full beard (Figure 57). He has a pipe in his hand and points to the audience in a manner which recalls the First World War recruitment poster 'Your country needs YOU'. Above his head the slogan 'Support the Empire!' is emblazoned. Here, a white settler from the colonies encourages and almost demands the consumer to show his belief in Empire through the consumption of Digger. The man represented was a 'type' who appeared repeatedly in Digger advertising, and in fact was representative of the Digger logo, which can be seen in the bottom right-hand corner of the showcard. This logo, like the late-nineteenth-century ones depicting black men, is styled like an engraving and recalls those earlier images. Here, however, the black figure is replaced by the image of the 'settler colonial', who is not just referred to in the image, but also in the name of the tobacco – 'Digger'. Players Centenary Brochure outlines the reason for the name: 'One interesting sidelight on the war was the presence of a large number of Australian soldiers in the country which led to the trade name "Digger" for the all-Empire tobacco blend introduced in 1917'.[36]

The image of the 'digger' acts as a representative not only of the producer, but also of the consumer. With the increasing habit for brands to be advertised with transferable symbolic values, this figure was offered to the working-class and lower-middle-class white male consumer as an image with which he could identify with and which could offer him what appeared to be a degree of glamour and adventurism. While the image of the 'settler colonial' was clearly established well before the EMB came into existence, brands such as these undoubtedly benefited from the general imperial drive. The specific promotion of Empire tobacco in 1928 and 1929 encouraged this image further. Out of the seven extant showcards for Digger in the Players collection, three date from 1928, 1929 and 1931, the period during which the EMB launched support for Empire tobacco. While not dependent on the sentiment created by the EMB for its launch, the level of Digger's success must partly have been the result of the EMB's work. As an article in a 1929 issue of Tobacco highlights:

7 Digger Tobacco showcard, 1932

58 W. D. and H. O. Wills Empire Grown Tobaccos advertisement, *Tobacco*, November 1927

'London and provincial cities and towns are enjoying a pictorial reminder and an exhortation to "Smoke Empire Tobacco" emanating from the Empire Marketing Board, whose activities in this connection should give Empire brands a fillip'.[37]

Later brands such as Stockrider Fine Rhodesian Blend and Adkin's Rhodesian Mixture, marketing themselves after the crisis in the Rhodesian tobacco trade, adopted similar kinds of imagery (Figure 55). The image of the settler colonial/planter even formed a kind of trademark for Wills's Empire-grown brands (Figure 58). Advertisements such as these popularised what was often seen as the esoteric nature of the EMB's publicity, which many accused of being ineffective, believing 'the masses' could not understand the messages of the EMB posters. The 'imperial self-consciousness' which the EMB had deliberately fostered, however, clearly had some effect on commercial advertising.

While the rugged planter/settler was used to appeal to the lower-middle-class and working-class consumer, in 1928 Lambert and Butler tried to attract a higher-class consumer with the launch of 'Rhodian' cigarettes. The difference in image may also partly be the result of the fact that they were marketing cigarettes rather than pipe tobacco. Introduced in 1928, it seems clear that Imperial, to which Lambert and Butler belonged, must have launched this cigarette in the wake of the collapse in trade for Rhodesian tobacco. The EMB and other government departments were in constant negotiation with Imperial to encourage the purchase of Empire leaf. There are numerous references to the need for its assistance and acknowledgement of its support in minutes for meetings by the EMB tobacco committee, formed in 1930:

> The Imperial Tobacco Company supply about two-thirds of the products smoked in the United Kingdom ... Hence it is important for Empire producers to have the sympathy and assistance of Imperial, which now appears prepared to make a much bigger effort in the interest of Empire-grown tobacco than formerly.[38]

The relationship between government policy and the Imperial Tobacco Company's expressed reasons for launching Rhodian can be seen in *The Times* on 4 December 1928. On the same page as the EMB press advertisement for Southern Rhodesian tobacco discussed above is one for Lambert and Butler's Rhodian. The advertisement for Rhodian does not discuss its quality or any symbolic attribute which it may offer the consumer, but simply the benefits to unemployment and Britain. It is titled 'How to reduce unemployment – How to sell more British goods'. Following this is a statement by the former Governor of Southern Rhodesia, who discusses the increase in settlers over the last year, the increase in tobacco production and overseas trade, and the increase in the amount of British goods which white Rhodesians buy. He ends by urging: 'Britishers at home should reciprocate by buying and smoking Rhodesian Tobacco'. The advertisement was clearly developed to compliment the EMB advertisement for Southern Rhodesian tobacco, since it appears to be a one-off image that was not used in another context. This Rhodian advertisement is almost like an extension of EMB advertising. Other Rhodian advertisements discussed quality as well as the economic benefits to the consumer, indicating that there was more tobacco and less duty. None of the advertisements represented Rhodesia or the planters, but concentrated on middle-class, male Britishers. The connection between these consumers and the Rhodesian planters, however, was made early on in an advertisement in *The Times* on 12 October 1928. The advertisement depicts two men, one clearly older than the other, discussing the taste of Rhodian cigarettes. The older gentleman indicates his interest in Rhodesian tobacco: 'I, like many Britons, have a boy out there, I have made many converts to RHODIANS and I don't hesitate to tell them that the flavour is different'.

Through advertisements such as this, the irrevocable link between Britain and white settlers in Rhodesia was established, and even seemingly mundane images of two men smoking are imperialised. M. Corina indicates that Imperial was doubtful about the idea of all-Rhodesian cigarettes because it believed that they would always be regarded as inferior. Yet Amery put pressure on Imperial to help tackle the Rhodesian tobacco crisis.[39] The launch of Rhodian in direct response to EMB pressure indicates the degree of persuasion that the EMB applied to private companies and may explain why the brand's advertising recites almost verbatim the ideology of the EMB. Apart from persuading manufacturers to create Empire brands, the EMB also pushed traders to stock these brands by printing persuasive articles in trade journals such as *Tobacco*. On 1 July 1929, for instance, an article entitled 'Stock and Sell Southern Rhodesian Tobacco and Cigarettes' informed traders that the EMB had produced an Empire tobacco list and was also inserting advertisements in support of Empire tobacco in many papers in the UK. It mentioned that the 'fine quality of Southern Rhodesian leaf was being appreciated more and more' and described it as a 'Purely British product, grown by British farmers in Southern Rhodesia'. 'Bring these facts to the notice of your customers', the article declared, 'the campaign for Empire buying has created a goodwill which any enterprising trader can turn to his own advantage by stocking and pushing Empire produce.'[40] Piling on the pressure, the Secretary for the Southern Rhodesian High Commission also advertised in *Tobacco* two months later, encouraging traders to show their imperial preference.[41]

Imperialising and patriotic imagery, however, was not simply limited to brands within Imperial that used Empire tobacco. Wills's Woodbine, for example, was advertised in 1935 with a series of showcards depicting 'British industries'. The series included scenes of steel forging, aeroplane manufacture and agriculture (Figure 59). Earlier, as we have seen, the EMB had brought British industry within the wider ambit of Empire. British industries were Empire industries, and in 1928 the EMB had even had a series of press advertisements entitled 'British industries' which depicted and promoted industries such as iron and steel, motor construction and cotton (Figure 60). In developing its series of showcards, Wills must been aware that it was recalling the EMB ideology without even mentioning Empire. These men were also Empire men.

In developing its ideology, the EMB had also created a problem. The patriotic and imperial image could easily be used to service any

59 'British industries: aeroplane manufacture', Wills's Woodbines showcard, 1920s

product. Selling the abstract imperial idea did not necessarily lead to more Empire buying, for the image could not be restricted to Empire produce. By the 1920s, the shifts in advertising techniques meant that symbolic values were advertised more than product qualities, as I have already mentioned, and this must have also encouraged advertisers to employ an imperial image as a general characteristic rather than as reflective of the products' origin.[42]

Barneys and Craven tobacco and the image of Empire

While Wills's Woodbine used images of British patriotism within its advertising, a number of non-Empire brands also exploited the image of Empire. Two brands of pipe tobacco which produced a stunning series of imperial images were Barneys Tobacco and Craven Mixture. Significantly both brands developed their advertisements after the establishment of the EMB. The advertisements for Barneys in *Punch*

BRITISH INDUSTRIES

MOTOR VEHICLES
AND BICYCLES

Rows of lathes and machines . . . at each the mechanic
is moulding, turning and finishing one of the many parts,
which, when fitted and-assembled, produce British cars
and bicycles for the markets of the world.

Fifty years ago bicycles were almost unknown and motor-
cars unheard of. To-day the Motor Industry of the United
Kingdom produces over 350,000 motor vehicles a year.

In 1927 the Empire Overseas took two-thirds of the motor
vehicles and bicycles exported from these islands.

¶ EVERY TIME you buy Empire Goods
you are helping the Empire to place an
order with one of our Industries at home.

ISSUED BY THE EMPIRE MARKETING BOARD

Z.E.I.L.

60 'British industries: motor vehicles and bicycles', EMB press advertisement,
The Times, 12 November 1928

began in June 1927, three months after the EMB had started to advertise in *Punch*. Unlike the 'Digger' brand, which depicted the ruddy-cheeked planter, these two tobaccos, and Barneys in particular, emphasised the slightly higher-class civil servant or merchant in the Empire. As the context of the advertisements in *Punch* indicate, these brands were intended for a middle-class consumer. It is hard to identify the *Punch* readership, since no audience surveys of the magazine exist, but what is clear is that the men reading this magazine were obviously interested in politics and, judging from the content of the cartoons of this period, held establishment views. *Punch* was also a magazine that was distributed amongst British workers in the Empire. The political importance of the *Punch* readership was recognised by the EMB, which perceived its relationship with *Punch* as 'special' and inserted a vast number of advertisements in the magazine which was disproportionate to that in any other paper. Even some special advertisements appeared in *Punch* that were not used elsewhere, such as the 'Smoke Empire tobacco' advertisement from November 1928. The special relationship that *Punch* had with the EMB makes it all the more interesting that two non-Empire brands were able to advertise so profusely in *Punch* with an imperial image, at the precise moment when the EMB was also advertising.

The advertisements for Barneys Tobacco began in *Punch* in June 1927 and continued throughout the period of the EMB's existence. The first advertisement, which features a merchant from Baghdad and is titled 'Factory freshness in Baghdad: in summer' sets the tone for the whole series (Figure 61). The gentleman depicted is the imperial archetype, with moustache, pipe and pith helmet. Even in the height of summer, he wears a tie and jacket, codes of white bourgeois masculinity and, in the context of Empire, European 'civility'. In the background is an image of Baghdad, as much imaginary as actual, scattered with minarets and domes. Larger than even the male imperialist consumer is a photographic depiction of a tin of Barneys Tobacco, which contrasts with the line drawings of the scene behind. The thrust of the text indicates that even in hot, dry and humid places, Barneys Tobacco remains fresh because of the vacuum seal on the tin. While the text talks about the freshness of tobacco, the graphic indicates something different. The prominence of the tin makes our eye gravitate towards it first and the element on the tin which is highlighted is the vacuum seal. An arrow towards the rubber tab is marked 'PULL This releases the vacuum and allows tin to open'. The tab is in fact placed at an ideal angle for us as viewers to reach out and pull. It is as though when we activate this photographically realistic tin by opening it, we will activate or 'realise' the scene behind.

61 'Factory freshness in Baghdad in summer', Barneys Tobacco advertisement, *Punch*, 1 June 1927

In this sense, visually, when the vacuum is released, the promise is not just of sweet and fresh tobacco, but a taste of Empire.

These advertisements must have both encouraged and affirmed the image of the imperial pipe smoker which began to appear in films and popular culture of the period. Finally, in constructing its symbolic identities, Barneys aimed to attract both those who wished to be associated with what must have been regarded as the glamour of imperial duty, and those actually out in the field. At the bottom of the page, in all the advertisements, are listed details of how to obtain duty-free despatches for abroad. While the glamour of imperial travel may have appealed to the middle-class male consumer in Britain, it was the assurance of home comforts and the tobacco as a symbol of 'civilisation' which was needed for the white man abroad. Letters from apparent customers abroad were frequently printed in the advertisements, telling of the sense of comfort and relaxation the tobacco offered, and the familiar tin persisted in the advertisements:

> On my return I shall be going out into the Provinces, where a regular supply of the 'baccy' will be of even more vital import than here in the comparative civilisation of Khartoum . . .
>
> Being a 'teak-wallah' in a sorely troubled land, a satisfying and friendly smoke is a great boon . . .

As time went on, Barneys appeared like a faithful companion, accompanying the white man on his travels, a mark of his 'civilisation' and his distinguished and superior status. Appearing in all corners of the earth, these advertisements recall the Pears advertisements of the 1890s to some degree. Yet, while Pears in the 1890s was represented as a product to civilise and conquer, as a product that would encourage commodity culture, Barneys is not presented as a product to be left behind, to be consumed by Africans or Asians, but as a product to distinguish the white imperialist from others. The product symbolically represents the development of consumer identity. It was not simply Barneys that sold itself in this way. During this period, even Pears employed a similar imperial image in *Punch*, emphasising the availability of Pears for the white male Empire-builder in various areas of the world. In this sense these images were not about the development of mutual trading links, but about the imaging of a mythical masculine imperial hero. This 'hero' was also depicted on Austin Reed's advertisement for its tropical kit department (Figure 62). The man represented stands in tropical kit with his knee propped up in a posture of relaxed control, in a similar style to that of the Empire-builder in Adrian Allinson's EMB poster discussed earlier. The eulogising of Empire by the EMB lent these images a moral

East
of Suez
via
The New
AUSTIN
REED'S

IF it's Eastward Ho ! for the first time in your life, there's one
man you should see before you go—the expert in charge of our
Tropical Kit Department, whose job it is to place his experience
at the disposal of all who care to consult him. He's lived in the
East. So he can give some useful tips.
And if you know the ropes, you will find here everything you need
to replenish your kit before setting out again. This Department
maintains the Austin Reed tradition. It is a complete service,
offering the widest possible choice in the right things for the right
climate—from China to Peru.

AUSTIN REED'S
of REGENT STREET

TROPICAL KIT DEPARTMENT

AUSTIN REED, LTD., LONDON

62 'East of Suez', Austin Reed's tropical kit department advertisement, *Punch*, 11 May 1927

righteousness. They were also clearly intended for a middle-class consumer. Between 1927 and 1932, thirty different Barneys advertisements appeared in *Punch*. Each one represented Barneys in a different part of the world, from markets in Nigeria to the Sind desert. They became a travelogue transporting the viewer/consumer to different exotic locations. Another tobacco brand which exploited a similar type of imagery, but this time with even more clearly marked postcard-style imagery, was the cigarette brand 'State Express – 555'. During the 1920s, the main form of advertising to focus on black people was travel advertising, which exoticised colonial and foreign locations, presenting them as a spectacle for the white consumer.[43]

In none of the advertisements for Barneys is there any suggestion that the tobacco was produced from Empire tobacco, but there is also no indication of the origin of the tobacco either. In two advertisements for 1932, Barneys is described as 'the Empire's *most-recommended* tobacco', but this appears to refer entirely to consumption rather than production. Barneys did eventually produce an Empire blend but there are no advertisements for it in *Punch*. It is interesting that although traversing across various parts of the Empire, there is no advertisement for Barneys in Rhodesia. Instead an advertisement references Barneys as being more generally available in Central Africa, declaring 'East of Benguela, West of Zanzibar, North of Bulawayo' (*Punch*, 14 January 1931).

From July 1931 Craven Mixture also advertised in *Punch* and exploited the image of Empire without referencing the tobacco's origin. While Carreras launched Craven Empire-de-luxe and Craven Empire-de-luxe Curly Cut in 1932, it was not the Empire variety that was advertised in *Punch* with an array of imperial imagery. The similarity of image between Barneys and Craven Mixture was probably the result of Mr Sinclair, of John Sinclair Ltd (which manufactured Barneys), becoming sales director of Carreras Ltd in 1931. In 1929 the two companies had undergone capital integration after Mr Sinclair became a director of Carreras and a financial arrangement between the two companies came into being in 1930 through which they traded as associated companies before a complete merger in 1935.[44] Drawing on the Barneys imperialist style of advertisements, Craven Mixture exalted the Empire even more jingoistically, employing phrases such as 'The sun never sets'. While Barneys had represented the white male consumer in various parts of the Empire with letters from consumers expressing the comfort and satisfaction which they received through smoking the brand, in Craven Mixture advertisements the tin and tobacco are almost personalities experiencing the exploits of its consumers, and practically supplanting them. The men are not represented, it is only the tin that is depicted larger than life in the imperial scene. The advertisements depict scenes of both England and the Empire, linking 'home' and Empire in a similar way to the campaign of the EMB (Figures 63 and 64).

In the first Craven Mixture advertisement, reproduced in *Punch* in 22 July 1931, the text suggests:

> If Craven tins could speak, what tales would they not tell; what epics of endurance and fortitude, now part of History. There is something about Craven Mixture in tune with the pioneering spirit, something which *appeals* to the men who *do* things . . .

Here Craven tobacco is presented as experiencing the history of all those who have smoked it, and these men are perceived as active, 'real' men. This first advertisement depicted a photograph of the Mawson expedition that had recently reached Antarctica and carved out areas for scientific investigation. The photograph appears to have been constructed after the event. There is no background and the ladder in the middle of the image looks particularly bizarre. Yet the event marks a moment of triumph for British imperialism and the text speaks of endurance and fortitude. The concept of men who *do* things was used repeatedly. One advertisement from 21 December 1932 depicted an aeroplane flying through the rugged mountains of the North West Frontier, and was titled 'Men like these' (Figure 64). The implication was obvious: men like the ones flying the plane and carrying out brave and pioneering tasks smoke Craven Mixture. Images of the air force and navy were used repeatedly. On 2 June 1938 another advertisement depicted the rock of Gibralter with the commanding presence of both the British navy and air force. Images such as these eulogised British forces and their role as policemen of the Empire and emphasised the masculinity of such a task.[45] These men were 'real' men with traditional values.

Through the advertisements, Craven was described as a tobacco that 'invites trust', contains 'the spirit of dependability' and is 'a tobacco to live for'. In advertisements such as these, the tin looms large over the scene portrayed. The gigantic tin assumes a personality and force which goes beyond simply offering consumers an attribute which may enhance them to actually representing them and their identity – something that was very new in advertising at this time. For Craven Mixture, this identity was entirely imperial, with no room for any other way of living. This imperial vision was both racialised and entirely masculine. Hand in hand with discussions about men and tobaccos that you can 'trust' were images of military heroism and the pioneering spirit. Repeated reference was also made to white men

63 'The sun never sets', Craven Mixture Tobacco advertisement, *Punch*, 22 July 1931

On the N.W. Frontier.

Men like these

They have spread the friendship for Craven Mixture Tobacco from end to end of the Empire . . . soldiers, sailors, sportsmen all, putting so much *into* life, expecting much from it in the matter of smoking-joy.

In every Garrison Town, in every Port and City, in almost every frontier post . . . *wherever the Flag flies* . . . that homely famed old Craven Tin will give you greeting ; a symbol of something animating the very fabric of the Empire—dependability and character.

Character brought Craven its distinguished patronage, for it was first blended for the third Earl of Craven's personal smoking. *Dependability*—which is character tested against circumstance —has made the chosen blend of one mid-Victorian smoker trusted wherever white men go.

The Craven Mixture we commend to the discriminating smoker of to-day is the same steadfast old Craven . . . unchanged in its goodness . . . cool, fragrant and so wonderfully satisfying, revealing, above all, that intangible, inexpressible charm which makes it, in Barrie's own words, "*A Tobacco to live for.*"

★ 'ARCADIA'

immortalised by Sir James M. Barrie in "My Lady Nicotine," is Carreras' Craven Mixture.
Fine Cut, Double Broad Cut, Extra Mild.
1 oz. 1/3, 2 oz. 2/6, 4 oz. 5/-, in Airtight Tins. (The 1-oz. size is not exported.)

CRAVEN MIXTURE TOBACCO

MADE BY CARRERAS LTD., (FOUNDED 1788) ARCADIA WORKS, LONDON, N.W.1.

64 'Men like these', Craven Mixture Tobacco advertisement, *Punch*, 21 December 1932 as consumers of Craven. In an advertisement entitled 'A little bit of England', the text begins: 'wherever white men go good tobacco is sure to follow'. This phrase was repeated in other advertisements. Craven, like Barneys, was clearly demarcated as a product which would create 'difference' between its consumers and other members of the Empire. Its consumers were men on active service, the 'men on the spot' who had often been criticised by politicians. The eulogising of these men at a time of rising criticism of Empire is notable. A sense of superiority and control was also established through the frequent presentation of a bird's eye view of places, suggesting possession, surveillance and control.

While I have highlighted the imperial image used to sell some tobacco products, it would be incorrect to perceive this image as the most dominant identity in tobacco advertising, since it is clear that by the 1920s consumer identity had become an important issue and the beginnings of market segmentation had begun. A variety of identities were therefore sold through a range of brands. The imperial identity was one that was particularly strong in pipe tobacco, and seemed to reflect on imperial propaganda produced by the government through the EMB. In advertisements produced for Barneys and Craven Mixture, the Empire was perceived as masculine, full of adventure and just.

During the inter-war period the idea of Empire as a benign family with each member playing a complimentary role was pushed by the government through the EMB. This was a marked shift from the previous period in which private enterprise appeared to have more influence on representations during a time when government policy was ill-defined. Tobacco advertising in particular exploited the image of the white male Empire-builder in the hope of encouraging consumers to buy products which used Empire tobacco. However, the image of the imperial consumer was not only present in tobacco advertising. It was used on many other products including soap, alcohol, clothing and even Shredded Wheat. Apart from government policy, which saw the answer to Britain's economic problems being solved through Empire, one reason for this was the shift in advertising during this period from an emphasis on the product and its uses to a focus on imbuing products with symbolic attributes and qualities desired by consumers. A substantial amount of British tobacco advertising, from both brands that used imperial tobacco and those that did not, rode on the bandwagon of the imperial dream. They offered their consumers a way of partaking in the supposed glamour and masculinity of Empire-building through a smoke.

Notes

1 M. Havinden and D. Meredith, *Colonialism and Development: Britain and its Tropical Colonies 1850–1960* (London, 1993), p. 147.
2 From a speech by Amery, 1906, cited in S. Constantine, 'Bringing the Empire Alive: The Empire Marketing Board and Imperial Propaganda 1926–1933', in J. MacKenzie (ed.), *Imperialism and Popular Culture* (Manchester, 1987), p. 196.
3 The Coalition Manifesto, 1918, cited in *ibid.*, p. 149.
4 *Hansard* (House of Commons) 5th series CLXXIX, 17 December 1924, col. 1665, cited in *ibid.*, p. 150.
5 Annual Reports of the Empire Marketing Board, 1927–28; 1928–29; 1929–30.
6 Constantine, 'Bringing the Empire Alive', p. 199.
7 *Ibid.*, p. 200.
8 Annual Report of the Empire Marketing Board, 1927–28.
9 PRO, CO 760/26, Minutes of the Poster Sub-committee, 27 October 1926; 1 December 1926; 9 December 1926.
10 W. Crawford, 'Making the Empire Come Alive', *Commercial Art*, 1:6 (1926), pp. 241–6; W. Crawford, 'The Poster Campaign of the Empire Marketing Board', *Commercial Art*, 6 (1929), pp. 128–35.
11 Cited in G. Abbott 'A Re-examination of the 1929 Colonial Development Act', *Economic History Review*, 2:24 (1977), p. 68.
12 D. Meredith, 'Imperial Images: The Empire Marketing Board 1926–1932', *History Today*, 37 (January 1987), p. 35.
13 See posters 'Colombo Ceylon' 1928, PRO, CO 956/13 and 'Empire Builders' 1927, PRO, CO 956/529.
14 J. Grierson, 'The EMB Film Unit', *Cinema Quarterly*, 4 (1933), p. 204, cited in S. Constantine, *Buy and Build: The Advertising Posters of the Empire Marketing Board* (London, 1986), p. 17.
15 F. Clements and E. Harben, *Leaf of Gold: The Story of Rhodesian Tobacco* (London, 1962), p. 100.
16 Minutes of the Poster Sub-committee, PRO, CO 760/26, 14 June 1928.
17 PRO, CO 760/26, 28 June 1928.
18 PRO, CO 760/26, 30 August 1928.
19 The representation of a sanitised image of labour has also been discussed by Jonathan Woodham in 'Images of Africa and Design at the British Empire Exhibitions between the Wars', *Journal of Design History*, 2:1 (1989), pp. 15–34.
20 PRO, CO 760/23, 25 October 1928.
21 *Punch*, 28 November 1928.
22 PRO, CO 760/25, 18 November 1928.
23 D. Meredith, 'The Colonial Office, British Business Interests and the Reform of Cocoa Marketing in West Africa 1937–1945', *Journal of African History*, 29 (1988), pp. 285–304.
24 One exception appears to be 'Old Friend', which conforms to the 'sambo' stereotype.
25 This image is reproduced in Clements and Harben, *Leaf of Gold*, p. 48.
26 D. Janiewski, *Sisterhood Denied: Race, Gender and Class in a New South Community* (Philadelphia, 1985), p. 16.
27 W. Leiss, S. Kline and S. Jhally, *Social Communication in Advertising: Persons, Products and Images of Well-being* (Scarborough Ontario, 1988), p. 124.
28 J. Richards, *Visions of Yesterday* (London, 1973).
29 A. Allinson, 'East African Transport – New Style' 1930–31, PRO CO 956/215.
30 Cited in MacKenzie, *Propaganda and Empire*, p. 110.
31 For histories of black people in Britain during this period, including their resistance to racism, see D. Frost, 'West Africans, Black Scousers and "the Colour Problem" in Inter-war Liverpool', *Journal of the North West History Labour Group*,

20 (1995/6), pp. 50–7; J. Jenkinson, 'The Race Riots in Britain: A Survey', in R. Lotz and I. Pegg (eds), *Under the Imperial Carpet: Essays in Black History 1780–1950* (Crawley, 1986); R. Ramdin, *The Making of the Black Working Class in Britain* (Aldershot, 1987).

32 J. N. Pieterse, *White on Black: Images of Africa and Blacks in Western Popular Culture* (New Haven, 1992), p. 157.

33 B. W. E. Alford, *WD and HO Wills and the Development of the UK Tobacco Industry 1786–1965* (London, 1973), Chapter 15; M. Corina, *Trust in Tobacco: The Anglo American Struggle for Power* (London, 1975), Chapters 8 and 9.

34 Corina, *Trust in Tobacco*, p. 138.

35 See PRO, Imperial Economic Committee, 'Report on the Methods of Preparing for Market and Marketing within the United Kingdom of Tobacco Produced within the Empire', July 1928, p. 22.

36 Players Archive, Nottingham Castle Museum, *John Players and Sons Centenary 1877–1977* (leaflet), p. 14.

37 *Tobacco*, 1 July 1929, p. 83.

38 Summary of the Imperial Economic Committee's Report on Tobacco, presented to the Tobacco Committee on 28 February 1930, in CO 760/30. A paper on Southern Rhodesian tobacco presented to the Tobacco Committee on 1 May 1930 also talks about Imperial's support for Empire tobacco.

39 Corina, *Trust in Tobacco*, pp. 156–7.

40 *Tobacco*, 1 July 1929, p. 82.

41 *Tobacco*, 1 September 1929, p. 60.

42 See Leiss *et al.*, *Social Communication*, and A. Marchand, *Advertising the American Dream* (Berkeley, 1985).

43 W. O'Barr, *Culture and the Ad: Exploring Otherness in the World of Advertising* (Boulder, 1994). O'Barr dedicates a chapter to travel advertising from the *National Geographic* for 1929.

44 'History of John Sinclair Ltd', 2 December 1963, unpublished and unauthored essay in Newcastle Libraries.

45 By 1930 the use of air power to police and pacify the Empire was well established, since it could cause maximum devastation with minimum casualties on the British side. For a discussion on air policing see David E. Omissi, *Air Power and Colonial Control: The Royal Air Force 1919–1939* (Manchester, 1990).

CHAPTER SIX

Corporate advertising, decolonisation and the transition to neo-colonialism

In the immediate post-war period, the general belief that the economic basis of British independence 'required the energetic defence of far-flung colonial and semi-colonial commitments' continued to hold sway.[1] At the same time, however, anti-colonial feelings in many parts of the Empire were at their height, leading to the establishment of political sovereignty for India and Pakistan in 1947, followed by independence for Burma and Ceylon a year later. This was to have a profound impact on the general belief in the legitimacy of Empire. It was a period of intense flux and political change in the colonies and the producers of commodities for mass consumption shied away from representing black people to the British consumer. Many corporate advertisers, however, chose to represent the peoples and lands of the colonies and emerging Commonwealth. Through these images we can trace the attitudes of companies to changing and conflicting colonial policy, as they attempted to defend their overseas interests at a time of relative uncertainty.

Advertisements in establishment papers such as the *Illustrated London News* represent the corporate companies as bringers of so-called progress and development. Within these images, development is closely associated with industrialisation and consumption. Such images continue to persist in corporate advertisements of the 1990s. The rise of these representations during the 1950s, however, is significant and represents the corporate companies' backing of 'modernisation theory' popular in the 1950s and 1960s. I do not intend to suggest that the images of the colonial/ex-colonial world were the only or even the most prominent of images for these corporate advertisers. What is significant is that a sizeable proportion of images did represent these territories and that corporate advertisers were the main group to represent the image of black people during this period. The existence of so many of these images in the *Illustrated London News*

may have been a result of the large number of expatriates that sub-
scribed to the magazine. This meant that there was a significant
number of readers anxious about the changes that decolonisation was
to bring. The *Illustrated London News* was also an establishment
paper whose readers must have included shareholders with interests
in the colonies. We can see these advertisements as appeals by the
companies to appease shareholders and also pacify the conscience of
the expatriate class, who may have begun to question their colonial
role.

For corporate companies who had clearly benefited from systems
of imperial preference, the process of decolonisation in many parts of
the Empire brought uncertainty. At a time when expatriate companies were also out of favour in many areas of growing nationalist
resistance, these companies clearly wished to construct a new image
for themselves as organisations that were involved in development
and 'progress', rather than exploitation. Large corporate firms had
even come under attack and scrutiny in Britain with the establishment of the Monopolies and Restrictive Practices Commission in
1948 and the Restrictive Practices Court and Restrictive Trade Practices
Act in 1956. For their image in Britain and abroad, it was essential
for firms to present themselves as caring concerns. The effect of the
war had been 'to encourage a leftward shift in British opinion across
the whole range of political and social issues'.[2] Even an article in
The Times in 1940 demanded greater equality and freedom:

> If we speak of democracy, we do not mean a democracy which main-
> tains the right to vote but forgets the right to work and the right to live.
> If we speak of freedom, we do not mean a rugged individualism which
> excludes social organisation and economic planning. If we speak of
> equality, we do not mean a political equality nullified by social and
> economic privilege. If we speak of economic reconstruction, we think
> less of maximum production . . . than of equitable distribution.[3]

Such opinions impacted on attitudes to Empire. 'Imperial supremacy
and the assertion of racial superiority were no longer an appropriate
rhetoric.'[4] This made it imperative for companies to re-construct their
corporate identities. They looked for representations which would
suggest their concern for world-wide economic development. While
representing Commonwealth and colonial nations, none of the companies mentioned the term 'Empire' in any of their advertisements.

In some ways we can see these advertisements as representing a
negotiated political change while maintaining economic interests.
These interests needed to be represented as benefiting both Britain
and the 'developing' nations. Their images represent the ideological

interests of companies that wished to maintain their economic interests through a Commonwealth economic union or other structures and systems of preference, in the face of growing competition. As Darwin notes:

> The economic meaning of decolonisation . . . has not been the collapse of 'imperialist exploitation', but rather the rise of the branch plant and the multi-national company which could trade safely inside the defences of the closed economy, largely immune from the hostility displayed by post-colonial governments to foreign enterprise proper.[5]

In establishing a space for themselves within new political systems, the corporate firms with colonial and ex-colonial interests threw themselves behind 'modernisation theory' popular in the 1950s and 1960s and articulated this support in their corporate image-making.

Modernisation theory

Modernisation theory presented a teleological approach to development. It held the position that all societies could be laid out at different points on the same evolutionary scale, with the Western world at the top. Based on the ideas of social scientists such as Talcott Parsons and economists such as Walter Rostow, this theory formed the basis of much Western policy in the 'third world' during the 1950s and was directed at bringing the necessary conditions for Western-style development and growth into existence as rapidly as possible.[6] Parsons's *The Social System* represented society and social change as gradual and evolutionary. He saw society and people as constantly adjusting through 'a voluntary theory of action', which emerged through the application of 'shared values'. Parsons's theory of the social system was based on the idea of a constant search for equilibrium. He ignored the inherent contradictions that exist within a class-based society and the possibility of competing value systems and radical or revolutionary change.[7] Rostow's *Stages of Economic Growth* also theorised change as evolutionary. He defined five stages of economic development: the traditional society; the pre-conditions for take-off; take-off; the drive to maturity; and the age of high mass-consumption. In this system, while underdevelopment may have existed in parts of the world, it was not seen as a result of exploitation but as a condition that all societies had to pass through and was a pre-condition for development.

The image of British corporate firms propelling 'third world' nations from traditional society into 'pre-conditions for take-off' made them appear like honest brokers aiding former colonies. As Webster indicated, the 'diffusionist thesis explicitly argued that the developed countries could have nothing other than a benign influence in the "developing" countries'. Such ideas were seen as 'a great source of justification for the activities of the development agencies' during this period.[8] Rostow, for example, outlines the second stage as either taking place through internal change or as 'prepared by external forces'.[9] According to Rostow, colonialism itself is part of the process of development and the result of two societies at different stages within the development process. He describes decolonisation as part of the process towards the pre-condition period. These arguments therefore undermined the socialist and anti-imperialist arguments about colonial exploitation continuing in a neo-colonial form.[10]

Apart from representing Western business interests as benign, modernisation theory's focus on the 'third world' was also the result of the desire of politicians and businessmen 'to show countries pushing for independence that sustained development was possible under the western wing (rather than that of the Soviet Union)'.[11] Rostow's subtitle to *The Stages of Economic Growth – A Non-Communist Manifesto* – asserts this theory as part of the Cold War project. Therefore we can see these images as part of the Cold War's attack on communism. Modernisation theory can be regarded as a theoretical development in support of processes that would lead to the establishment of a neo-colonial structure, where despite political independence, the economic strings would still be held by the West. As Nkrumah put it:

> The essence of neo-colonialism is that the state which is subject to it is, in theory, independent and has all the trappings of international sovereignty. In reality its economic system and thus its internal policy is directed from the outside.[12]

The representation of neo-colonialism through the espousing of modernisation theory is apparent in all the images produced by corporate firms during the 1950s and early 1960s.

Dominant representations

Four particular types of imagery dominate corporate advertising during this period. The first could be described as the image of complementary economics, which was articulated from the late nineteenth century onwards. The second, much newer representation was that of an industrialising Africa. The third reworked the image of infancy with which non-European nations had been represented. The fourth, less dominant, but still significant image was of a new African middle-class consumer. I shall discuss each of these representations in turn and highlight the ways in which they asserted a notion of development that modernisation theory espoused.

Complementary economics

Shell, the most prolific corporate advertiser for this period, repeatedly used imagery which represented the philosophy of complementary economics. Anglo Iranian Oil, which became British Petroleum (BP) in 1954, also used similar imagery. Shell's advertisements appear in almost every other issue of the *Illustrated London News* from the mid 1950s onwards. The advertisements from the early 1950s describe the use of chemicals in all parts of world agriculture, from Britain and France to South East Asia and Guatemala. The advertisements from the late 1950s discuss the use of Shell Chemicals in agriculture as well as industry, and present the 'third world' as a series of agricultural units that contrast with industrialised Britain, in which research and development take place. Two separate advertisements from 1957 show the difference. An advertisement entitled 'An army routed' from 16 February 1957 for Shell Endrin depicts an agricultural scene in Africa, in contrast to the scientific scene in the 27 July 1957 advertisement from the series 'I'll tell you something else about Shell'. Later in 1959 and 1960, Shell produced double-paged advertisements which represent Shell in both agriculture and industry. The sense of complementary economics is particularly strong in these images, where scenes of agriculture in places such as Africa and Mexico contrast with scenes of an industrialised, 'modern' world within which consumption also appears to take place (Figure 65). The contrast between the non-European and European world is also naturalised. For example, the representation of the adult male coffee grower in Africa contrasts with the image of young British boys making go-carts – mechanical and industrial skills are presented as though they are inherently white, rather than as skills that are acquired.

While maintaining this contrast, however, there is a new tone in some of the images. This deliberately conflicts with representations from the past in order to enhance the image of Shell as a philanthropic and modern-thinking company. The advertisement for Shell Endrin entitled 'An army routed' is a good example (Figure 66). This advertisement appeared not only in the *Illustrated London News*, but also in *Punch* in both February and March 1957. Through the title of the advertisement, the stereotype of Africa as a series of warring tribes, as well as the memory of British wars and conquest in Africa, is evoked. This representation, however, contrasts with the quietness of the image as well as with the smaller text, which describes what Shell must have regarded as a new type of African:

Coffee line

From Bonabéri, on the wide estuary of the Wouri river, the Chemin de Fer du Nord runs just 160 kilometres to its terminus at N'Kongsamba. A short line, in the immensity of Africa, but a picturesque one. Winding first through evergreen rain forest and the humid zone of oil palm and banana, it then climbs steadily into a land of black volcanic earth where, in March, the air is sweetly scented and every tree a foam of blossom. Here, in the Mungo district of Cameroun, is grown the country's biggest tonnage of *Robusta* coffee. And here, an insect pest struck recently with unexpectedly vicious force.

Normally, damage by the coffee clear wing moth (*Cephonodes hylas* L.), known in most of the coffee growing areas of Africa, is reasonably easy to control, and hand destruction of the big green and white caterpillars is sufficient. In May 1957 however, very heavy infestations caught the planters by surprise; hand picking failed to check the pests, and in some plantations trees were quickly stripped of two-thirds of their foliage. An immediate appeal for aid was made to the N'Kolbisson Entomology Laboratory near Yaoundé.

The answer was swift, effective, and based on Shell *endrin*. A formulation of 19.5% *endrin* applied at a rate of 3 litres per hectare in 500-1000 litres of water was recommended, and results were spectacular. Even the largest caterpillars

were rapidly killed, and 100% control was achieved within 12 hours—yet another example of the killing-power of this important foliage insecticide developed by Shell. With the aid of *endrin* the coffee line to Bonabéri carried full loads in 1957; with the aid of *endrin* many other crops come safely to harvest year by year in many parts of the world

Cephonodes hylas L.

Shellendrin

Endrin is one of six Shell pesticides for world-wide use. Between them, endrin, aldrin, dieldrin, Phosdrin, D-D and Nemagon offer control of virtually every significant pest, both above and below the soil. In addition, dieldrin has important uses in public health. Have you a pest problem in your area? Your Shell Company will gladly advise you on methods of control or eradication.

IN AGRICULTURE...YOU CAN BE SURE OF CHEMICALS

65 *also facing* Shell Chemicals advertisement, *Illustrated London News*, 24 October 1959

Bright beginnings

Cars without engines need a smooth run to the finishing line. The smoother the flow, the finer the finish. And not only for 'soap-box fliers', but for every car on the production line. Car-proud owners today look for higher-gloss finishes—and more colours to choose from—than ever before, and an answer to this (as any manufacturer of paint will tell you) lies in the quality of the aromatic solvents used. With their evaporation rate chosen for the purpose, together with the highest standard of purity, you get the best 'flow' and gloss in the paint when using these solvents.

By the Shell range of aromatics—benzene, toluene, xylene and the higher-boiling-point products—the requirements of many industries are covered. Materials as diverse as synthetic rubber, detergents, plastics, textile fibres and dye stuffs all find a call for aromatics—just as do many surface coatings including paints, lacquers, enamels and printing inks.

Have you a problem concerning finer finishes? If your process includes stoving, 'Shellsol' A is probably the aromatic you need. With an evaporation rate adjusted to the requirements of stoving finishes and brushing paints, and an aromatic content of almost 100%, 'Shellsol' A ensures exceptional 'flow' and gloss and is a product of great potential.

Solvents, resins, intermediates, plastics, base chemicals, additives, detergents, glycols, synthetic rubber . . . Shell chemical production serves every industry. Ask your Shell Company for details.

Shell Aromatic solvents

High aromatic solvents are also necessary to produce agricultural sprays containing high concentrations of chlorinated insecticides. Shell aromatic solvents are frequently employed to produce high quality formulations containing the Shell insecticides aldrin, dieldrin and endrin. Ask your Shell Company also about the range of aliphatic as well as aromatic hydrocarbons. The Shell solvent range covers many industrial and agricultural needs.

Issued by Shell International Chemical Company Limited and Bataafse Internationale Chemie Mij. N.V.
For further information apply to your Shell Company (in the U.K. apply to Shell Chemical Company Limited).

IN INDUSTRY . . . YOU CAN BE SURE OF **SHELL CHEMICALS**

[179]

An Army routed

Kweheli is a peace loving man. His tribe no longer goes to war—in the ways his forefathers knew. Yet, throughout his life, regularly year by year (and sometimes several times a year) Kweheli has had to fight —and just as regularly lose—a battle which has threatened his very livelihood. Today, that battle has been won. For Kweheli. By Shell.

In the sun-soaked lands of the Rhodesias, maize is a staple food. It is also a favourite target of the voracious army worm—caterpillar of the moth *Laphygma exempta*. The army worm, so called because of its vast numbers, appears suddenly, unexpectedly and devastatingly. It comes like a thief in the night and in a few short hours can destroy every young and promising plant in its path . . . pasture, forage grass or cereal. For generations, when the army worm struck, hunger came close.

Today, however, the army worm has been routed—and the livelihood of millions of Kwehelis protected. Tests have conclusively proved that even when followed by continuous and heavy rain, a complete kill of the army worm can be obtained by a dilution of endrin 19.5% emulsifiable concentrate applied by knapsack sprayer.

Endrin, developed by Shell, is the most effective insecticide ever used against this voracious pest. It is also a most persistent method of control, economical and easy to apply.

Shell endrin

ENDRIN, ALDRIN AND DIELDRIN

ARE SHELL **INSECTICIDES**

FOR WORLD-WIDE USE

66 'An army routed', Shell Endrin advertisement, *Illustrated London News*, 16 February 1957

Kweheli is a peace loving man. His tribe no longer goes to war – in the ways his forefathers knew. Yet, throughout his life, regularly year by year (and sometimes several times a year) Kweheli has had to fight – and just as regularly lose – a battle which has threatened his very livelihood. Today, that battle has been won. For Kweheli. By Shell.

Interestingly, Shell does not suggest past representations to be wrong, but rather represents the colonial philosophy of an African who has developed into a 'civilised' man. In this image, the white man's burden appears to have paid off, through the representation of an African who appears to be taking responsibility. He appears to represent Rostow's idea of a culturally altered figure, stimulated by the preparation for 'take-off'. The picture continues this assessment, with the image of a man checking his damaged crop with some care. Here, Africans appear to have been given control over agricultural development, in contrast to the EMB images from the inter-war period, in which work of a technical or scientific nature was depicted as carried out by Europeans.

In Shell's advertisement, however, while the image appears to contrast with inter-war representations, the text asserts Kweheli's continuing dependence. Shell is endowed with the role of philanthropist who preserves the livelihood of Kweheli and others. The image also depicts Kweheli dominated by a stalk of maize. He looks up at the damaged leaves and the scientific enlargement of the army worm is also placed above him in the advertisement. His physical positioning, despite his ponderous pose, still encourages us to assess him as the grateful recipient of the bounty of Western science. This dependency is interpreted as the way forward, as W. A. Lewis commented:

> It is historically true that all countries have depended on foreign enterprise to help them along in the early stages of their development, but for most countries this enterprise has been as important for its value in training the native people and showing them the way, as it has been for its direct contribution to output.[13]

While Lewis later suggests that for 'racial reasons' this training does not appear to have taken place in tropical colonies in the same way, the Shell image suggests that it has taken place in areas under Shell's jurisdiction. Such images not only legitimised Lewis's main concepts but represented Shell in an almost philanthropic role.

While such colonial policy was affirmed in Shell's British advertising, its images in *West Africa*, a magazine that was distributed amongst both expatriates and the African middle classes and emerging elites on the African continent, were more appropriately liberal. In *West Africa* images of African men and women as skilled labourers and

Nothing left to chance

CIVIL AVIATION is of first importance to Nigeria.

A network of rapid air communication has been extended

over this vast country where distances are great and roads few.

In the air travellers rely upon the skill and careful calculations of the

Airways staff. On the ground, Shell Aviation Service ensures that every gall

of fuel and oil delivered to the aircraft is of consistent quality

and purity. A complex system of quality control ensures that

variations do not occur. Nothing is left to chance. This member of a Shell fuelli

crew knows that he is part of a valuable service — a service of great

importance to Nigeria's future development.

SHELL **PART OF NIGERIA'S LII**

THE SHELL COMPANY OF WEST AFRICA LIMITED, LAGOS

67 'Nothing left to chance', Shell West Africa advertisement, *West Africa*, 26 May 1956

staff are depicted. There is a much greater sense of African involvement in the process of change and an acknowledgement of individual
workers' skill and experience, despite the relatively menial positions
of most of the people depicted in the *West Africa* advertisements
(Figure 67). Comparing these two sources of Shell advertising indicates the politics of representation. While in *West Africa* Shell needed
to represent itself as not having discriminatory recruitment policies,
in Britain and amongst British expatriates Shell clearly wished to
reinforce an image of European dominance and control, and the right
of the company to maintain its overseas interests despite increasing
African nationalism.

An industrialising 'third world'
While Shell's images of 'complementary economics' represent the
negotiated difference of a much older image, a key representation
during this period which marks a striking shift from previous images
of Africa and Asia is contained in the scenes of apparent industrialisation of 'developing' nations. Previously, industrialism had always

been used to signify the metropolis, yet in images by BP, Associated Electrical Industries (AEI), English Electric, Vacuum Oil and Holman Pneumatic Equipment during the 1950s, this ceases to be the case. The image of industrial development in Africa appears in advertisements as early as 1954 and expresses unequivocal support for the project of modernity. Two advertisements, one by the Vacuum Oil Company Limited and the other by AEI depict a new dam at Owen Falls in Uganda (Figures 68 and 69). Both advertisements discuss the importance of electricity for the development of Uganda, and highlight their companies' involvement in the building of the dam.

What is significant about both images, however, is that the Africans represented watch the scenes of development from a distance. Unlike Kweheli in the Shell advertisement, they are not involved in any form of production. In the Vacuum Oil advertisement, an African woman and her son look down on the dam from the countryside above it. They are little more than a pictorial device used to frame a scene of industrialism below. They are from a pre-industrial world in which water and other goods are collected in buckets and carried home on foot. They contrast with the scene of modernity below them in which water is harnessed in enormous volume for, as we are told, the future development of Uganda and Kenya. There is clearly a sense of past and future in the image, with the Africans representing the past in contrast to the image of the future which pans out below them. The vision for the future, however, is attributed to the British Prime Minister of the time, Sir Winston Churchill, who is recorded as having dreamt of harnessing the headwaters of the Nile to generate electricity. While there is no mention of the word Empire or colony in the advertisement, there is an inherent imperialising vision, which appears to be legitimised by the 'power' – harnessed for Uganda. Images such as these, even more than Shell's scenes of African control over agriculture, legitimated the ideas of W. A. Lewis and others who believed that developing nations were dependent on industrial nations for economic progress.

The second advertisement, for AEI, depicts a young African man playing a flute by the banks of the dam. Three more African men are depicted on the bank looking at this feat of engineering. They are also uninvolved in its production. Although this time the central figure, the man with a flute, is named as Mukasa and we are told that he has watched the dam being built for four years, we are given no indication of what he does for a living. The image of him playing a flute suggests that he does nothing productive, although it is implied that he understands the benefits of electricity, which are in Mukasa's words 'for the benefit of Man'. In both these images, it is clearly the Western

POWER for UGANDA

Vacuum helps to make

a Statesman's Dream come True

"It is possible that nowhere else in the world could so enormous a mass of water be held up by so little masonry."
— Sir Winston Churchill,"My African Journey" 1908.

In 1908 Sir Winston Churchill dreamed of harnessing the headwaters of the Nile to generate electricity. In 1954 Her Majesty Queen Elizabeth II inaugurates the Owen Falls hydro-electric scheme and brings to life a majestic project that will provide electricity for the future development of Uganda and parts of Kenya. Started in 1948 by the Uganda Electricity Board, the Owen Falls plan includes a main dam 2,725 feet long and 85 feet high; also a powerhouse to be equipped with ten 15,000 k.w generating units — Boving "Kaplan" hydro-turbines and British Thomson-Houston Ltd. "umbrella" type alternators.

These generating units will be lubricated, like many others in power stations all over the world, with Vacuum D.T.E. Turbine Oils.

GARGOYLE LUBRICANTS

A lubrication service for everything mechanical

VACUUM OIL COMPANY LIMITED

MAKERS OF MOBILOIL, MOBILGAS

GARGOYLE LUBRICANTS   MOBILAND   DELVAC AND SOVAC OILS   MOBIL DIESEL AND VACUUM FUEL OILS

68 'Power for Uganda', Vacuum Oil Company advertisement, *Illustrated London News*, 1 May 1954

OLWOBULUUNGI BWABANTU!

FOR OVER FOUR YEARS Mukasa has watched the great dam being built at Owen Falls, to make more electricity for Uganda.

Mukasa has seen much good come from electric power.

In this new hydro-electric scheme he sees a brighter future for his people. " Electricity," says Mukasa, "is *olwobuluungi bwabantu*—for the benefit of Man."

Her Majesty the Queen, homeward bound on her world tour, recently opened the Owen Falls dam. The six 16,770-kVA waterwheel alternators, which make the electricity, are being supplied by one of the. nine famous British companies that together make up A.E.I.

A.E.I. (Associated Electrical Industries) make everything electrical from a turbine to a torch bulb.

AEI
for everything electrical

Associated Electrical Industries are a family of companies:
The British Thomson-Houston Co. Ltd.
Metropolitan-Vickers Electrical Co. Ltd.
The Edison Swan Electric Co. Ltd.
Ferguson Pailin Ltd.
The Hotpoint Electric Appliance Co. Ltd.
International Refrigerator Co. Ltd.
Newton Victor Ltd.
Premier Electric Heaters Ltd.
Sunvic Controls Ltd.

69 'Olwobuluungi Bwabantu', AEI advertisement, *Illustrated London News*, 12 June 1954

world and the corporate companies in particular that are represented as harnessing the natural resources of Africa for the benefit of humanity. This task even appears to have been given spiritual assent if we are party to the knowledge that Mukasa is in fact the god of Lake Victoria. While on a superficial level these scenes of industrialism appear to suggest a new path for African development, the notion of the West as responsible for or inevitably involved in harnessing the resources of various colonies, which modernisation theory supports, dates back to the turn of the century, and seems to echo Lugard's notion of Britain's 'dual mandate' in Africa. Bearing this in mind, it is important to note that these images of industrial 'development' were not ones which suggested dramatic change for Africans, but were geared towards the more efficient extraction of African resources.

Infancy and dependence

The distance represented between African industrialisation and African people's involvement also enabled an old image of African and Asian infancy to be moulded into a new form that was acceptable for the politics of the 1950s. The image of infancy fitted neatly into Rostow's argument, since he and his followers saw Africa as being at an early stage of its economic development. Hawker Siddeley Group and Shell both use images of African and Asian children in their advertisements (Figure 70). While the images are in some senses enchanting, they present these children as helpless creatures dependent on the bounty provided by corporate conglomerates. This is also the kind of image which we have seen frequently in the late twentieth century on both corporate and charity advertising. Shell's use of this image, along with that of complementary economics, asserts a fairly traditional imperial philosophy, despite its appearance of concern for world hunger. The idea of 'third world' dependency is also encouraged by the child in the advertisement looking upwards. Resonances of the Shell image can be found in contemporary charity adverting.

One aspect of these two advertisements that is worthy of comment is that they present a visual image which is not based on discussing the actual production with which the corporation is concerned (such as involvement in a particular hydro-electric project or mining construction). Instead they concentrate on images which evoke a kind of general humanism. The evocation of general images of humanism within the context of the rest of these images of neo-colonial development can also be analysed as supportive of the modernisation thesis, since according to the arguments of Parsons and his followers, it was the application of general shared values that was a key driving force within society. Arguments such as these depoliticised the relationship

world in a hurry

What is Hawker Siddeley doing here?

In a world excited by its own technical mastery, the problem has become not "If only . . ." but "How soon?". How fast can we produce the thousand things that will allow all the world's people to live in happiness and dignity? How soon replace the last oxen with the diesel-driven harvester, how soon give a giant's strength to the work of men's hands with electric power plants? In the race for a better life Brush Electrical has an active role. ☐ Think of almost any kind of power equipment and you'll find that Brush has a part in it. Power to speed ships and trains, power for factories and townships or power for an entire electric generating plant . . . this is the work of Brush Electrical, one of the companies of the world-wide Hawker Siddeley Group. Whenever, wherever you wonder "Who can do this?" it will pay you to tap the enormous resources of the Group for information. ☐ There is a representative in your part of the world who can speak for the Group—call him.

HAWKER SIDDELEY GROUP
International Sales: Duke's Court, St. James's, London, S.W.1

HAWKER SIDDELEY INDUSTRIES: BRUSH ELECTRICAL · FULLER ELECTRIC · HAWKER SIDDELEY BRUSH TURBINES · HAWKER SIDDELEY NUCLEAR POWER · MIRRLEES ENGINES · NATIONAL ENGINES · PETTERS · HAWKER SIDDELEY HAMBLE · HIGH DUTY ALLOYS · MCLAREN FABRICATIONS · KELVIN CONSTRUCTION · NOKSTEL & TEMPLEWOOD HAWKSLEY

70 'World in a hurry', Hawker Siddeley Group advertisement, *Illustrated London News*, 5 March 1960

between the 'first' and 'third world'. Such representations have been critiqued more recently as maintaining the image of a passive 'third world' in need of Western support and 'aid'. yet 'aid' to a neo-colonial state was, as Nkrumah noted in 1965, 'merely a revolving credit, paid by the neo-colonial master, passing through the neo-colonial state and returning to the neo-colonial master in the form of increased profits'.[14] Aid programmes, with which many of these corporate firms were or were to be connected, were in effect to follow on from the kind of projects that colonial 'development' policies produced earlier.[15] The policies surrounding the distribution of aid were also part of the development of modernisation theory.

In assessing the Hawker Siddeley image, it is important to note that while the photograph lends a sense of humanity to these poor children, it is a highly voyeuristic image, which does not suggest any possibility of these children taking their lives into their own hands (Figure 70). They run after the photographer. The implication is that they are running after his way of life, which is situated as the future. Although we cannot see him, he is clearly established as an outsider and a privileged figure, but not one who appears to pose a threat, since there is no implication of violence or exploitation. This is a key transformation from earlier colonial images of domination. Metaphorically, these children are running with excitement and glee towards 'development' and modernity, which only appear obtainable through one path in the advertisement – that of the corporate firm. The continuing extraction of primary materials for the benefit of Europe, which Nkrumah discusses in some detail,[16] would in fact increase the poverty of such children, but this appears unreal in the face of advertising's reality.

The representation of the African middle classes

This final representation, although not as prominent in papers such as the *Illustrated London News* and *Punch*, was an image that was fostered by companies advertising in magazines such as *West Africa* and further legitimised modernisation theory, since it suggested that Western-style economic development would lead to prosperity and increased consumption. The representation of an emerging African middle class can be particularly well understood through a look at the advertisements for the United Africa Company Ltd in *West Africa*. While advertisements from the early 1950s still discussed Africans in terms such as the 'colonial harvester' or 'colonial consumer',[17] by 1955 these images had altered to represent professional Africans such as a graduate, i.e. the newly educated African on 'the road to responsibility' as the title of one image outlines. By 1957, the year of Ghanaian independence, the United Africa Company was promoting itself with images which emphasised the idea of black and white co-operation, with advertisements such as 'Progress through teamwork', which depicted black and white hands pulling together on a rope. In 1959 many images represented the middle-class African professional. An advertisement entitled 'Men of tomorrow', for example, published on 14 November 1959, depicted the sales manager (Figure 71). The United Africa Company positioned itself as the trainer and producer of an African middle class. While its advertisements represent business in Africa being conducted by Africans, they also represent the emerging neo-colonial relationship of an indigenous elite working for the benefit of the foreign corporate firm. The sales manager in particular, as a mediating figure between industrial production and the African marketplace, epitomises this relationship. The creation of an indigenous elite, which would take over the reins of authority without destroying the economic interests of major firms, was a deliberate policy of both the colonial government and British companies working towards political decolonisation. As Goldsworthy notes, by 1959 the acceleration of African nations towards independence meant that 'all that mattered was that an indigenous political elite, with some degree of local support, should exist and be willing to take over'.[18]

The fact that this kind of image did find space in the pages of British papers, through an advertisement by BP called 'West Africa on wheels', is significant (Figure 72). The advertisement appeared in the *Illustrated London News* on 15 March 1958, and also in *Punch* on 19 March 1958. It presented an image of a middle-class African family filling up their car at a BP petrol station in West Africa. It presented a rare image of a middle-class African family to a middle-class British audience. By 1958, the representation of Africans as a homogenised mass without class difference was fragmenting. The BP advertisement is slightly different from the United Africa Company images, in that it represents African middle-class consumers rather than individuals involved in some part of the production process. It asserts the increasing value of the African market for British conglomerates – here consuming, not cloth and beads, but expensive imported cars and fuel. The family, while distinguished from the British middle-class family by such things as the slightly uncomfortable tightness of the young girl's dress, which acts as a form of symbolic disfunctioning or disorder, are still clearly from a middle-class background since they own a relatively modern car. The young girl has been deliberately positioned to fill the tank in order to establish ownership of the car as a family vehicle, since the man could have been confused with an attendant by the British public. This image appeared shortly after BP established

men of tomorrow

THE SALES MANAGER

Progress and expansion are the driving forces of the country today! *Trained* men are needed for tomorrow's important business developments. The Sales Manager controls the sales team, and his expert knowledge of marketing is vital to commercial success. The United Africa Company is proud to play an important part in the training of such highly-skilled 'Men of Tomorrow.'

Training

FOR THE FUTURE

In office or workshop, at the docks or store or wherever he works, it is the trained man who makes progress—the man who knows his job thoroughly. U.A.C. trains its staff in many different skills and has many comprehensive training schemes and schools for this purpose.

Hundreds of Africans every year qualify for positions of authority in U.A.C. in this way. U.A.C. training produces technicians, salesmen, clerical and secretarial staff, transport and lighterage staff and management—men with a future, 'Men of Tomorrow.'

THE UNITED AFRICA COMPANY LIMITED

71 'Men of tomorrow', United Africa Company advertisement, *West Africa*, 14 November 1959

[190]

BP MAPS THE FUTURE

The British Petroleum Company is establishing hundreds of service stations, and training local talent to operate them in West Africa, where twice as many motorists are now fuelling at BP stations as three years ago.

West Africa on Wheels

IN AN AREA larger than Europe – where one's next door neighbour may live hundreds of miles away – roads are West Africa's vital arteries, and petrol its life blood. Anyone who helps transport along in West Africa to-day is contributing in a vital way to its economic and cultural future.

Operating in more than twenty West African countries, whose combined area exceeds 5,000,000 square miles, BP is making three great contributions to transport

development: by supplying petrol and lubricating oils that withstand the extremes of West African weather; by steadily extending its network of service stations; by training local talent to operate them safely and skilfully.

Oil is helping to raise West Africa's standards of living and will increasingly do so. There, as elsewhere throughout the world, The British Petroleum Company is speeding the wheels of progress.

THE British Petroleum
COMPANY LIMITED
BP

72 'West Africa on wheels', BP advertisement, *Illustrated London News*, 15 March 1958

service stations in West Africa. It formed part of a series of images entitled 'BP maps the future'. While producing an image which appears different from previous representations, it is interesting that this image also acted to represent Africa as benefiting from the labour and scientific knowledge of Europe. (Another advertisement from the same series, for instance, depicts white hands involved in skilled scientific work in a laboratory.) It sets up a contrasting relationship of production and development in Europe with beneficial consumption in Africa, implying that this example of increased consumption will eventually be accessible to all Africans. BP's involvement with Shell in prospecting for and extracting oil in Nigeria is not mentioned in the advertisement, which ignores one of the key grievances by nationalist politicians: the lack of investment in Africa and other 'third world' nations for secondary industries to refine and develop their own raw materials. It is interesting that this advertisement was not to be found in the magazine *West Africa*, where it might have been read by the growing African elite as a clear indication of BP's desired neo-colonial relationship.

These four representations did not all have the same impact nor were they all as numerous as each other. Taken together, however, they highlighted modernisation theory as part of a process that justified a neo-colonial system, to which all the images confer support. There is no doubt that in terms of the kinds of images of Africa and Asia with which the British public were familiar, the images of an emerging industrialism in the colonial/ex-colonial world must have had an enormous impact. This representation is also that used by the largest number of corporate advertisers. The British public would not have read these images as indicative of more efficient extraction, but as evidence of British involvement in development. For these reasons, it is important to give this representation further consideration in an attempt to analyse why it may have been dominant and in what ways it served the ideological interests of the companies concerned.

The image of industrialisation and the advertising of the British electrical companies

Concentrating on images produced by the British electrical firms is appropriate for two reasons. Firstly, the series of images by English Electric from 1958 to 1961 represents the most consistent use of the image of an industrialising 'third world'. Secondly, concentrating on the advertising images from the major electrical companies of Britain enables us to consider a set of representations which reflect the close ideological relationship between these companies and the government of that time. Oliver Lyttleton, chairman of AEI from 1945, was appointed Secretary of State for the Colonies in 1951 when the Conservatives won the general election. His position in AEI was only temporarily filled by George Bailey of Metrovick until his return to the company in 1954.[19] Finally, the electrical companies represent an industry that was acutely concerned with the Empire and the protected markets that it provided. As John Stopford notes:

> In electrical machinery, for example, by means of merger and wrangling over patent rights, English Electric, Associated Electrical Industries and others were attempting to catch up on the lead of the US General Electric, Westinghouse, and others. With respect to foreign investments, their competitive position was different from that of the pioneers, who had been part of the creation of new international industries. The followers had to face competition from firms already well established abroad. In these circumstances, Empire territories often provided investment sites with the least competitive disadvantage.[20]

According to Stopford, firms that expanded abroad between 1920 and 1959 tended to prefer Commonwealth markets. Stopford continues by describing the engineering industries as 'the most loyal Empire supporters'.[21]

In assessing these images it is important for us to consider (i) the changing and conflicting government policies on colonial development and decolonisation in the post-war period and their relation to modernisation theory discussed above; (ii) the role of nationalism in shaping images which, while still representing the interests of Britain, were forced to present Africans, for example, with a great deal more dignity than previously; (iii) the role of British public opinion; and lastly (iv) the overseas interests of British corporate firms and their role in development and underdevelopment. I will not deal with each of these issues separately as I would like to take a more chronological approach at this stage in order to discuss the advertisements effectively.

Although the images which we are assessing all fall within a period of Conservative rule, it is worth considering Labour's colonial policy after the Second World War, since all of its developments were not scrapped automatically by the Conservative government. In 1946 George Hall, Secretary of State for the Colonies, declared:

> It is our policy to develop the colonies and all their resources so as to enable their peoples speedily and substantially to improve their economic and social conditions, and as soon as may be practicable, to attain responsible self government . . . a goal towards which His Majesty's Government will assist them with all means in their power.[22]

Despite this rhetoric, and that of Arthur Creech Jones who followed him, Labour policy was far from altruistic and in fact shared the support of the Conservative Party. Although Labour and the Conservatives conflicted on issues surrounding decolonisation during the 1950s, the Conservatives continued Labour's main experiment in state enterprise – the Colonial Development Corporation – after the 1951 general election. In 1962, it was renamed the Commonwealth Development Corporation. Therefore, this government department existed throughout the period when the advertisements appear, and was renamed just one year after the advertisements cease.

In 1947–48 the Labour government sought to alleviate Britain's balance of payments problem by drawing on colonial resources. The colonies were asked to build up their currency reserves in London to strengthen the position of the sterling area, as well as limit dollar expenditure. They were also asked to maximise the production of goods that could be sold to the dollar area. While the needs of Britain were paramount, the already rising nationalist sentiments meant that these interests needed to be presented as ones that were in the interests of the development of colonial peoples. As Butler notes, in this period the term 'colonial development' was an ambiguous one, which implied both the imperial vision of developing 'underdeveloped estates' and the humanitarian ideal of improving the living conditions for the colonial population.[23] When the Colonial Development Corporation (CDC) was established in 1948, to 'promote in every possible way increased colonial production on an economic and self-supporting basis with an eye to the production of foodstuffs, raw materials and manufactures whose supply to the UK or sale overseas will assist our balance of payments',[24] Norman Brook, Secretary to the Cabinet, also advised 'that some care and preparation would be needed' in order to argue convincingly that the 'colonial development' envisaged was as good for the colonies as it was anticipated it would be for Britain.[25]

It was intended that the CDC would fund projects to help 'build up good living conditions'. It aimed to do this by supporting projects which would increase colonial output, in order to help territories earn funds to purchase commodities and supplies which they currently lacked. Documents such as *The Colonial Territories* stated:

> The more of them [foodstuffs and raw materials] they can export, the more money they will earn with which to purchase consumer goods, improve their social services, and further expand their production through the provision of better or more extensive basic services – roads and railways, water and power supplies, irrigation schemes, and so on.[26]

From statements such as the above, it is clear that the interests of Britain were paramount, since this strategy potentially provided a market for British goods and raw materials for production, and the development schemes suggested were all in the interests of the export sector. These government policies were similar to the ideas laid down by the modernisation theorists, who saw industrialisation and increased consumption as primary ways in which economic development would take place. The CDC – with the aid of public and private funds – was the main instrument through which development of the kind discussed above was supposed to be stimulated. Yet the kinds of projects supported were selective. Small-scale projects which needed little investment were ignored by the colonial administration, as were many industrial projects. In the twelve years of its existence, it supported only six industrial projects, one of which was abandoned. This was perhaps partly due to the fact that the CDC would only support projects that did not undermine British industry, so development, whether industrial or not, was always partial and privileged British capital abroad. As Havinden and Meredith note, 'the economic development effort of the colonial authorities was directed to large-scale transportation and communications works to benefit chiefly the export sector, or grandiose and wasteful agricultural projects like those of the OFC [Overseas Food Corporation] and CDC'.[27] The actions of the CDC indicate the way in which British efforts to 'modernise' Africa were neither benign nor neutral.

Although the Owen Falls Dam was not directly funded by the CDC, it did receive funding from the colonial government in Uganda, through reserves from its Marketing Board, which had been established during the Second World War for the bulk purchase of agricultural commodities for export. It was the kind of project which the CDC would have supported if funds had been available. The two Owen Falls advertisements certainly represent the attitudes of the CDC with regards to development. Such enormous hydro-electric projects were symbolic of the beginnings of industrialisation, and acted as symbols of modernity and the key to 'progress'. Critics of the kind of industrialisation encouraged in the colonies at this time did not emerge until much later[28] and industrialisation was a form of development which many nationalist groups were also keen to foster.[29] These projects appeared to represent the benevolent involvement of both private companies and the British government in Africa's preparation for 'take-off' (to use Rostow's term). They appeared to legitimate their presence in the colonies for the British public at a time of growing uncertainty. Yet, as Geoffrey Kay and others have argued, industrialisation in the 'third world' often brought further 'underdevelopment', since wherever it did take place it was partial, uneven, and was primarily in the interests of the export sector and foreign firms.

The development of hydro-electric power could be viewed as beneficial to both foreign companies and indigenous economic and social development. However, the lack of interest in sustainable development by major multinationals can be seen through contemporary documents such as *Power in Uganda*, prepared for the Economist Intelligence Unit Ltd in 1957. The document outlines Uganda's economy and while acknowledging the development of some industrial production suggests that agriculture will remain dominant. It goes on, however, to discuss the demand for electrical power, which is clearly the main reason for the research, describing power supplies as not only the *'sine qua non* of economic development', but also its major stimulus. In the document development is associated with the belief in not only industrialisation but also urbanisation. In Geoffrey Kay's analysis of underdevelopment, however, he highlights how urbanisation in the 'third world' often brought increased deprivation. Urban areas have seen high unemployment, since production has tended to remain capital-intensive rather than labour-intensive despite a large workforce, and hardship has increased through the marketing of luxury consumer goods where basic needs have still not been met. The availability of such goods in urban centres has also encouraged urbanisation without providing jobs or an infrastructure for people to sustain themselves. In an urban environment even subsistence farming cannot take place, as in rural areas.[30] The Economist Intelligence Unit's document highlights the interest in so-called 'development' by British businesses in terms of their own economic interests, as well as in terms of the cultural changes which modernisation theory had outlined would take place. Following on from discussions about the effect of electric power on industrialisation and urbanisation, it also discusses 'the domestic scene' and highlights the way in which electricity will also bring a desire for irons, radios and other electric goods as well as provide a better workforce:

> The attraction of after-dark lighting, the ease of heating water, the possibilities of radios, electric irons, and other electric goods, all these material benefits come within reach of the African when mains electricity is introduced in his neighbourhood. And in this respect, the African woman looks as though she will emulate the American woman, who is largely responsible for the purchase of her family's day-to-day wants. It may well be the woman in Uganda who presses for the material benefits that electricity offers; certainly there is a great deal of evidence that the womenfolk are as much if not more interested in these possibilities as the menfolk.

[196]

There is no question about the Africans' desire to possess such things as electric power and light, and other domestic services and goods; and as these become more widely available, there can be little doubt that the incentives to work harder and to earn more, will be accordingly strengthened. For one of the main factors tending to restrict incentives to work is the lack of spending opportunities for the African in rural Uganda.

Thus, in industry, in townships and community centres, and in the home, the stimulating effect of increasing electricity supplies must not be under-emphasised – for there is ample evidence that power supplies are far more than a *sine qua non* of economic development; they are in fact its major stimulus.[31]

Documents such as these maintained the legitimacy of modernisation theory and more specifically the 'trickle down', diffusionist arguments used by theorists such as W. A. Lewis. Paul Baran's ground-breaking article 'The Political Economy of Growth' was to provide a viewpoint which challenged arguments such as these in the same year. Baran noted that not only did Western capitalism destroy the self-sufficiency of the rural communities of the 'third world' countries, which was the mainstay of their pre-capitalist economies, but that this removal had a devastating effect on the prospect of future economic growth.[32]

If we read the Owen Falls Dam advertisements in the light of the ideas presented by the Economist Intelligence Unit document, the position of the African woman and child does not simply indicate a contrast between development and underdevelopment and past and future. The world of ordinary Africans is also perceived as changing through the involvement of outside firms. The 'hunter-gatherer' society represented in the advertisement looks at the future, at industrialisation (which is associated with a Western capitalist economy), and in the terms of the Economist document, it will transform their desires and wants. This transformation, equated with economic progress, however, did not consider the devastation caused by Western capitalist enterprise in the 'third world'. The slogan in the AEI advertisement rings differently after reading *Power in Uganda*. Electricity is 'for the benefit of man'. This benefit includes Mukasa easily, without involving him in production, because his transformation, it is presumed, will come through consumption. He symbolises the developing workforce that will work hard through changed wants. Advertisements such as these affirm the arguments of modernisation theory, which was capable of presenting a colonial economy as benefiting everyone.

Produced in 1954, these advertisements also reflect Conservative Party resistance to the promotion of political change in the colonies.

Although the Conservatives recognised its inevitability, they followed what Goldsworthy describes as a policy of containment between 1951 and 1957. The conflict between an image of development in Africa, which is how the dam would have been viewed by most people at both ends of the political spectrum, and the lack of involvement and initiative attributed to Africans within the image, clearly asserts the notion that the time is not yet ripe for self-rule. For Uganda certainly, the moment of self-rule is a long way off. Appearing in 1954, the image of Ugandan Africans as living in a pre-industrial, underdeveloped world is also significant, in relation to the political conflicts in Britain over the issue of an East African Federation. Ugandans had already expressed their dissatisfaction with such a proposal, which they saw as leaving them under the political control of white settlers in Kenya. These advertisements, although not referring to the issue of Federation, certainly express the unlikelihood of an independent Uganda, and the disquiet of many is ignored in the AEI advertisement, which presents Mukasa's contentment at the development of electrification in his country without his involvement in production. It is important to note that this AEI advertisement was from a series which also depicted AEI's investments in Turkey and Spain. In the latter advertisements, in contrast to Mukasa, the Turkish man is depicted as working in a power station and the Spanish woman, although not involved in industry, is depicted as using electricity in productive work.

The image of Africans watching industrial development taking place around them is also apparent in the first advertisement by English Electric that uses images of the colonies and Commonwealth as part of its corporate image-making during this period (Figure 73). In the advertisement an African man looks at a railway line, which carries an English Electric locomotive hauling the Johannesburg Mail in Natal. His distance from actual industrialisation and electrification is asserted by the fence, which divides him from the railway line. His association with nature is also increased by the leopard skin design on his clothes. While he is on one side of the wire fence, just behind the fence, on the side of the train, is a stone which we are told marks the spot where Sir Winston Churchill was captured during the Boer War. A fragment of European history in Africa is placed with the train, clearly affirming Europe's role in Africa. As in the Uganda advertisement, there is an appeal to a major political icon of the day.

Before discussing this advertisement further, it is important to note that most of the advertisements which I have discussed, or will be discussing, actually appear in or after 1957. The exceptions are the two advertisements featuring Owen Falls, which date from 1954. By

The world is crying out for more POWER

The composite armature for a large English Electric motor during manufacture for a steel-works. Steel is one of the basic requirements of any industrial country and comprehensive contracts for steel rolling-mill drives have been carried out by English Electric all over the world for over half a century.

Rival ideologies are competing for the future of the world. The one that wins will be that which offers more people a better life.

The key to a better life is to use more of the power that is within our grasp. Power to develop barren wastes; to produce more food; to manufacture both necessities and luxuries; to make communications quick and simple.

Creating the means to produce, distribute and use power is the business of The English Electric Company. It designs and builds power equipment on every scale, from giant hydro-electric schemes to electric cookers.

For us in Britain such projects as the new atomic power station, the world's largest, now being constructed by English Electric (in association with Babcock & Wilcox Ltd. and Taylor Woodrow Construction Ltd.) at Hinkley Point, Somerset, will mean more abundant power. Faster electric trains, and better refrigerators and washing machines in the home—also made by English Electric —will use it more efficiently.

But how can a power station in a foreign country you may never see affect you? First, because it brings in large amounts of currency, to import goods we all want. Second, it raises living standards in that country, and people there will have more money to spend on the things we make.

Lastly, the lessons learned and the knowledge gained in projects abroad can be applied directly to your benefit at home—just as English Electric's home experience benefits the company's work abroad.

Better living in Britain; better living abroad; in the final analysis, a worthwhile existence for everyone—*the business of English Electric now.*

Power is the business of

'ENGLISH ELECTRIC'

. . . bringing you better living

THE ENGLISH ELECTRIC COMPANY LIMITED, MARCONI HOUSE, STRAND, LONDON, W.C.2

73 'The world is crying out for more power', English Electric advertisement, *Illustrated London News*, 13 December 1958

1957, dramatic political change in Africa was taking place. On 6 March 1957, Ghana won its independence and this was to have a profound impact on national struggles in other African countries. Just two years earlier, in 1955, Eden had set up a colonial committee 'to assist the Cabinet in controlling development in colonial territories'.[33] By 1957, however, it was clear that a policy of 'containment' was virtually impossible, nor was it necessarily in the interests of the Western world as a whole. One key concern for Britain and Europe was the rise of Soviet influence on the African continent, which demanded careful diplomacy. The Suez Crisis of 1956 had already provided an unprecedented blow to imperialist interests and marked the collapsing of Britain's imperial role. In Julian Amery's words, it had been 'the hinge of our Imperial strength'.[34] The British establishment recognised that it must not only 'assist the economic progress of the underdeveloped countries' through development policy, but 'if the Commonwealth was to provide an effective counter to the growth of world-wide Marxism friction between Britain and the new member states – above all over the issue of self government – must be reduced to the minimum'.[35]

As I mentioned earlier, modernisation theory was part of the attack on communism in the 1950s as well as a response to a changing political climate in the colonial world. These advertisements legitimised a neo-colonial partnership through the affirmation of images of benign industrialism. Images of conflict or exploitation were eliminated and replaced with scenes of apparent mutual development. The conflict with communism is made manifest in this English Electric advertisement. The text begins: 'Rival ideologies are competing for the future of the world. The one that wins will be that which offers more people a better life.' This text is printed in slightly larger typeface than the text following it and its position just below the image encourages us to consider the main image in relation to it. On reading the text, the African man here, unlike Mukasa and others noted previously, is not simply watching naïvely. He looks on at the scene in front of him in an almost contemplative manner. He is divided from it, but the implication of text and image together is that he can choose to embrace the world in front of the fence (and its history) or he can turn away. He is at a pivotal point in his own history. It is as though he stands in a no man's land, since we cannot see anything in the space where he stands except barren land. The fact that this land is barren suggests lack of productivity in his present and past world. The future that we can see embraces elements of industrialisation that the West brings. The signification of Africa and the 'third world' as the 'past' in contrast to European-fostered industrialism as the 'future' is encouraged by the image of 'third world' people's looking on at 'development'. It acts as another signifier in support of Rostow's thesis.

This format is used in another English Electric image from the same series, in 1959. This time, English Electric is depicted bringing 'progress' to Argentina, as the 'gaucho' on his horse watches and waits for the future form of transport to pass. The meanings in both these images are all the more significant, since neither advertisement uses straight documentary photography, but photomontage in order to construct reasonably unambiguous meanings in the advertisements. The image of an African in leopard-spotted clothes watching development was a representation which the company must have felt reflected its ideas effectively, since a photograph from the December 1956 issue of the company magazine *English Electric and its People* uses an image of the same man watching industrial development (Figure 74). This magazine was distributed to all English Electric's staff. In the magazine image, the man is looking at the Vierfontein Power Station in South Africa and has a pipe in his mouth. That type of pipe clearly signified imperial culture as well as increased consumption. In the advertisement, English Electric appears to have wanted to create a greater sense of opposition between past and present, development and underdevelopment, African 'nature' and Western 'industrialism'. The pipe resting in the African man's mouth as he watches activity and work is an ambiguous image, since as I have

74 A view of Vierfontein Power Station, photograph, *English Electric and its People*, December 1956

[201]

discussed earlier, it was often used to signify relaxed white imperial control.

It is also worth considering why English Electric reworked the image to depict him watching a train. Transport could effectively signify a sense of movement and change. The railway track and train are used repeatedly throughout the series of English Electric advertisements under discussion. Apart from acting as a symbol of rapid movement and change, the train ironically reflects the kind of industrialisation which took place in the colonies. Railways were built to increase the efficiency of raw material extraction for export, and not to aid local development.

In the English Electric advertisement, the use of the term 'power' is also significant. The word 'power' is situated right above the African man's head and forms part of the title of the advertisement – 'The world is crying out for more power'. His authority and decision-making can no longer be ignored, even when he is represented as peripheral to the industrial development depicted. The word 'power' rings with multiple meanings – the African's struggle for political power, the conflict between communism and capitalism, the desires of English Electric for greater market share and economic power, and its literal meaning of the need for more electricity. In the advertisement, the delivery of electrical power is attributed to the work of English Electric, which has situated itself as part of the capitalist/Western world which the train represents, since its locomotive pulls the train. As there is no alternative represented in the image, it is the ideology of capitalism that is seen to offer a better life, whether in colony or Commonwealth. 'Power is the business of English Electric . . . bringing you a better life' is the advertising slogan, which summarises the arguments at the bottom of the page. While their role in supplying electrical power is the literal meaning of the slogan, it is impossible to disengage the other meanings of the word 'power' from it and therefore English Electric's role in fostering the ideologies of capitalism and the Commonwealth/colonial system. While Commonwealth and colony are not referred to directly, an economic argument which was effectively the policy of the CDC is outlined for the British reader:

> But how can a power station in a foreign country you may never see affect you? First, because it brings in large amounts of currency, to import goods we all want. Second, it raises living standards in that country, and people there will have more money to spend on the things we make.
>
> Lastly, the lessons learned and the knowledge gained in projects abroad can be applied directly to your benefit at home – just as English Electric's home experience benefits the company's work abroad.

[202]

Better living in Britain; better living abroad; in the final analysis, a worthwhile existence for everyone – *the business of English Electric now.*

The word 'power' is not just significant in this advertisement, but was also played on in the Vacuum Oil Company image, with its title 'Power for Uganda'. However, the meanings of the term power were here generally inferred rather than developed as in the English Electric advertisement. The slogan 'Power is the business of English Electric ... bringing you a better living' was also used in the advertisement from 1959 set in Argentina. It is important to note that the slogan 'English Electric, bringing you a better living' was the original slogan that was used in earlier advertisements in the 1950s which featured British scenes showing the convenience of fridges and other electrical appliances. The first part of the slogan, 'Power is the business ...', only appears after 1958 on the advertisements that represent the company's overseas trade. The inferences of the term 'power' must have been recognised by English Electric, which later changed the slogan in 1960 to 'Power for peace'. This was also the slogan which it used in advertisements in 1960 and in the Commonwealth exhibition of 1961. Considering the timing of its appearance, it was clearly introduced to acknowledge an embracing of decolonisation, as well as an affirmation of the idea of the Commonwealth.

The significance of the Commonwealth as a trading group and the possible trading preferences which this 'community' could provide were important to English Electric. They were probably more significant for English Electric than for any of the other electrical firms, since it was a company that relied almost completely on the heavy electrical trade. It was English Electric that secured more contracts in this field during the late 1950s than the other electrical companies. Its concern with Commonwealth trade and preferences can be seen in the speech delivered by George Nelson, chairman of the company, at the 1957 Annual General Meeting, by which time negotiations between European nations for a European trading block were beginning to get under way:

We as a company have derived great benefit from Commonwealth orders, and I believe Commonwealth countries have derived great benefit from our engineering technique and the equipment we have been privileged to supply. But I do not think of this matter solely in terms of this company, nor do I think of it exclusively as a matter of Commonwealth Preference, important though that is. I am thinking in wider terms of the great economic resources developed and still to be developed in the Commonwealth which, taken as a whole with those of Great Britain, can provide an economic trading entity comparable with the economic units of the USA, Europe and in the future, Soviet Russia and China. If we break up the integration of trading in the British Commonwealth, then its various countries will probably ultimately be absorbed in one or other of these competing blocks; this I do not think will be in the best interests of the Commonwealth or the world.

If the countries of the Commonwealth work together to develop these resources, as they can be developed, then great advantages – political as well as economic – would accrue to all these countries and, I believe, to the world.[36]

It should be noted that the English Electric advertisements which I am discussing begin the year after this public declaration of interest in the Commonwealth as a trading group. Over the next four years, in its corporate advertising as well as through direct negotiation, English Electric worked hard to maintain the Commonwealth/colonies as a trading block. While the first two advertisements in 1958 and 1959 represent an image which is much more suggestive of opposition and the struggle for political power, the images after 1960 tend to suggest collaboration and partnership, and it was at this point that the slogan 'Power for peace' was introduced. This change reflects English Electric's recognition of the altered political and economic climate. By 1960, the processes towards decolonisation were advancing rapidly. Ghana had already achieved independence, the date for Nigeria had been set for October of that year, and by 1964 Uganda, Kenya, Sierra Leone, Tanzania and Zambia had won political independence. English Electric's corporate image-making during 1960 and 1961 included advertisements featuring the Sudan, Brazil, India, West Africa, Australia and Rhodesia. A dominant proportion of its advertisements were therefore based around the newly independent colonies and Commonwealth countries (Figures 75 and 76).

A significant change between the 1960s images and the two previous advertisements is the shift away from the representation of 'third world' peoples looking on at development in their own nations. The main photomontages of the 1958 and 1959 advertisements were altered for straightforward documentary images of, for the most part, grandiose modernist schemes of industrial 'progress'. These images, reflecting the optimism of 1950s industrialism, gave a sense of the ability of human beings to harness and control nature at their will. There was a feeling of self-confidence, which had not yet been shattered by the future knowledge of natural and human devastation that many of these projects were to cause. Only the advertisement for Rhodesia depicts a scene of untamed nature as its key image. Titled 'Power from the Zambesi', it depicts the thundering waters of the Victoria Falls. The inference, however, is the ability of human beings

The mammoth new steelworks at Durgapur, built for Hindustan Steel Ltd., by ISCON, a British consortium of 13 of the largest engineering firms in the U.K., including English Electric.

THE NEW FORGES OF INDIA
—and the power that drives them

An English Electric 38-MVA, 132-kV transformer at the Delhi grid substation. English Electric is now supplying three 125-MVA, 200-kV transformers, which are the first to be ordered for India at this voltage.

INDIA is fast becoming a great industrial nation. Three new steelworks are nearly complete and many big projects —for heavy machinery, ball bearings, boiler plant—are proposed in the recently published Third Five-Year Plan.

These new "forges" will demand an enormous supply of power. The new plan sets India the great task of *doubling her electric power production in the next five years*. Fortunately the country is exceptionally rich in hydro-electric resources: present estimates put her potential at around 35 million kilowatts. Dams will be built, many of them providing irrigation as well as electricity, helping to solve India's food problems. From all points of view, the power programme is crucial in India's future.

English Electric in India. Well known for its world-wide success in the export field, The English Electric Company is actively engaged in Indian development, and has been since the 1920's. Generating and distribution plant for power projects, electrical equipment for industry, and extensive railway work including India's first electrification

scheme 1924-28—these are some of the Company's activities in India. Now English Electric has installed rolling mill drives at Durgapur's huge new steelworks; power equipments are being made for the first Indian-built electric locomotives; complete turbine generating plant is going in at the 385,000 h.p. Rihand hydro-electric site; and plant for India's largest rectifier installation, for a fertilizer factory, is on order. English Electric has recently built a factory producing electrical equipment in Madras. Besides all this, in the sphere of technical education the Company trains Indian graduates who return home as qualified engineers.

These are some of the many ways in which English Electric is helping to develop and use India's power resources.

The relationship is mutually fruitful. India knows she can depend on the store of technical knowledge, skill and research which lie behind every contract with The English Electric Company, while English Electric gains in India further valuable experience, which it can use in other countries and at home.

Seen leaving Bombay's Victoria railway terminus, this English Electric 3,600-h.p. locomotive is one of the most powerful in India. Alongside is an old steam engine built by The Vulcan Foundry (member of the English Electric Group) who made the first locomotive ever to run in India.

POWER FOR PEACE

'ENGLISH ELECTRIC'

The English Electric Company Limited, English Electric House, Strand, London, W.C.2.

One of the many hydro-electric schemes, at Sengulam, includes these four 18,000-h.p. generating sets which, together with transformers and switchgear, were supplied by English Electric under a comprehensive contract.

75 'The new forges of India', English Electric advertisement, *Illustrated London News*, 26 November 1960

76 'The Sudan pulls ahead', English Electric advertisement, *Illustrated London News*, 2 December 1961

to harness and control the power of these waters, since the text refers to the new Kariba Dam built further down the Zambesi, which at its completion was the largest hydro-electric dam to have ever been built. The smaller images on the right-hand side of the advertisement also illustrate the harnessing of the Zambesi's power through technology. The reference to Kariba is also important in highlighting the relationship between government initiatives and those of private enterprise, since Kariba was funded by the CDC and was upheld as an exemplar of great industrial 'progress'. Politically too, Kariba represented what the government saw as the benefits of federation between the agriculture and mining of Northern Rhodesia and the industry of Southern Rhodesia. Kariba, as the advertisement highlights, would provide electricity for the extraction of raw material from the northern copper belt, while also providing power for the expanding industrial south. The image of north and south as complementary units may explain why an image of raw nature is used as a key representation in the advertisement. Juxtaposed with the smaller images of technology, it represents nature and industry as complementary, echoing what was seen as the complementary nature of the Federation.

Some of the English Electric advertisements also represent scenes of potential change. The advertisement for Sudan, for example, depicts the irrigation dam at Sennar, which was to be developed into a hydro-electric dam, while the advertisement for Brazil features an image of part of Brazil's future city – Brazilia. There is a crucial sense of future development and modernisation and this is affirmed by the titles of many of the advertisements too: 'The Sudan pulls ahead'; 'Brazil-giant on the march'; 'The new forges of India'; 'Rhodesia's dynamic thrust ahead'. This emphasis on the future ensures that we read the images as moments of transition. We do not therefore read the image of workers in loin cloths at the steelworks in Durgapur as a representation of contradictory relations (Figure 75). We do not see these workers as exploited, since the text directs us to assume that these workers' lives will be transformed in the future through Fordist principles and that wants will be satisfied through high productivity and industrialisation. As the text indicates, 'Dams will be built, many of them providing irrigation as well as electricity, helping to solve India's food problems. From all points of view, the power programme is crucial to India's future.' The sense of the future and of modernity is also continued in advertisements, which do not strictly represent industrialisation. The central image on the advertisement featuring West Africa is of students walking out of a new college. Visually the emphasis is on education as the potential for change, and the sense of modernity and optimism for the future is partly carried through the image by the representation of a modernist architectural college building.

English Electric's emphasis on the future can partly be understood by its clear desire not to associate itself with an imperial culture. It never uses the term Empire or colony, even in the advertisements which depict South Africa and Rhodesia, but rather emphasises itself as operating in a transformed modern world in which it works 'in partnership' with the newly independent states. The text for advertisements featuring Sudan, India and West Africa all draw attention to the economic planning of the new governments, and in the case of the African nations, the more recent acquisition of political independence. In the advertisement featuring the Sudan (2 July 1960), for example, the text explains:

> With the peaceful revolution of 1958, General Abboud's government made careful and far-reaching plans and put them in order of priority ... [D]evelopment plans centre on cotton, power and the railways.

The advertisement depicting West Africa (10 June 1961) highlights:

> two of Africa's most progressive states, are throwing themselves energetically into the development of their new nationhood ...
> ... Both countries are keenly aware of the need to diversify their economies – to build up new industries rather than depend so much on agriculture.

The text for the advertisement on India (26 November 1960) affirms a Nehru-style vision of transformation, in which Western firms could find a niche:

> India is fast becoming a great industrial nation. Three new steelworks are nearly complete and many big projects – for heavy machinery, ball bearings, boiler plant – are proposed in the recently published Third Five Year plan.

The texts then continue by highlighting English Electric's involvement in the industrial development of these nations, describing the relationship as 'mutually fruitful' and recognising how in the case of India, for example, the country 'can depend on the store of technical knowledge, skill and research which lie behind every contract with the English Electric Company, while English Electric gains in India further valuable experience, which it can use in other countries and at home'. It is clear that the technical expertise still lies in the West. The idea of partnership is still based on a complementary relationship, which encourages dependency. The images themselves, while removing the representation of Africans and others as looking on at development in their nations, still affirm a sense of English Electric as a provider. In the Sudanese advertisement from 1960, one of the smaller photographs depicts the arrival of the first of fifteen English Electric 1,850 h.p. diesel electric locomotives at Khartoum. The photograph shows the locomotive surrounded by a crowd of local people looking at it. While there is a much greater sense of their relationship to the locomotive, there is still a degree of distance and there is no visual representation in any of the advertisements (unlike those in *West Africa*) of 'third world' peoples in positions of leadership or control. In fact, in images representing locomotives, both in the company magazine *English Electric and its People* and in the advertisements, there is a continuing feeling of the locomotive and by inference the West and industrialisation as the future, and African culture and peoples as the past. Interestingly, when the Sudanese advertisement reappeared in 1961, the locomotive train was not shown crowded by Sudanese, but instead in juxtaposition with a camel (Figure 76). This image was also reproduced in *English Electric and its People* in June 1961 and in the company magazine its meaning for company employees was made transparent: 'The camel train waits for its successor to pass. The goods train is drawn by one of the 1,840 h.p. diesel electric locomotives supplied by our company.'[37]

These advertising images, while representing a seemingly new image of industrial development in the 'third world', still privileged the requirements of Western capital. In this sense, they maintained the notion of complementary economics overtly depicted in Shell and BP advertising. Despite the seeming euphoria that these images depicting crucial moments of change present, English Electric and other corporate firms were sensitive to their loss of control over Empire markets and the disintegration of the Commonwealth as a trading block. As George Nelson's address to the 1961 English Electric AGM makes clear:

Political and economic changes occurring in all parts of the world are affecting British business in two principal ways. In the first place, many countries had been industrialised in the past by British finance and enterprise and many of their undertakings were staffed by British engineers, who naturally had a tendency to accept automatically British standards and British equipment. In modern conditions these ties have been greatly loosened and what were previously regarded primarily as British markets are now scenes of intense international competition.

In the second place, many countries wish to move from an economy based mainly on primary industries to one including an increasing element of manufacture. As part of this process they progressively manufacture goods that formerly were bought from Britain and other industrial countries. I, personally, welcome these changes because I believe that they offer us even greater opportunities for export of capital goods in the future.

For this and other reasons your Company has played its part in developing overseas manufacture having established factories in Canada, Australia, South Africa and India. These activities also enable us to maintain a selling organisation ready to meet these countries' needs and able to deal with special projects involving the importation of British equipment.[38]

Mira Wilkins also points out that while UK multinational enterprises increased their share of the total capital stake of Commonwealth countries in the 1930s to around 50 per cent, by 1960 it was over 70 per cent.[39] In trying to maintain and expand its overseas trade and investment, English Electric also recognised the importance – at least for itself – of a degree of industrialisation in the 'third world'. Three years before 1961, in an article in the August 1958 issue of *English Electric and its People* entitled 'The Role of Britain in World Progress', George Nelson's speech to the British Electrical Power Convention is summarised as noting:

> Although local industrialisation might stop our exports of certain goods the usual effect was to stimulate the exports of other goods. With the growth of factories came demands for factory machinery, including electric motors and transformers for electric power supplies; for generating and distributing equipment, for railways and other services.
>
> But the growth of local industries did not only create a demand for industrial equipment and electric power; it also led to the creation of towns, cities and wage-earning populations.
>
> From this stemmed a powerful demand for amenities. They would want consumer goods and shops to sell them, electric lights to illuminate these shops, trams or electric trains to carry workers and shoppers, electrical appliances in the homes, television sets and so on.[40]

The arguments here are similar to those found in the document *Power in Uganda* referred to earlier (see pp. 196–7). As noted in my discussion of the Owen Falls Dam and Uganda, the development that was encouraged was partial, unbalanced and primarily in the interest of foreign firms. For the export of heavy industrial equipment, which was a key part of English Electric's business, some industrialisation had to take place, yet many of the company's projects involved the development of transport for the more efficient export of raw materials. Similarly, the Kariba project was highlighted for the benefit that it would provide the copper mines, i.e. the extraction of raw material for export. Only in the advertisement for India is reference made to Indian-built items, yet the major industrial projects are still clearly under British control, and will demand the future importation of

British-built technology, which in turn will encourage the consumption of luxury electrical goods, as Nelson indicates. While a degree of political independence is acknowledged in these advertisements, a continuing economic dependency is visualised as the future.

Why did these images stop after 1961 in the *Illustrated London News*? While Heath declared in 1961 that 'Commonwealth trade is one of the strongest elements in maintaining the Commonwealth association', Britain's application to join the European Economic Community in the same year certainly signalled a reorientation in trade policy, and was to affect the thrust of English Electric's corporate image-making. Images of an industrialising Commonwealth ceased to appear in English Electric advertisements in the *Illustrated London News* after this date. This kind of image, however, did not simply disappear in 1961. In his analysis of neo-colonialism, Nkrumah referred to a corporate advertisement for General Electric, displayed in an issue of *Modern Government* from 1962:

> When the countries of their origin are obliged to buy back their minerals and other raw products in the form of finished goods, they do so at grossly inflated prices. A General Electric advertisement carried in the March/April 1962 issue of *Modern Government* informs us that 'from the heart of Africa to the hearths of the world's steel mills comes ore for stronger steel, better steel – steel for buildings, machinery, and more steel rails'. With this steel from Africa, General Electric supplies transportation for bringing out another valuable mineral for its own use and that of other great imperialist exploiters. In lush verbiage the same advertisement describes how 'deep in the tropical jungle of Central Africa lies one of the world's richest deposits of manganese ore'. But is it for Africa's needs? Not at all. The site, which is 'being developed by the French concern, Compagnie Minière de l'Ogoone, is located on the upper reach of the Ogoone River in the Gabon Republic. After the ore is mined it will first be carried 50 miles by cableway. Then it will be transferred to ore cars and hauled 300 miles by diesel-electric locomotives to the port of Point Moire for shipment to the world's steel mills'. For 'the world' read the United States first and France second.[41]

The English Electric advertisements, like the General Electric advertisement discussed by Nkrumah, provide us with classic representations of neo-colonialism. In the first English Electric advertisement discussed above, which declared 'The world is crying out for more power', for 'the world' we can read Great Britain first and English Electric second. In asserting the value of the Commonwealth for the company, also euphemistically Nelson declared: 'If the countries of the Commonwealth work together . . . then great advantages – political as well as economic – would accrue to all these countries and, I believe to the world'.

In the post-war climate of decolonisation the corporate advertisements discussed in this chapter reveal the overseas interests and concerns of companies that were attempting to grapple with the inevitable changes that they could see taking place across the world. It is worth noting that the firms which resisted the political shifts taking place, such as the Ashante Goldfields, do not appear to have used such images. Many of the advertisements discussed are striking because of their representation of industrialisation in Africa and Asia, previously only represented as providers of raw material. Yet the modernisation and industrialisation of the third world is presented as only possible by the intervention of European firms passing down their knowledge and expertise. They affirm support for neo-colonialism through a projection of diffusionist rhetoric. The image of a neo-colonial relationship as benevolent and peaceful continues in corporate advertisements today. In the late 1980s and early 1990s, for example, BP employed the slogan 'For all our tomorrows' and ICI the slogan 'World problems, world solutions, world class'. The visual construction of these images, like the ones from the 1950s, presents a vision of development as only possible through Western enterprise, enabling the ideology of neo-colonialism to continue to appear as benign and almost altruistic.

Notes

1 J. Darwin, *Britain and Decolonisation: The Retreat from Empire in the Post-War World* (London, 1988), p. 62.
2 *Ibid.*, p. 64.
3 Quoted in C. J. Bartlett, *A History of Post-war Britain 1945–1974* (London, 1977), p. 3.
4 Darwin, *Britain and Decolonisation*, p. 64.
5 *Ibid.*, p. 15.
6 For outlines of modernisation theory see A. Webster, *An Introduction to the Sociology of Development* (London, 1984) and the introduction of S. Hall and G. Bram (eds), *Formations of Modernity* (Cambridge, 1992).
7 T. Parsons, *The Social System* (London, 1991); S. Savage, *Theories of Talcott Parsons* (London, 1981).
8 Webster, *Sociology of Development*, p. 56.
9 W. Rostow, *The Stages of Economic Growth: A Non-Communist Manifesto* (New York, 1971), p. 17.
10 *Ibid.*, pp. 108–12.
11 Webster, *Sociology of Development*, p. 49.
12 K. Nkrumah, *Neo-colonialism: The Last Stage of Imperialism* (London, 1965), p. ix. Other authors who discuss neo-colonialism include W. Rodney, *How Europe Underdeveloped Africa* (London, 1972); S. Amin, *Eurocentrism* (London, 1989).
13 W. A. Lewis, *Colonial Development* (Manchester, 1949).
14 Nkrumah, *Neo-colonialism*, p. xv.
15 The concept of aid as an extension of imperialism is discussed in Webster, *Sociology of Development*, pp. 163–7.

16 Nkrumah, *Neo-colonialism*. Most of the book is devoted to discussing this exploitative relationship, and references to Hawker Siddeley can be found on pp. 95 and 101.

17 See advertisements from *West Africa*, 7 February 1953, p. 110, and 7 March 1953, p. 206.

18 D. Goldsworthy, *Colonial Issues in British Politics 1945–1961: From 'Colonial Development' to 'Wind of Change'* (Oxford, 1971), p. 361.

19 For a history of the electrical firms and their eventual merger, which focuses on the business acumen of individual chairmen, see R. Jones and O. Marriott, *Anatomy of a Merger: A History of GEC, AEI and English Electric* (London, 1970).

20 J. Stopford, 'The Origins of British Based Multinational Manufacturing Enterprises', in M. Wilkins (ed.), *The Growth of Multinationals* (Aldershot, 1981), p. 184.

21 *Ibid.*, p. 190.

22 Quoted in Goldsworthy, *Colonial Issues*, p. 15.

23 L. J. Bulter, 'The Ambiguities of British Colonial Development Policy 1938–48', in A. Gost *et al.* (eds), *British Contemporary History* (London, 1991).

24 J. Kent, *British Imperial Strategy and the Origins of the Cold War 1944–49* (Leicester, 1993), p. 132.

25 Note by Brook, 16 January 1948, cited in M. Havinden and D. Meredith, *Colonialism and Development: Britain and its Tropical Colonies 1850–1960* (London, 1993), p. 233.

26 *The Colonial Territories* (1948–49 PP. 1948–49 XIII Cmd 7715 pp. 1–2), cited in Havinden and Meredith, *Colonialism and Development*, p. 299.

27 Havinden and Meredith, *Colonialism and Development*, p. 303.

28 The building of such massive hydro-electric projects has been criticised in recent years. E. F. Schumacher's *Small is Beautiful* (London, 1973) was the beginning of a projected attack on the grandiose schemes supported by the modernisation thesis. The crescendo of criticisms that these types of projects have received more recently can be seen through the organised resistance to the Narmada Dam project in India. See W. Fisher (ed.), *Towards Sustainable Development* (New York, 1995).

29 In India, for example, despite Gandhi's call for the use of the handloom, Nehru instituted a process of rapid industrialisation through a series of five-year plans. Nehru's policies were directed towards the partial development of Indian capital; some expatriate firms were nationalised or were forced to work in partnership with nationalised industries.

30 G. Kay, *Development and Underdevelopment: A Marxist Analysis* (London, 1975), pp. 125–30.

31 *Power in Uganda 1957–1970: A Study of Economic Growth Prospects for Uganda with Special Reference to the Potential Demand for Electricity* (London, 1957), p. 151.

32 Baran's thesis is discussed by A. Zack-Williams, *Tributers, Supporters and Merchant Capital* (Aldershot, 1995), pp. 14–15.

33 D. Goldsworthy, 'Keeping Change within Bounds: Aspects of Colonial Policy during the Churchill and Eden Governments 1951–57', *Journal of Imperial and Commonwealth History*, 18:1 (1990), p. 84.

34 Quoted in Goldsworthy, *Colonial Issues*, p. 296.

35 Darwin, *Britain and Decolonisation*, p. 227; see also J. Darwin, *The End of Empire* (Oxford, 1991), p. 27.

36 *The Times*, 15 March 1957, p. 15.

37 *English Electric and its People*, June 1961, p. 15.

38 *The Times*, 28 February 1961, p. 19.

39 Wilkins (ed.), *The Growth of Multinationals*, p. 101.

40 *English Electric and its People*, August 1958, p. 14.

41 Nkrumah, *Neo-colonialism*, p. 14.

CHAPTER SEVEN

Conclusion

> When representation is understood in terms of the production of defini-
> tions rather than the simple reflection of pre-existing ideas, then a
> number of questions can be asked of any given image: What meanings
> are produced and how? And in which ways does the image relate to
> society as a whole? The latter question does not imply a form of eco-
> nomic determinism in which meaning is reduced to an 'effect' of an
> economic 'cause', rather, it involves dismantling ... complex relations.
>
> (Lynda Nead, *Myths of Sexuality*, 1990)

The representations of black people explored in this book demonstrate the value of the social, political and economic contextualisation
of imagery and the limitations and uses of stereotyping theory. In the
late nineteenth and early twentieth centuries colonialism provided a
political logic for capitalism and almost all the images of black people
in advertising gave expression to the ways in which we were dehuman-
ised, diminished and naturalised as servants and inferior beings.

However, if we simply concern ourselves with this binarism it is
difficult to understand the more specific ways in which colonialism operated and the conflicts and contradictions of companies and
governments struggling to preserve their own vested interests. By
contextualising images of black people in advertisements it has been
possible to reveal the interests of manufacturers and governments in
maintaining or developing specific colonial ideologies. Black people
were never intended as consumers of these products; their images
were therefore symbolic. Unlike the majority of advertising, which
hides relations of labour, images of black people – perceived as natural labourers – reveal company interests in particular relations of
production.

In pre-1920 imagery, the lack of governmental direction to colonial
policy can be seen in the sometimes conflicting concerns of the soap,

cocoa and tea firms. This was a period in which forms of colonial government were not fully established. Those with interests in the colonies made their voices heard, not just through influence in government or Chambers of Commerce, but also through the mass media, including their own advertising. Visual imagery in advertising was a new and powerful weapon with which to express a company's outlook on the world. Lord Lever and William Cadbury's conflicting opinions on how West Africa should be governed and developed are openly expressed in their advertising. Perhaps Lever's declining use of the image of Africans after 1910 was the result of his failure to establish support for direct rule and plantation production in West Africa. For all the companies, colonial labour relations appeared natural and are represented as ideal. Lipton's and other tea firms represent the order of plantation life as idyllic.

In the inter-war period, the Empire Marketing Board was instrumental in forming a national policy and strategy for British colonialism. The Empire was represented as a harmonious family – the colonies would provide the raw materials and Britain the industrial muscle. The colonies would also provide food for British consumption. Companies responded by repeating the rhetoric of the Empire as a benign family. By the 1920s advertising was also changing and Leiss, Kline and Jhally have discussed the way in which advertisements began to suggest that products could resonate with qualities desired by consumers. Being imperial became a desired quality. Advertisers exploited the imperial image and message to sell their products. In tobacco advertising we can see the way in which even products that did not use imperial tobacco exploited the image of imperial grandeur and adventurism.

In the post-war period, as decolonisation became a reality, and immigration from the colonies began to change the face of Britain, consumer advertising stopped using the image of black people to sell products. Corporate advertisers, however, with interests in the colonies, could not simply ignore the changing scene. The conflict was not simply between coloniser and colonised, but also between capitalism and communism. In projecting their involvement in the former colonies, the corporate advertisers presented themselves as catalysts of change. In line with modernisation theory and Rostow's stages of economic growth (an anti-communist manifesto), the corporate firms from the 'developed' world presented themselves as stimulating change in the 'developing' countries on their road to modernity. The possibility of any other road to development was denied.

By contextualising these images of black people in advertising we are also able to reveal the way in which manifestations of racism shift and change over time. Racism as an ideology has been exploited by capitalism and imperialism in order to maintain hegemonies. At moments images of aggression appear appropriate and dominant as they did in the late nineteenth century. During other periods, resistance and internal conflicts lead this to change; although images of inequality persist, the gloss of familial care presents exploitation as a form of nurture.

All the representations discussed in this book can be found in late-twentieth-century advertising. The reasons for their use are not the same, since in the late twentieth century they are clearly not involved in negotiating colonial policy in the same way. What they do express is a nostalgia for Empire and imperial relations. The notion of black people washing themselves white has been referenced as late as 1989, through the editorial 'From Yazz to Daz' in the *News of the World*, which discussed the black singer's transformation of her skin colour (Figure 77). The happy-go-lucky sambo caricature no longer signifies a peasant producer in contemporary images, but still persists through the use of, for example, the golliwog on Robertson's jams and marmalades. Tea advertising has been the one product that has persistently maintained the image of plantation production. Although permanently exoticised, it represents a rare image of labour within contemporary advertising. Contemporary PG Tips and Twinings packaging draw on historical tea advertising as well as the images of black labour from the EMB posters of the late 1920s and early 1930s (Figure 78). The image of assertive masculinity employed to represent the white male imperial hero so prevalent in inter-war tobacco advertising also continues to be used when patriotism – seen as male – is fostered. An Ariel advertisement from 1998, released to coincide with the Football World Cup, depicts a young boy in England strip, who stands against the image of green pastures, symbolically evoking the green and pleasant land. Significantly, he puts one foot up on the packet of soap powder, and strikes a pose of control similar to that used in Adrian Allinson's EMB poster of East African transport – new style (Figure 78).[1] The resonances of imperial grandeur in the construction of masculinity can be denied, but there are traces of Empire everywhere, as Bill Schwarz has discussed. Finally, the neo-colonial relationship of dependency continues to be evoked in corporate as well as charity advertisements of the late twentieth century (Figure 79).

In post-1960s advertising, images of black people are not confined to those that echo imperial relations. The changing political climate, the increase of immigration by black people into Britain and the civil rights movement in America led to shifts in representations as disapproval of overt racist ideas began to grow in all sectors of society

77 The same old story

78 Resonances

and black people began to resist subordination. As a result there has been an increase in the diversity of images of black people in advertising and all visual culture in the post-1960s period. Advertising as an industry also changed dramatically after 1960, with increasing market segmentation and the development of a more outwardly consumer-oriented society.[2] Television also altered the frame. Many have described the 1960s as the beginnings of a 'post-modern' advertising –

79 'People shouldn't have to choose between dying of thirst and dying from cholera', ICI advertisement, *Time Magazine*, 15 June 1990

an era in which advertising images rapidly change, representing a succession of ever-shifting lifestyles and conflicting perspectives.[3] In the late twentieth century, advertising has certainly become more sophisticated. We live in 'a cultural economy of signs', where signs gain value from vast marketing exploits. Product properties are no longer a defining factor in consumption. The signs and symbols with which a product is associated are often more important. It is hard to contextualise contemporary advertisements in quite the same way as I have done here, since advertisers exploit diverse kinds of imagery to increase their market share, and the mystification of production and the fetishisation of the commodity have increased beyond what Marx could ever have imagined.

However, while many advertising images today *may* reveal less about the production context of products in the fight for niche markets, they still represent the ideological interests of imperialism, which at its base is dependent on exploiting the third world in the interests of the first. Advertising is the poetry of imperialism. Let me highlight one example to show this continuity. When the clothing company Benetton developed from a national to a multinational company, it began to exploit an image of multiculturalism. It was an image that also exposed the company's support for Western/capitalist hegemony.[4] This is particularly clear in an advertisement for Colors perfume from October 1988 (Figure 80). It depicts a black and a white hand holding

80 *Constructing Globalism*

a bottle of perfume. Although the hands interlock, the positioning of the two hands (we can see the palm of the black hand, whereas we see the back of the white hand) suggests that a white man is giving perfume to a black woman. Whites are therefore put into the position of givers and blacks are the receivers. It is not an image of mutual exchange. The titling of the advertisement encourages the underlying sense of charity that permeates the image: 'Her first perfume by Benetton'. It seems to recall the charity advertisements that are titled with such phrases as 'her first shoes', or 'her first smile' etc., juxta- posed with images of appropriately satisfied children. In this Benetton advertisement, the bottles of 'Colors' perfume and toiletries are also situated under the white hand. The white hand of Benetton, the West and the metropolis are the owners of capital and the world. The word 'world' in the top title even touches the top of the perfume bottle that rests on the white hand. The line of toiletries below the white hand seems to suggest a skyline of skyscrapers, an image frequently asso- ciated with 'progress' and Western modernity. Under the black hand there is nothing but information about stockists – the only role for black people is consumption. In this simple image, the diffusionist rhetoric of modernisation theory is advocated again and Benetton appears to be offering not just perfume, but a symbol of modernity to the 'third world'. Western hegemony is represented once again with a moral righteousness. Imperialism and capitalism, as this advertise- ment indicates, are essentially about inequality, and racism continues to be used by capitalism in its imperialist stage to promote and pro- tect its interests.

What will twenty-first-century advertising and marketing bring? Racism in its more aggressive manifestations is on the rise again and has targeted a new scapegoat – Islam. The conflict is discussed as 'the clash of civilisations'. Racism as before is condoned in its new form in the interests of what is defined as 'progress'. The multicultural imagery of the 1970s and 1980s appears to have diminished in this raw new climate of aggressive racism. Anti-imperialist struggle and at times even the political conflict between the haves and have-nots has been renamed as support for terrorism in the mass media. At the end of 2001 following the events of September 11 and the American bombing of Afghanistan, fashion stores such as Next, FCUK and Adams produced clothing and advertising featuring the American flag and its colours fostering support for the system which nurtures and feeds them – imperialism.

The social, cultural and political meanings advocated in advertise- ments can never contradict an advertiser's economic interests. In the main, these social and cultural meanings naturalise capitalism as the only logical system and present commodities as things that actually hold particular ideological value. Issues of 'race' and ethnicity are frequently irrelevant to this process, but not always. Imperialism today could not survive without the cheap labour of the 'third world'. Imperialism of which advertising is a cultural expression is therefore incapable of expressing true equality. During the days of direct colonialism, advertisers were able to express the labour and power relationships that existed with impunity. They also constructed and reconstructed images of Africans and Asian people to suit their own political and economic interests. In this way they were involved in the construction and manipulation of racist ideologies. In the late twentieth century the representations of inequality and racism in advertising and culture were frequently less overt, although the changing political and economic climate in Europe and America may lead to this changing in the twenty-first century. Even the images that appear to represent global harmony can be deconstructed to reveal support for systems of global inequality.

Notes

1 John Gabriel also refers to the evocation of white nationalism in football during Euro 96 in *Whitewash: Racialized Politics and the Media* (London, 1998), pp. 25–9.
2 Leiss, Kline and Jhally date the fourth phase of market segmentation and lifestyle advertising as beginning in 1965. *Social Communication in Advertising: Persons, Products and Images of Well-being* (Scarborough Ontario, 1988), pp. 125, 210–15.
3 For a discussion of the term postmodern see D. Kellner *Media Culture: Cultural Studies, Identity and Politics Between the Modern and the Postmodern* (London, 1995), pp, 43–9.
4 For a more extensive discussion see my chapter 'Photography and Commodity Culture', in L. Wells (ed.), *Photography: A Critical Introduction* (London, 1997), pp. 188–96.

SELECT BIBLIOGRAPHY

PRIMARY SOURCES

Newspapers and magazines

Daily Mail 1928
Daily Mirror 1928
English Electric and its People 1950–61
The Graphic 1880–1930
Illustrated London News 1920–65
Pears Annual 1896–1925
Punch 1880–1910, 1920–40, 1950–61
The Times 1928–29
Tobacco 1926–33
West Africa 1950–60

Advertising ephemera and scrapbooks

Cadbury Collection, Birmingham Central Library
Books of Advertisements: MS466/7–13; MS466/15–19; MS466/32; MS466/218

Cadbury's Archive, Bournville
Advertising Albums: 520–003587; 520–003589; 520–003371; 520–003372; 520–003579; 520–003370
Labels and Packaging: 450–003291

John Johnston Collection, Bodleian Library
Soap Boxes 1–8
Cocoa, Chocolate and Confectionery Boxes 1–3
Exhibition Catalogues Boxes 24–25
Tea and Coffee Boxes 1–4
Tobacco Boxes 1–3
Tobacco Papers 1–2

Empire Marketing Board Posters, Public Record Office (CO 956)
CO 956/5–10; CO 956/13–18; CO 956/60; CO 956/90–95; CO 956/181–186; CO 956/211–216; CO 956/241–246; CO 956/274–278; CO 956/324–330; CO 956/352–355; CO 956/360–363; CO 956/374–375; CO 956/424–427; CO 956/439–444; CO 956/499–504; CO 956/558, CO 956/649; CO 956/678; CO 956/722; CO 956/725; CO 956/629; CO 956/643

Unilever Historical Archives, Port Sunlight
Lipton's Collection: Lipton's Advertising Boxes 1 and 2
Pears Collection: Advertising AFP 12/02; AFP 12/03; AFP 12/04
Pears Cuttings Books AFP 10/1/1–6; AFP 10/3/3

W. D. and H. O. Wills, Bristol Record Office
Press Cuttings Books 1923–28

Exhibition catalogues and related literature

British Empire Exhibition, ed. G. C. Lawrence, London, 1925
Colonial and Indian Exhibition: Empire of India (Special Catalogue of Exhibits by Government of India and Private Exhibitors), London, 1886
Colonial and Indian Exhibition: Official Catalogue, London, 1886
Colonial and Indian Exhibition: Official Guide, London, 1886
Colonial and Indian Exhibition: Reports on the Colonial Sections, ed. Trueman H. Wood, London, 1887
'Colonial and Indian Exhibition', *Westminster Review*, July 1886
Empire Exhibition News: The Organ of the British Empire Exhibition 1924, Nos 1/2, 1922–23
Empire Exhibition Official Guide, Glasgow, 1938
Empire Exhibition, Scotland 1938, Bellahouse Park, Official Photographs, Glasgow, 1938
'The Empire Exhibition: Wembley 1924' unpublished paper by R. A. Combes, Victoria and Albert Museum, London
Exhibition 1862: Catalogue of the Ceylon Court, London, 1862
Exhibition 1862: The Penny Guide, London, 1862
Exhibition 1874: Official Guide, London, 1874
Franco-British Exhibition Guide, London 1908
Franco-British Exhibition Official Guide, London, 1908
Franco-British Exhibition: Report on the India Section (a booklet prepared by James Buckingham), London, 1909
The Pageant of Empire: Souvenir Volume, London, 1924
Reminiscences of the Colonial and Indian Exhibition, ed. Frank Cundall, London, 1886
Sketches at the Colonial and Indian Exhibition, London, 1886
Times Special Numbers: The Empire Exhibition, 1924

Minutes of meetings, reports and correspondence

W. D. and H. O. Wills, Bristol Record Office
Reports of the Advertising Sub-committee 1930–34, 38169/M/10

Empire Marketing Board, Public Record Office
EMB Indian Tea Association Correspondence, CO 758/24
Minutes of EMB Publicity Committee, CO 760/23
Minutes and Papers of the Education Sub-committee, CO 760/25
Minutes of the Poster Sub-committee, CO 760/26
EMB Tobacco Minutes, CO 760/30
'Note on the Work and Finance of the Board and Statement of Research and Other Grants Approved by the Secretary of State for Dominion Affairs from July 1926–Mar 1928', 1928

EMB Annual Reports, 1928–33

'Report on the Methods of Preparing for Market and Marketing within the United Kingdom of Tobacco Produced within the Empire', July 1928

'Southern Rhodesian Tobacco', paper presented to the Tobacco Committee, 1 May 1930

Tea Documents, Public Recard Office

Colonial Office Registers of Correspondence from Ceylon 1885–1890: CO 337/015; CO 337/016; CO 337/017

Index to Proceedings of Dept of Industries for April 1921 – Tea Cess

Annual Reports of Indian Tea Association, 1881–93

Detailed Reports of the General Committee of the Indian Tea Association 1893–1898

Report on the General Committee of the Indian Tea Association 1908

Report of the General Committee of the Indian Tea Association 1915–16

Reports of General Committee of Indian Tea Association 1928–1938

Commercial brochures

Century of Progress 1831–1931, T. B. Rogers, 1931, Cadbury's Archive, Bourneville

John Players and Sons Centenary 1877–1977, Players Archive, Nottingham Castle Museum

Tarrant, Henderson and Co.'s Annual Ceylon Tea Report 1898, Colombo, 1899, School of Oriental and African Studies Archive

The Lipton Magazine, Centenary Issue, 1990, Unilever Archives, Port Sunlight

Cocoa: The Story of its Cultivation, 1927, Cadbury's Archive, Bournville

SECONDARY SOURCES

Ahmad, Aijaz, 'Orientalism and After: Ambivalence and Metropolitan Location in the Work of Edward Said', in *In Theory: Classes, Nations, Literatures*, London, 1992

Ajayi, J. F. A. and Crowder, M. (eds), *History of West Africa*, Vol. 2, London, 1987

Althusser, Louis, *Lenin and Philosophy and Other Essays*, New York, 1971

Amin, Samir, *Eurocentrism*, London, 1989

Balch Institute for Ethnic Studies, *Ethnic Images in Advertising*, Philadelphia, 1984

Baran, P. and Sweezy, P., *Monopoly Capital: An Essay on the American Economic and Social Order*, London, 1968

Barker, Frances, *Europe and its Others*, Vol. 2, Colchester, 1985

Barker, F., Hulme, P. and Iversen, M., *Colonial Discourse/Postcolonial Theory*, Manchester, 1994

Barker, George M., *A Tea Planter's Life in Assam*, Calcutta, 1884

Barthes, Roland, *Image, Music, Text*, London, 1977

Berger, John, *Ways of Seeing*, London, 1972

Bevan, Edwyn, 'The East, the West and Human Progress', *The Nineteenth Century*, August 1911, pp. 350–66

Bhabha, Homi, *The Location of Culture*, London, 1994

Bolt, Christine, *Victorian Attitudes to Race*, London, 1971

Bose, Sanat Kumar, *Capital and Labour in the Indian Tea Industry*, Bombay, 1954

Boskin, Joseph, *Sambo: The Rise and Demise of an American Jester*, Oxford, 1986

Brewer, A., *Marxist Theories of Imperialism: A Critical Survey*, London, 1980

Cadbury, William, *Labour in Portuguese West Africa*, London, 1910

Cain, P. J. and Hopkins, A. G., *British Imperialism: Innovation and Expansion*, London, 1993

Cave, Henry, *Golden Tips: A Description of Ceylon and its Great Tea Industry*, London, 1900

Chamberlain, M. E., *Britain and India: The Interaction of Two Peoples*, Newton Abbot, 1974

Constantine, Stephen, *Buy and Build: The Advertising Posters of the Empire Marketing Board*, London, 1986

Coombes, Annie, *Reinventing Africa: Museums, Material Culture and Popular Imagination*, New Haven, 1994

Crawford, W. S., 'Making the Empire Come Alive', *Commercial Art*, 1:6, December 1926, pp. 241–6

Crawford, W. S., 'The Poster Campaign of the Empire Marketing Board', *Commercial Art*, 6, 1929, pp. 128–35

Crossick, Geoffrey (ed.), *The Lower Middle Class in Britain*, London, 1977

Crowder, Michael, *West Africa under Colonial Rule*, London, 1968

Darwin, John, *Britain and Decolonisation: The Retreat from Empire in the Post-War World*, London, 1988

Darwin, John, *The End of Empire*, Oxford, 1991

Duffy, James, *A Question of Slavery*, Oxford, 1967

Dyer, Richard, *Gays and Film*, London, 1977

Economist Intelligence Unit, *Power in Uganda 1957–1970: A Study in Economic Growth Prospects for Uganda with Special Reference to the Potential Demand for Electricity*, London, 1957

Flint, Sir John, *Sir George Goldie and the Making of Nigeria*, London, 1960

Forrest, Denys, *A Hundred Years of Ceylon Tea 1867–1967*, London, 1967

Frank, Andre Gunder, *Latin America: Underdevelopment or Revolution, Essays on the Development of Underdevelopment and the Immediate Enemy*, New York, 1969

Fraser, W. H., *The Coming of the Mass Market 1850–1914*, London, 1981

Frith, Katherine Toland (ed.), *Undressing the Ad: Reading Culture in Advertising*, New York, 1997

Frost, Diane, 'West Africans, Black Scousers and "the Colour Problem" in Inter-war Liverpool', *Journal of the North West Labour History Group*, 20, 1995/6, pp. 50–7

Fuller, Bampfylde, 'East and West: A Study of Differences', *The Nineteenth Century*, November 1911, pp. 860–70

Gann, L. H. and Duignan, P. (eds), *Colonialism in Africa 1870–1960*, Vol. 1, Cambridge, 1969

Gardner, A. G., *Life of George Cadbury*, London, 1923

Gilroy, Paul, *There Ain't no Black in the Union Jack*, London, 1987

Goldman, Robert, *Reading Ads Socially*, London, 1992

Goldsworthy, David, *Colonial Issues in British Politics 1945–1961: From 'Colonial Development' to 'Wind of Change'*, Oxford, 1971

Goldsworthy, David, 'Keeping Change Within Bounds: Aspects of Colonial Policy during the Churchill and Eden Governments 1951–57', *Journal of Imperial and Commonwealth History*, 18:1, 1990, pp. 81–108

Goodman, Jordan, 'Fashionable and Necessary Consumption: The Culture of Tea, Coffee, Chocolate and Tobacco in Eighteenth-Century Europe', V&A Research Seminar, 1993

Gorst, A., Johnman, L. and Lucas, W., *Contemporary British History 1931–1961*, London, 1991

Green, David, 'Photography and Anthropology: The Technology of Power', *Ten 8*, 1:14 (1984), pp. 30–7

Greenhalgh, Paul, 'Art, Politics and Society at the Franco-British Exhibition', *Art History*, 8:4, December 1985, pp. 434–52

Greenhalgh, Paul, *Ephemeral Vistas: The Expositions Universelles, Great Exhibitions and World's Fairs 1851–1939*, Manchester, 1988

Grierson, John, 'The EMB Film Unit', *Cinema Quarterly*, 4, Summer 1933

Griffiths, Percival, *The History of the Indian Tea Industry*, London, 1967

Hall, Stuart, 'Cultural Identity and Cinematic Representation', *Framework*, 36, 1989, pp. 68–81

Hall, Stuart (ed.), *Representation: Cultural Representations and Signifying Practices*, London, 1997

Haug, W. F., *Critique of Commodity Aesthetics: Appearance, Sexuality and Advertising in Capitalist Society*, Cambridge, 1986

Havinden, M. and Meredith, D., *Colonialism and Development: Britain and its Tropical Colonies 1850–1960*, London, 1993

Hobsbawm, Eric J., *The Age of Empire 1875–1914*, London, 1987

Holland, P. *et al.* (eds), *Photography/Politics One*, London, 1986

Holland, P. *et al.* (eds), *Photography/Politics Two*, London, 1988

Hooks, Bell, 'Choosing the Margin as a Space for Radical Openness', *Framework*, 36, 1989, pp. 15–23

Hopkins, A. G., *An Economic History of West Africa*, London, 1975

Inden, Ronald, *Imagining India*, Oxford, 1990

Kabbani, Rana, *Europe's Myth of Orient*, London, 1986

Kay, Geoffrey, *Development and Underdevelopment: A Marxist Analysis*, London, 1975

Kellner, Douglas, *Media Culture: Cultural Studies, Identity and Politics Between the Modern and the Postmodern*, London, 1995

Kiernan, Victor G., *The Lords of Humankind*, London, 1969

Kumar, Krishna, *Transnational Enterprises: Their Impact on Third World Societies and Cultures*, Boulder, 1980

Leab, Daniel J., *From Sambo to Superspade: The Black Experience in Motion Pictures*, London, 1975

Leiss, W., Kline, S. and Jhally, S., *Social Communication in Advertising: Persons, Products and Images of Well-being*, Scarborough Ontario, 1988

Lele, Jayant, 'Orientalism and the Social Sciences', in C. A. Breckenridge and P. Van der Veer (eds), *Orientalism and the Postcolonial Predicament*, Philadelphia, 1993

Lenin, V. I., *Imperialism: The Highest Stage of Capitalism*, Peking, 1975

Leverhulme, W. H., *Viscount Leverhulme, by his Son*, London, 1927

Liddle, J. and Joshi, R., 'Gender and Imperialism in British India', *South Asia Research*, 5:2, November 1985, pp. 147–65

Lorimer, Douglas, *Colour, Class and the Victorians: English Attitudes to the Negro in the Mid-Nineteenth Century*, Leicester, 1978

Lotz, R. and Pegg, I., *Under the Imperial Carpet: Essays in Black History 1780–1950*, Crawley, 1986

Lugard, Lord, *The Dual Mandate in Tropical Africa*, London, 1965

McClintock, Anne, *Imperial Leather: Race, Gender and Sexuality in the Colonial Contest*, London, 1995

MacKenzie, John, *Propaganda and Empire: The Manipulation of British Public Opinion 1880–1960*, Manchester, 1984

MacKenzie, John (ed.), *Imperialism and Popular Culture*, Manchester, 1987

MacKenzie, John, *Orientalism: History, Theory and the Arts*, Manchester, 1997

McPhee, Alan, *The Economic Revolution in British West Africa*, London, 1926

Mack, John, *Emil Torday and the Art of the Congo 1900–1909*, London, 1990

Madras Mail, 'Legislative Abetment of Slavery', 11 September 1890, p. 4

Mani, Lata, Review of Ronald Inden's *Imagining India, Journal of Asian Studies*, 50, 1991, pp. 435–6

Marchand, Roland, *Creating the Corporate Soul: The Rise of Public Relations and Corporate Imagery in American Big Business*, Berkeley, 1998

Marx, Karl, *Capital*, London, 1954

Meredith, David, 'Imperial Images: The Empire Marketing Board 1926–1932', *History Today*, 37, January 1987, pp. 30–6

Miles, Robert, *Racism*, London, 1989

Morel, E. D., *Affairs in West Africa*, London, 1902

Morel, E. D., 'Free Labour in Tropical Africa', *The Nineteenth Century and After*, 75, March 1914, pp. 629–43

Morel, E. D., *The Black Man's Burden: The White Man in Africa from the Fifteenth Century to World War One*, London, 1920

Nead, Lynda, *Myths of Sexuality*, Oxford, 1990

Nevinson, H. W., 'The New Slave Trade', *Harper's*, October 1905, p. 674

Nevinson, H. W., *A Modern Slavery*, London, 1906

Nkrumah, Kwame, *Neo-colonialism: The Last Stage of Imperialism*, London, 1965

Nworah, K. K. D., 'Humanitarian Pressure Groups and British Attitudes to West Africa 1895–1915', unpublished Ph.D. thesis, University of London, 1966

Nworah, K. K. D., 'The Politics of Lever's West African Concessions 1907–1913', *International Journal of African Historical Studies*, 2, 1972, pp. 248–64

Nye, David, *Image Worlds: Corporate Identities at General Electric 1890–1930*, Cambridge MA, 1985

O'Barr, William, *Culture and the Ad: Exploring Otherness in the World of Advertising*, Boulder, 1994

Page, Jesse, *The Black Bishop: Samuel Ajai Crowther*, London, 1908

Pannikar, K. M., *Asia and Western Dominance*, London, 1959

Phillips, Anne, *The Enigma of Colonialism: British Policy in West Africa*, London, 1989

Pieterse, Jan Nederveen, *White on Black: Images of Africa and Blacks in Western Popular Culture*, New Haven, 1992

Ramamurthy, Anandi, *Black Markets: Images of Black People in Advertising and Packaging in Britain 1880–1990*, Manchester, 1990

Ramamurthy, Anandi, 'Photography and Commodity Culture', in L. Wells (ed.), *Photography: A Critical Introduction*, London, 1997

Richards, Thomas, *Commodity Culture in Victorian England: Advertising and Spectacle 1851–1914*, London, 1991

Rodney, Walter, *How Europe Underdeveloped Africa*, London, 1972

Rostow, Walter, *The Stages of Economic Growth: A Non-Communist Manifesto*, Cambridge, 1971

Ryan, James, *Picturing Empire: Photography and the Visualisation of the British Empire*, London, 1997

Said, Edward, *Orientalism*, London, 1978

Said, Edward, 'Orientalism Reconsidered', in F. Barker *et al.* (eds), *Europe and its Others*,Vol. 1, Colchester, 1985

Said, Edward, *Culture and Imperialism*, London, 1993

Sinha, Mrinali, *Colonial Masculinity: The 'Manly European' and the 'Effeminate Bengali' in the Late Nineteenth Century*, Manchester, 1995

Southall, R. J., 'Cadbury on the Gold Coast: The Dilemma of the "Model Firm" in a Colonial Economy', unpublished Ph.D. thesis, University of Birmingham, 1975

Steadman, John, *The Myth of Asia*, New York, 1969

Taylor, Miles, 'John Bull and the Iconography of Public Opinion in England 1712–1929', *Past and Present*, 134, February 1992, pp. 93–128

Thomas, Nicholas, *Colonialism's Culture: Anthropology, Travel and Government*, Cambridge, 1994

The Times, *Through the Chairman's Eyes*, 1952, 1955–59, 1961

Wilkins, Mira (ed.), *The Growth of Multinationals*, Aldershot, 1991

Williams, Iolo, *The Firm of Cadbury 1831–1931*, London, 1931

Williams, Patrick, and Chrisman, Laura, *Colonial Discourse and Postcolonial Theory: A Reader*, London, 1993

Williams, Raymond, 'Advertising, the Magic System', *Problems in Materialism and Culture*, London, 1980

Williamson, Judith, *Decoding Advertisements*, London, 1978

Willis, Susan, 'I Want the Black One: Is There a Place for Afro-American Culture in Commodity Culture?', *New Formations*, 10, 1989, pp. 77–98

Wilson, Charles, *The History of Unilever*, Vol. 1, London, 1954

World Development Movement, *The Tea Trade*, London, 1979

Zack-Williams, Alfred, 'Merchant Capital and Underdevelopment: The Process Whereby the Sierra Leone Social Formation Became Dominated by Merchant Capital 1896–1961', *African Review*, 10:1, 1983, pp. 54–73

Zack-Williams, Alfred, *Tributers, Supporters and Merchant Capital*, Aldershot, 1995

INDEX

Tariq, Gibral 30
Tarrant Henderson and Co. 112–14,
    117, 124, 125
Taylor Brother's 66
tea
  Ceylon 96–7, 98–103, 99, 106,
      109–15, 119, 121–6, 126–9
  China 94, 95, 96–7, 98–100, 103,
      115
  imports 96, 98
  India 96, 97, 98–9, 103, 105, 109,
      115, 116–17, 117–19, 122
  planters 105, 108, 109
  production in India 94–6
  workers 108, 109, 122–3, 216, 217
    women tea-pickers 122–6
  see also Indian Tea Association;
      Liptons; Orientalism;
      Planters' Association of
      Ceylon; United Kingdom Tea
      Company
Third Party 63, 86
  political ideology of 70–3
  racism of 71
Thomas Barratt 26
tobacco
  early tobacco advertising 145–9
  Empire Marketing Board 136–45

female labour 148–9
  Rhodesian trade 138
  settler colonial 154–9
Torday, Emile 41–2

Uganda 183–6, 195, 196–7, 198, 204
Union of Students of Black African
    Descent 151
United Africa Company 29, 35,
    188–90
United Kingdom Tea Company 99,
    100, 101, 106

Vacuum Oil Company 183, 184
Vinolia Soap 48, 49, 58, 60

West Africa 25, 29–30, 46, 53, 55,
    58–9, 68, 71–3
  land policy 69–70, 85
West Africa 181–2, 188–9, 192
West African Lands Committee 83,
    86
West African Students Association
    151
Wills' tobacco 147, 157
  Old Friend 146
  Ricketts and Co. 148
  Woodbine 159, 160